From Forbidden Fruit to Milk and Honey

FROM FORBIDDEN FRUIT TO MILK AND HONEY

A Commentary on Food in the Torah

DIANA LIPTON

URIM PUBLICATIONS
Jerusalem • New York

From Forbidden Fruit to Milk and Honey:
A Commentary on Food in the Torah
by Diana Lipton

Printed in Israel

First Edition

ISBN 978-965-524-252-2

Published by
Urim Publications
P.O. Box 52287
Jerusalem 9152102
Israel
www.UrimPublications.com

Library of Congress Cataloging-in-Publication Data

Names: Lipton, Diana, editor.
Title: From forbidden fruit to milk and honey : a commentary on food in the Torah / Diana Lipton.
Description: First Edition. | Jerusalem : Urim Publications ; New York : Ktav Publishing House, [2017]
Identifiers: LCCN 2016057349 | ISBN 9789655242522 (hardback)
Subjects: LCSH: Food—Biblical teaching. | Food—Religious aspects—Judaism. | Bible. Pentateuch—Commentaries. | BISAC: RELIGION / Biblical Commentary / Old Testament. | COOKING / Essays.
Classification: LCC BS1199.F66 F76 2017 | DDC 221.8/6413—dc23
LC record available at https://lccn.loc.gov/2016057349

In loving memory of

Joseph Gross
(1935–2013)

He loved food and Jews

Contents

Contents

Acknowledgments

Many people helped me in different ways to write and edit this book, and it's my great pleasure to acknowledge some of them here. First and foremost, I'm immensely grateful to the 51 academics and Jewish educators from Israel, the US and the UK who contributed individual commentaries to what began as an online project in English and Hebrew to benefit the food rescue charity, Leket Israel: Dan Baras, Al Baumgarten, Malke Bina, Athalya Brenner, Robert Brody, Laliv Clenman, Paula Fredriksen, Uri Gabbay, Yehuda Galinsky, Ian Gamse and Tamra Wright, Tova Ganzel, Deena Garber, Shira Golani, Simon Goldhill, Ed Greenstein, Amit Gvaryahu, Chaim [Harvey] Hames, Susan Handelman, Rachel Havrelock, Joel Hecker, Sandra Jacobs, Alex Kaye, Lynn Kaye, Ariel Kopilovitz, Melissa Lane, Suzanne Last Stone, Hanne Løland Levinson, Itay Marienberg-Milkowsky, Adi Marili, Amira Meir, Chaim Milikowsky, Noam Mizrahi, Alicia Ostriker, Yitzhak Peleg, Nehemia Polen, Meira Polliack, Jonathan Price, Stefan Reif, Gary Rendsburg, Gilla Rosen, Jeremy Rosen, Jennie Rosenfeld, Ishay Rosen-Zvi, Pinchas Roth, Marc Saperstein, Jack Sasson, George Savran, Eliezer Segal, Shani Tzoref, Nili Wazana, Harlan Wechsler, Susan Weingarten, and Linda Zisquit.

Thanks to Sara Tova Brody, who translated ably between English and Hebrew for the Leket project; to Deena Fiedler and Anat Friedman-Coles, who oversaw the project from Leket's end; and to the many cooks and food writers who contributed recipes for the project. Special mentions go to Rachel Davies, Miriam Kresh, and Denise Phillips, and to Clarissa Hyman for a great JC write-up. I'm grateful to Cory Shulman Brody, who pointed me towards Urim Publications when I was in search of a publisher; to Tzvi Mauer and Sarit Newman at Urim Publications, who saw this book into print; and to Tikva Blaukopf Schein for excellent copy-editing and collegiality. I thank Linda Zisquit, my partner in texts and double-espressos, for weekly intellectual stimulation; similarly, the participants in my shiurim at Beit Moses and Neveh Shulamit; and the students at Hebrew University's Rothberg International School who participated enthusiastically in "Famine and Feast," a course on food in the Tanakh that emerged from my preparatory work on this book and inspired the final product: Agazi Desta, Stefanie Gedan, Kathleen Getaz, Benjamin Ginsburg, Alexander Guzy-Sprague, Katherine Hartman, Samantha Lindgren, Lianna Mendelson, Claire Rostov, Thomas Rush, Lilliana Shvartsmann, Ethan Smith, and Penina Torn Broers. Thanks go too to Eddy Breuer, who welcomed my new course at Rothberg. I'm indebted to many friends with whom I've shared inspiring shabbat and festival table talk while this book was in progress: Paula Fredriksen and Fred Tauber, Toby Freilich and Moshe Halbertal, Yehuda Galinsky, Deborah Harris and George Eltman, Shosh and Josh Levinson, Estelle and Abraham Levy, Ruth and Asher Ostrin, Meira Polliack and Itzik Genizi, Gene Rogers and Derek Krueger, Naomi Schacter and Jonathan Price.

For indelible food memories, I'm grateful to Hyman Gross and Joseph Gross *z"l*, Marcie and Dick Sclove, Mort and Mimi Schapiro, Simon and Shoshana Goldhill, Jonathan and Joan Harris, and Andrew Lovett and Melissa Lane. I've loved sharing recent food (and wine!) journeys with Sonja Abracen. I'm grateful to my extended family for the many significant meals we've shared: Noa and Itay, Yehonadav, Neta, and Atira; Elisheva and Eyal; and Natani and Noa, and all the brothers and sisters and nieces and nephews. A special mention to Subby; we talk a lot about food! Finally, gratitude beyond gratitude to my sons Jacob and Jonah and to Emily: you make everything so easy; and to my husband Chaim, my love, my life: I love rising to your challenges.

Introduction

A Torah Commentary on Food?

If you're even thinking about buying this book, it's probably not the first time you've thought about the distinctive relationship between Jews and food. Your grandfather's favorite herring or hummus; your savta's kubeh; oma's leibkuchen or bubbe's lemon cake; the deli where your uncle would or wouldn't eat; your mother's bottomless serving plates ("Take some more"); your great-aunt's fridge full of food past the sell-by-date ("It still tastes fine . . ."); latkes versus hamentashen debates; the lament that's also a joke ("The food at the kiddush was terrible and there was so little of it"); the joke that's also a lament ("Nine words that sum up all Jewish festivals: They tried to kill us. We won. Let's eat") . . . All this is familiar and, especially in the past decade, the subject of many excellent studies.

Shockingly unfamiliar is the idea that the Torah anticipates almost every twist and turn of the distinctive relationship between Jews and food. I'm not referring to the dietary laws, which, in spite of their role in Jewish life, take up very little space in the Tanakh. I have in mind food as the basis of a rich and subtle language with which God communicates to Israel, Israel addresses God, and people speak to each other. It's a language that expresses love, hate, anger, control, guilt, gratitude, appreciation, despair, exclusion, inclusion, trust, pain, generosity, deception, difference, belonging, identity, transformation, illusion, disguise, guilt, sex, desire, value, status, celebration, hope, natural order, social justice, obligation, responsibility, life, death, memory, loss, the passage of time . . . the list goes on.

What's on (and off) the menu

At the core of this volume is a collection of short essays written by fifty-two internationally renowned scholars and their students on the theme of food in the *parashat ha'shavua*, the weekly Torah portion. All the authors hail from the world of academia and Jewish education and are trained in textual interpretation. They reflect a broad Jewish religious spectrum; half are women and half men; half are Israeli (about a third of the essays were originally written in Hebrew and ably translated into English by Sara Tova Brody); and half are Diaspora Jews. Although none was invited to contribute to the volume based on the strength of his or her culinary expertise, many are passionate about food – as readers, writers, teachers, cooks, and, of course, eaters.

Each short essay on the parasha is followed by my own verse-by-verse commentary on references to food, drink, and eating and drinking that the essays did not cover. While the menu, so to speak, is diverse, this book is by no means a "shmorgasbord." It is not, for example, a compendium of everything anyone has ever written about food in the Torah. One reason for starting afresh is that the observations scholars tend to make about food when it's just one among many other interests are not always . . . tempting. More importantly, there's a big difference between how we analyze what we see as merely incidental – say, a bowl of soup or a plate of meat in a story about fathers and brothers, birthrights and blessings, the chosen and the not chosen – and how we understand what we choose to regard as a story's main focus, such as the role of food in family dynamics. Focusing on food breathes new life into well-known narratives, and some are completely transformed. For example, it was only when I read the familiar story of Joseph, the cup-bearer, and the baker through a culinary prism that I understood how the dreams of Pharaoh's servants might have revealed which of them was innocent and which was guilty, why Pharaoh was willing to release one of them on his birthday, and why they were in prison in the first place.

As for what's not on the menu, this commentary does *not* discuss what ancient Israelites ate or trace the identity of edible plants and animals in the Bible. It does not deal with sacrifices, unless they are discussed explicitly in relation to eating, and the same goes for farming and agriculture. It almost never touches upon the laws of kashrut as expounded by the rabbis. Indeed, it rarely interprets any texts with reference to post-biblical commentators, whether traditional Jewish or contemporary academic. And it does not address textual questions, fascinating as they might be, that have no direct connection to food. All this can be found elsewhere, and there is no need to replicate it here.

Do I Like this, Mimi?

Some potential readers may be wondering if this volume is for them. Is it hot, spicy, green, made from animal products, made from unfamiliar ingredients, smoked, pickled, raw . . . ? Does it have a *hekhsher*, a certificate of kashrut? In answer to the first question, if you enjoy Ottolenghi recipes, you'll probably enjoy reading this book. If you don't know who (Yotam) Ottolenghi is, Google him. If you don't have access to the internet, even via your grandchildren, maybe this book is not for you. As for the second question, if this book were a restaurant, not everyone would eat here, and it's certainly not *mehadrin* (glatt kosher). That's less a matter of ingredients (for example, there's no trace of that tired old sacred cow, the documentary hypothesis) than of presentation and atmosphere. But those are not trivial when it comes to eating and drinking.

Other potential readers may wonder if there's anything here for people who don't habitually seek out kosher or even kosher-style restaurants. The answer is that even though the ingredients are kosher – it is, after all, a book about the Torah – it aims to shed light on that timeless and universal question: What are we talking about when we're talking about food? In the words of the famous ad that my late husband Peter Lipton *z"l* remembered from his youth and loved to quote, "You don't have to be Jewish to love Levy's real Jewish rye."

Still on the theme of kosher and kosher-style, it's not just the food that is served that indicates a restaurant's identity; the names of the dishes are also a guide. When potato pancakes are called latkes or *levivot*, beetroot soup is called borscht, and smoked salmon is called lox, the restaurant is likely to be Jewish, if not kosher. Terminology is likewise a reasonable indication of religious outlook. To take a leaf from Lenny Bruce's book, or better a bite from his jelly doughnut: Leviticus, goyish; VaYikra, Jewish; Isaac, goyish; Yitzhak, Jewish; Yitzchok (ArtScroll), very Jewish. For reasons including the preferences of most contributors, I decided to follow the spellings and transliterations of the *Jewish Publication Society Tanakh*, from which citations in this volume are mainly drawn.

Only in the case of the name of God have I preserved each contributor's personal choice.

The Time Is Ripe

The time is ripe for a Torah commentary on food. In the last decade or so, eating and drinking have become global obsessions. In many countries, celebrity chef television shows top viewer popularity rankings. Hollywood does chefs and restaurants. Cookbooks are one of the few categories in publishing that still make money. There's a food blog for every day of the year, every meal, and some of them (smitten kitchen!) are quite fabulous. Luxury ingredients are no longer the exclusive domain of gourmet chefs, but available in ordinary supermarkets. Vacations are built around eating and drinking. You can meet your partner at a sushi-making workshop, celebrate your Bachelor or Bachelorette night at a pasta-making class, and enjoy locally-sourced organic produce at your wedding.

In the United States and beyond, intense interest in healthy eating is following on the heels of obesity epidemics. Governments around the world are, or should be, struggling to cope with food conglomerates that flood supermarkets with addictive junk food, sugar-laden confectionaries disguised as healthy breakfast cereals and yoghurt, and school lunch products that are less nutritious than their containers. There's no Western society that can afford to ignore eating disorders, and by necessity we are more aware than ever before about food intolerances and allergies, some of them life-threatening. Paradoxically, while many in the West are suffering in one way or another from the consequences of eating too much of the wrong food, entire populations continue to starve. We have yet to address this major ethical challenge: alongside war and natural disasters, the international corporations that fill our supermarket shelves are contributing significantly to hunger in other parts of the world.

The number of vegetarians, and even vegans, is growing in response to the cruelty to animals that's inherent to large-scale, industrialized farming, and fears about how human health is affected by the medication required to keep mass-farmed animals alive for long enough to be worth slaughtering. Consumers, especially among the middle-classes, are increasingly sensitized to the ecological and environmental dangers of over-fishing and over-farming. In North America, in particular, Jewish organizations have been among the front-runners in the ethical eating movements.

Food is the subject of a burgeoning academic field populated by scientists, economists, urban planners, anthropologists, philosophers, lawyers, sociologists, historians, literary critics, gender theorists, classicists, culture theorists, and others. Cookbooks are no longer just collections of recipes, but cultural guides to life as it was once or should be lived. (You only have to read the comments on food blogs to see how aspirational food can be: "I can't wait to try this . . .") There are cookbooks in which relevant recipes feature alongside *parashat ha'shavua* commentaries (though none, as far as I know, focused on food), as well as academic treatments of food in the Bible (what people ate, how they grew and stored it) and companions to food in the Bible (the identity of this plant or that animal, how they were prepared and eaten). This book, I believe, is the first dedicated to a systematic exploration of where it all began: From Forbidden Fruit to Milk and Honey.

I'm Diana – I'll be Your Waitress

I think the seed of this book was planted in March 1996, when I brought home a bound copy of my Cambridge University doctoral thesis on dreams in the book of Genesis and put it on the shelf next to my cookbooks. It stood for all the recipes I hadn't followed and the three years of home-cooked food I'd sacrificed in favor of Marks and Spencer ready-made meals (except for Shabbat) in order to write a Ph.D.

I have been a vegetarian for most of my adult life. I stopped eating meat in 1984, shortly before my first marriage, and a few years later we stopped eating fish as a family. My late husband, Peter, was a philosopher of science by training, but his first academic job, at Clark University, required him to teach a course on ethics. The syllabus included animal rights and Peter Singer's *Animal Liberation* was on the reading list. Peter (Lipton) used to say that this was the only time that a philosophical argument changed his life; he decided it was unethical to raise animals in suffering only to kill them, and became a vegetarian. I followed suit, partly in solidarity – knowing that Peter found meat distasteful, I did not want to have it in the house – and partly because it was an answer we both found acceptable to the kashrut question. We ate vegetarian food everywhere.

When Peter died, my religious orientation shifted; vegetarianism was no longer my answer to the kashrut question. Three years later, I married Chaim, for whom eating meat is akin to a religious obligation, but whose commitment to ethical practices in the raising and slaughtering of animals is immense. I remain vegetarian, but happily prepare meat as recommended by Abed, our local kosher butcher at Super Moshava in Jerusalem's German Colony. Our kitchen is more complicated than the one I was used to, where there was no meat to avoid mixing with milk, and my Shabbat cooking has been transformed by the need to prepare food that can survive being reheated on the *plata*, hot plate. With one or two glaring exceptions – I may never get my head around cholent – I've adjusted pretty well.

It is not only in the kitchen that the intersection of food and religion became prominent in my life in recent years. Since 2011, I've lived in the land where the seven species grow, where the rain will fall (or not) in its season, and where we will eat and be satisfied (or not). The laws of kashrut operate throughout the world, but the agricultural laws do not, as was particularly obvious last year in the *shemitah* (sabbatical) year, when the land takes its seven yearly break from producing.

In the Diaspora, certainly in the circles in which I was fortunate to move, Jewish food usually means excess – the Bar Mitzvah where you feel stuffed after the kiddush and then sit down for a huge lunch. Needless to say, that's not the only association with food in the Jewish State. As I write this, Israel's government has announced a plan to deal with the significant percentage of its population who live below the poverty line and don't have enough to eat. This book emerged from my thoughts about eating strictly kosher food in "the land," surrounded by Jews and others who cannot eat and be satisfied.

Leket Israel

This book began its life, in Hebrew and English and accompanied by recipes for each parasha, on the website of Leket Israel, Israel's National Food Bank. Serving as the country's largest food rescue organization, Leket Israel works to alleviate the problem of nutritional insecurity amongst the growing numbers of Israel's poor. In 2014, with the help of 55,000 volunteers, Leket Israel rescued and distributed over 25 million pounds of produce and perishable goods, 1.5 million prepared meals, and 1.2 million volunteer prepared sandwiches to benefit the underprivileged. Food that would have otherwise gone to waste is redistributed to 180 nonprofit partners caring for those in need. Leket Israel offers nutrition, education, capacity building, and food safety projects to further assist its partners. **All royalties from the sales of the book will be given directly to Leket Israel. You can also donate via their website: www.leket.org.**

Food and Memory

In *Remembrance of Things Past*, Marcel Proust describes famously how scenes from his childhood were unlocked by the taste of madeleines. In her introduction to *The Book of Jewish Food*, Claudia Roden writes movingly of food and the vanished Jewish Cairo of her youth. Moses seals the connection between eating and remembering: "Remember this day, on which you went free from Egypt, the house of bondage . . . Seven days you shall eat unleavened bread" (Exod 13:3,6). The Israelites added insult to injury when they remembered the fish they used to "eat free in Egypt, the cucumbers, the melons, the leeks, the onions and the garlic" (Num 11:5). Joseph Gross, to whom this book is dedicated in loving memory, did not communicate much about his early life, which began in his parents' New York home and ended in a home for people with mental disabilities. But I got a vivid glimpse of it once when Joseph and I were walking somewhere green in New York, and I asked if he remembered the Passover seders of his childhood. "Yes," he replied without hesitation. "We ate brisket, tongue, turkey, chicken soup, chopped liver, gefilte fish . . ." Most of my closest memories of Joseph are connected to food, from the pizza he scraped dejectedly into the waste bin after discovering that he didn't like it cold for breakfast after all, to the unofficial announcement he used to make in synagogue when the sermon-giver went on too long: "We're going to have a good, big kiddush." Here's to that.

Diana Lipton
Jerusalem

Abbreviations

Gen	Genesis
Exod	Exodus
Lev	Leviticus
Num	Numbers
Deut	Deuteronomy
Josh	Joshua
Judg	Judges
1,2 Sam	1,2 Samuel
1,2 Kgs	1,2 Kings
Isa	Isaiah
Jer	Jeremiah
Ezek	Ezekiel
Hag	Haggai
Ps	Psalms
Prov	Proverbs
Song	Song of Songs
Lam	Lamentations
Eccl	Ecclesiastes
Esth	Esther

Glossary

akedah	The near-sacrifice of Isaac in Genesis 22
aliyah	Immigration to Israel, literally "ascent"
amora	A Jewish sage (pl. amoraim) in Babylon and the land of Israel 200-500 C.E. who "told over" the Oral Torah
avodah	Service, worship
berakhah	Blessing
betayavon	Bon appetit!
birkat ha'mazon	Blessing said after having eaten a meal
challah	Bread eaten ritually on Shabbat, often plaited egg bread
chutzpah	Nerve, cheekiness
cholent	Casserole, usually of beans, potato and meat, traditionally kept hot overnight and eaten for Shabbat lunch
etrog	Lemon-like citrus fruit; one of the "Four Species," with willow, myrtle, and palm, used ritually at the festival of Sukkot, Tabernacles
gemara	Commentary on the second century C.E. Jewish law code, the Mishnah. Together they comprise the Talmud
gemilut chassadim	Deeds of loving-kindness
gezeira	Rabbinic ruling given to prevent breaking a Jewish law
gid hanasheh	The tendon in an animal's thigh
gomel	A survivor of danger; associated with the Birkat

	Ha'Gomel, the Gomel's blessing, recited in synagogue by the survivor
haftarah	Set reading from the prophetic books following the chanting of the Torah in synagogue
hag	Festival (pl. hagim)
haggadah	Liturgical book for use at the Passover seder that tells the story of the exodus from Egypt
halakhah	Jewish law
ḥametz	Leavened bread. Any substance containing a yeast mixture forbidden on Passover
haroset	Mix intended to resemble mortar, used on the Passover seder plate. Traditionally made by Jews of Northern and Central European origin with grated apples, red wine, cinnamon and chopped almonds, and by Jews with Mediterranean, Middle Eastern and North African origin with dates and other dried fruits and spices
ḥelev	Suet. Specific animal fat strictly prohibited for consumption
hasidism	Jewish movement that began in 18th century eastern Europe, characterized by heightened spirituality and attachment to mysticism
hullin	Tractate of the Talmud dealing with what is profane (versus sacred)
kasher l'Pesah	Kosher for Passover, permitted to be eaten at Passover, and therefore without leaven
kashrut	Jewish dietary laws
kezayit	Statutory amount of food that must be eaten to constitute halakhic consumption. lit. "like an olive [in size]"
kodashim	Things set apart for a sacred purpose, usually an animal
kohen	Priest (pl. *kohanim*)
korban pesaḥ	Passover sacrifice
leḥem hapanim	Two bread loaves kept in the Temple daily
l'ḥaim	Cheers! literally, "to life"
maariv	Jewish evening service

manhiga ruḥanit	Spiritual guide (fem.)
maror	Bitter herb, used on the seder plate, a ceremonial plate placed on the table at Passover: typically raw horseradish, traditionally lettuce
matzah	Flat bread without leavening agent, baked for no more than 18 minutes
midrash	Post-biblical Jewish commentary on biblical passages, typically bringing seemingly unrelated biblical verses to bear, and often featuring meshalim, parables (pl. midrashim)
minḥa	Jewish afternoon service
mishkan	Portable place of worship built by the Israelites in the wilderness to transport the Torah and serve as a focus for the divine presence
mishnah	2nd century CE Palestinian Jewish law code
mitzvah	Commandment (pl. mitzvot)
nazir	One who vows to take upon him or herself specified restrictions and thus becomes set apart, usually for a set period
omer	A biblical unit of measurement. The 49 day period between Passover and Shavuot (Festival of Weeks) is designated by "Counting the Omer"
parasha	Portion of Torah, divided into weekly readings (parashat, portion of)
peah	Corner of the field that must be left unharvested to feed those without land
Pesaḥ	Passover
seudot	Meals, often used with reference to the meals required on Shabbat and Hagim
semachot	Celebrations
shabbat	Sabbath, biblically-ordained day of rest
shaḥarit	Jewish morning service
shefa	Divine influence in medieval Jewish philosophy. Comparable to light in Jewish mysticism. Literally, "flow"
sheḥitah	Animal slaughter according to Jewish ritual requirements

shekhinah	Divine presence
shelamim	Peace or whole offerings, perhaps signifying repayment
shema	Jewish prayer comprised of three biblical paragraphs (Deut 6:4-9; Deut 11:13-21; Num 15:37-41). The central prayer of Judaism
shemitah	The last year in a seven year cycle during which agricultural produce grown in the land of Israel cannot be harvested and used by Israelites/Jews
shulchan arukh	Medieval Jewish law code written by R. Joseph Karo. It remains the central handbook of Jewish practice for orthodox Jews
tabernacle	See mishkan
Tanakh	The name by which many Jews know the Hebrew Bible; an acronym of Torah, Neviim ["prophets"] and Ketuvim ["writings"]
Targum of Onqelos	An Aramaic translation of the Hebrew scriptures, attributed to Onqelos, a 1st century Jewish convert
todah	Thanksgiving offering
tohu va'vohu	Primordial chaos
tosafot	Medieval Jewish commentaries on the Talmud
tumah	Ritual impurity
yahrzeit	Anniversary of a death
yishuv	Small Israeli rural community
yovel	The "Jubilee," the final year in every fifty year cycle, when debts were remitted, slaves released, and land that had been sold was returned to its original owners
zemirot	Liturgical songs typically sung at the Shabbat table
zenut	Sexual promiscuity, from the Hebrew *zonah*, prostitute

Bere'shit

Genesis 1:1–6:8

Creation and Sustainability

Melissa Lane

On the third day of creation of the world, God creates vegetation: "seed-bearing plants of every kind, and trees of every kind bearing fruit with the seed in it" (Gen 1:12). After human beings have been created on the sixth day, these seed-bearing plants and fruits are presented to them as "yours for food" (Gen 1:29). Fruit has a special resonance as a foodstuff in many cultures. The ancient Greeks also considered it as an aboriginal kind of food, for example in Hesiod's myth of the Golden Age and Plato's versions of the myth of Kronos. In both these narratives, humans enjoyed abundant fruits. As in these Greek texts, abundant fruit in the Torah embodies the dream of food without toil. Fruit is so seductive a foodstuff because, ripe, it may fall literally into our hands; we need not even till the earth to harvest it.

But is the Torah's vision in this parasha one of food without toil altogether? When the story of creation is telescoped into a second account of human beings who are placed in the Garden of Eden, we find a double role for artisanry. On the one hand, God again takes care to stock the garden with "every tree that was pleasing to the sight and good for food" (Gen 2:9). God is concerned to make trees beautiful in human eyes: we are not to see them only as producing the utility of human nourishment. On the other hand, the man is placed in the garden "to till . . . and tend" it (Gen 2:15). Although the soil is cooperative and the labor not painful – as it will become with the cursed expulsion from Eden – work must be done even in Eden.

This reminds us that in fact the dream of food without toil is a fantasy. Fruit trees need pruning if they are to flourish long term. Even fruitarian food requires a cooperative venture between nature and human craft, all the more so insofar as human activities come to disrupt the health of the self-reproduction with which divine creation originally endowed trees and plants. In its second creation story, the parasha recognizes this fact, acknowledging the partnership between humans and the natural world that sustaining food will require.

Yet if we return to the first creation story, we find one more thing to learn from the creation of "seed-bearing" plants and fruits on the third day, and their designation as "food" on the sixth. Seeds are the promise of a recurrent, perennial supply of food, one with self-renewing powers, even if they will do best when cultivated by human care. In other words, the creation of food – the first food that is created – is intrinsically sustainable. Human effort in the second creation story can enhance and support that sustainability, working with trees and plants. But to undermine or disrupt the self-renewing source of our food supply is to violate the order of creation itself.

MELISSA LANE is the Class of 1943 Professor of Politics at Princeton University. She was the founding director of Princeton's Program in Values and Public Life in the University Center for Human Values, and co-convenes the Princeton Climate Futures Initiative. Melissa's third book, *Eco-Republic* (2011/2012), is on Plato and sustainability.

And God said, "Let the earth sprout vegetation: seed-bearing plants, fruit trees of every kind on earth that bear fruit with the seed in it." And it was so. The earth brought forth vegetation: seed-bearing plants of every kind, and trees of every kind bearing fruit with the seed in it. And God saw that this was good. And there was evening and there was morning, a third day. (Gen 1:11–13)

We read this account of the third day knowing what happens on days four, five, and six. More to the point, we read it from an anthropocentric perspective, putting ourselves and our needs at the heart of the matter. So naturally, we assume that the seed-bearing plants and the fruit-bearing trees are ultimately intended as food for us. That assumption is supported on day six, when God tells the male and female He has just created that He is giving plants and trees to them as food. But it's worth noting the absence of an explicit reference to food on day three, along with the position of vegetation after the separation of water from dry land and before creation of the sun, moon, and stars. This suggests that food is not the *only* purpose of vegetation. Rather, plants and trees are as crucial as earth, water, and light to the fabric of the world. Each contributes to the others as well as benefitting from them. We have seen all too clearly, for example, what happens to a landscape when forests are cleared and, deprived of a protective canopy and roots that trap moisture and hold soil, it becomes arid and ultimately barren.

God said, "See I give you every seed-bearing plant that is upon all the earth, and every tree that has seed-bearing fruit; they shall be your for food. And to all the animals on land, to all the birds of the sky, and to everything that creeps on the earth, in which there is a breath of life, [I give] all the green plants for food." (Gen 1:29–30)

In addition to the emphasis on sustainability, discussed by Melissa Lane above, there is another striking feature: God's first explicit reference to food does not mention meat. Some would argue that eating falls under the umbrella of "ruling" in the preceding reference to the relationship between humans and all other living things: "Fill the earth and master it; and rule the fish of the sea, the birds of the sky, and all the living things that creep on earth" (Gen 1:28). Clearly though, the right to rule does not inevitably include the right to eat. More likely, as seems to be confirmed after the flood (Gen 9:3–5), God's original intention was that living things would not eat each other; meat-eating was a compromise made only once it seemed necessary.

> *The Lord God took the man and placed him in the garden of Eden, to till it and tend it. And the Lord God commanded the man, saying, "Of every tree in the garden you are free to eat; but as for the tree of knowledge of good and bad, you must not eat of it, for as soon as you eat of it, you shall die." (Gen 2:15–17)*

God's first negative command, His first threatened punishment, and His first references to death and evil, come in relation to eating. What does this signify? First, we learn that eating is more than a matter of sustenance. Man is free to eat from every tree in the garden, other than the tree of knowledge of good and evil. When he disobeys God and eats from that tree, it is not because he is hungry, but because he has an appetite for its fruit and its fruit alone. Second, appetites are neither rational nor easily controlled. It's very hard to avoid eating something tempting once it's in front of you, even if you know t°hat it's bad for you. Third, knowing that something is bad for you can sometimes be a temptation in itself. If God hadn't singled out this tree, there's a chance that Adam and Eve would never have eaten its fruit. Fourth, eating is in part about opposites. It entails what tastes good and what tastes bad; choosing constantly between what will sustain and what will harm, taking what's external and making it internal; demonstrating that we are not angels who live forever, but mortal beings who need food to survive.

> *. . . He [the serpent] said to the woman, "Did God really say: You shall not eat of any tree of the garden?" The woman replied to the serpent, "We may eat of the fruit of the other trees of the garden. It is only about the fruit of the tree in the middle of the garden that God said: "You shall not eat of it or touch it, lest you die."' And the serpent said to the woman, "You are not going to die, but God knows that as soon as you eat of it your eyes will be opened and you will be like divine beings who know good and bad." (Gen 3:1–5)*

This interaction between the snake and the first woman contains the seeds of two very familiar, very different food-related phenomena. The first, emanating from Eve, is the notion, advocated today by dieticians and nutritionists around the world, that it's not enough for those striving to lose weight to avoid *eating* unhealthy food; they must avoid contact with it altogether. If you keep chocolate chip cookies in the pantry and cheesecake in the refrigerator, sooner or later, you'll eat them. As many commentators have noted, God prohibited Adam from eating the fruit of the tree of knowledge of good and evil; He did not mention touching it. Eve adds that prohibition, the world's first "fence around the Torah," perhaps in the vain hope that it will protect her from the snake's temptations.

The second food-related phenomenon that this exchange seems to predict is false advertising. Food corporations spend vast amounts of money working out how to make their products hard to resist once we start eating them, and how to make us buy them in the first place. The truth is that junk food can cause heart-disease, morbid obesity, and death; the snake-like lie that its advertisers peddle is that it's a taste of heaven.

> *When the woman saw that the tree was good for eating and a delight to the eyes, and that the tree was desirable as a source of wisdom, she took of its fruit and ate. (Gen 3:6)*

Two points stand out here. The first is the role of visual aesthetics in food preparation. Contemporary cuisine is sometimes accused of privileging color and the arrangement of food on the plate over of taste, but Eve's response to the tree shows that there's nothing new in the desire to be delighted by the appearance of what we eat. The second is that food is linked to properties and benefits that extend far beyond simple nutrition. While plenty of highly intelligent people, for reasons beyond anyone's control, ate poorly as children, there seems to be little doubt that intellectual development is enhanced by a healthy childhood diet.

> *. . . She also gave some to her husband, and he ate. (Gen 3:6)*

This is not the place to spell out the consequences of the fact that Eve ate the forbidden fruit first and then gave some to Adam; the history of world religions makes it clear enough. Worth noting here, though, is the extent to which these words predict, if not predicate, the respective roles of men and women when it comes to food: usually, though not inevitably, women feed men.

> *Then the eyes of both of them were opened and they saw that they were naked . . . (Gen 3:7)*

Adam and Eve eat fruit and experience desire: food and sex. Commentators have disagreed about what kind of fruit grew on the tree of knowledge of good and evil. Perhaps because of its association with beauty (Lev 23:40), the etrog was proposed in some rabbinic texts, but it was the apple that entered the popular imagination. According to historians of food, this is a reasonable choice. Apples are believed to have been first cultivated in the same geographic region as the Garden of Eden. More plausibly, however, the first couple ate from a fig tree. There was certainly a fig tree at hand: aware for the first time of their nakedness, they sewed loincloths from fig leaves (v. 7). And whereas the sexual connotations of the apple are derived more from its traditional association with Adam and Eve than from its physical properties; ripe, soft, sweet, purple-red, seed-filled, juicy figs are evocative of so much. There's a pleasing poetic justice to the idea that Adam and Eve covered with fig leaves the nakedness of which they became aware by eating figs from the very same tree.

> *. . . Cursed be the ground because of you; by toil you shall eat of it all the days of your life: Thorns and thistles shall it sprout for you. But your food shall be the grasses of the field; By the sweat of your brow shall you get bread to eat . . . (Gen 3:17–19)*

Babies and young children are fed on demand or at set times. In normal circumstances, they need make no effort to get food; it simply comes their way. That changes when they reach adulthood, and must shop for food, store it, and plan and prepare meals. Pleasant as it is to eat without prior effort in someone else's home or a restaurant, most of us see the food preparation as a necessary responsibility, not a punishment. God's "curse" of the land because of Adam can be interpreted similarly, not so much a punishment as a transition from the childlike conditions of the Garden of Eden, where food literally grew on trees, to the harsh reality of an adult world in which food comes with hard work and you eat "by the sweat of your brow."

And the L*ORD* *God said, "Now that the man has become like one of us, knowing good and bad, what if he should stretch out his hand and take also from the tree of life and eat, and live forever!" (Gen 3:22)*

It turns out that, in one respect, the tree of knowledge of good and evil functioned as a kind of "fence around the Torah." Eating its fruit was a signal that man might now attempt to capture the real prize – immortality gained by eating from the tree of life. Or was the fruit of the tree of life rather an antidote for the fruit of the tree of knowledge, a second fruit with the power to reverse the threat of death that came with the first fruit? Either way, it's striking that, like a tempting piece of ripe fruit, the choice of sex and death versus immortality is at once man's for the taking and yet not fully within his control.

DIANA LIPTON

Noah

Genesis 6:9–11:32

Rav Kook's vegetarian vision

Dan Baras

Adam was commanded to keep a vegan diet: "God said, "See, I have given you every seed-yielding plant that is upon all the earth, and every tree that has seed-bearing fruit; they shall be yours for food" (Gen 1:29). Noah, on the other hand, was permitted to eat meat: "Every creature that lives shall be yours to eat; as with the green grasses, I give you all these" (Gen 9:3). This change, perhaps the most radical change regarding diet in the Bible, is never explained, and the biblical exegete must attempt to fill in this void on his or her own.

Following a declaration heard in the context of the first World Zionist Congress in 1897, that "Zionism has nothing to do with religion," Rav Abraham Isaac Kook, then the rabbi of Bauska, Lithuania, was inspired to take up the cudgels in defense of religion's role in Zionism. During the years 1903–1904, Rav Kook published a long treatise, in installments,* in which he entreated the Zionist Movement not to cut itself off from Jewish religion. In the minds of the leaders of secular Zionism, religion symbolized the unenlightened past of Judaism, in contrast to the forward-thinking Zionist

* Rav Abraham Isaac HaCohen Kook, *Afikim BaNegev*, Hapeles (1903). Excerpts from this and an additional article by Rav Kook, *Telalei Orot*, were later published by Rav David HaCohen (the *nazir*) as an independent publication entitled *The Vision of Vegetarianism and Peace*.

movement. Rav Kook, on the other hand, attempted to convince the readers of his treatise that religion was also mindful of the future, and that the particular halakhot of Judaism were the necessary means to raising the Jewish nation to a supreme level of moral perfection. This claim was backed by an example: the Torah's attitude toward animals.

Rav Kook developed an interpretation by Rabbi Yosef Albo (*Sefer Haikarim* 3:15), according to which the relationship between the *parshiyot* of Bere'shit and Noah was that of an idealized halakha and one that takes into account the current imperfect reality. According to Rav Kook, following the murder of Abel by his brother Cain, "*the Divine Wisdom saw that Man had fallen from his high moral plane, and that until he regained it . . . he was not deserving of that same high moral level of knowing the law of animals.*" Moral progress, Rav Kook argued, particularly collective moral progress, must be achieved gradually. Before man could learn to treat animals properly, it was necessary that he learn to treat his own kind in the appropriate manner. It was for this reason that the eating of animal flesh was temporarily permitted to Noah and his descendants. But the Torah never intended to leave us on this diminished moral plane. Its purpose is the moral advancement of human society, step by step. The many limitations the Torah imposed on human use of animals were intended to implant the idea of animals' moral worth, until such a time as humans were once again ready to ascend to the higher ethical plane of vegetarianism, presented to Adam in parashat Bere'shit.

It is easy to miss the extent to which these words of Rav Kook, overall conservative in tone, are based on assumptions which are different than those that many Jews consider "the normative stance of Judaism." I will point out three of these assumptions in what follows.

Firstly, regarding animals, we are familiar with the Rambam's opinion that "all the creatures under the moon were brought into being for the sake of man alone. And among all the species of animals, there are those that are for man's sustenance, such as sheep, goats, and cattle; and there are those that are for his use in other ways, such as the donkey, to carry loads that cannot be carried by hand, and horses, to travel long distances in fewer days . . ." (Maimonides,

Introduction to the Mishnah). In contrast to this opinion, Rav Kook assumes that the life of animals has an intrinsic value of its own. According to Rav Kook, even the taking of wool or milk from an animal for man's purposes "should, by reason, be recognized as theft!"

Secondly, the Rambam established as a principle of faith that the Torah is unchanging (Maimonides, Introduction to *Perek Ḥelek*), "And God will not change nor exchange his religion for another" (from "*Yigdal*"). Rav Kook, however, believed humanity was in a gradual process of moral progression, in which the Torah shared. Just as the Torah changed its opinion on the consumption of meat, we can expect it to continue to change in accordance with society's moral advancement.

Thirdly, a common conception in the Jewish world is dismissive of moral feeling on man's part. It views God's commandments as independent of human judgment, and believes that he who applies his feelings to them "must be silenced" (Babylonian Talmud, Berachot 33b). The positive model of this kind of behavior is Abraham, who overcomes his natural love for his son and agrees to sacrifice him; whereas Saul's behavior, in feeling compassion for Amalek, is viewed as the epitome of the fallacy of applying human feelings to God's commandments. It is interesting to note that, as a basis for his opinions regarding animals, Rav Kook states that "it is impossible to deny that which is sensed by any feeling heart." According to Rav Kook, moral sensitivity is an accurate and trustworthy indicator of God's true will.

In these opinions, coming from a figure so central to Israeli religious Zionism, there is a substantial challenge to what some view as normative dogmas of Jewish Orthodoxy. It appears that the "meat revolution" in parashat Noah may serve as a basis for discussion of central issues in Jewish philosophy.

DAN BARAS is working on a doctorate in the Philosophy Department of Ben Gurion University of the Negev, Israel, and is a Fellow in the Human Rights and Judaism program of the Israel Democracy Institute.

For your part, take of everything that is eaten and store it away, to serve as food for you and for them [the animals] (Gen 6:21)

Anyone who has lived through warnings of a major snow storm will have an inkling of how Noah must have felt when he heard these words from God. Other than his immediate family and two representatives of each member of the animal kingdom (a few more if they're fit for sacrifice), the entire world is about to be covered with water. Their collective survival in the ark will depend on Noah's ability to procure and store enough food of the right kinds. He has no idea how long they will be on the ark, and he probably has little idea of the various diets of the many species of animals whose extinction he has been commissioned to prevent. At least Noah had advance warning, and was not competing with his neighbors (who didn't know that unfortunately they wouldn't need food for long) once the rain began in earnest. In the big picture of things, Noah's part of the operation seems trivial: you bring snacks for the journey. We have only to recall the empty supermarket shelves before a national holiday weekend (or Shabbat plus two days of a festival in a Jewish neighborhood) to imagine how easily food could have become Noah's prime preoccupation, not just in advance of the flood but throughout it. And we have only to recall those tragic occasions on which people miraculously survived natural catastrophe or man-made disaster only to die of starvation, to realize that in Noah's case the preoccupation was extremely serious and more than justified.

So long as the earth endures, seedtime and harvest, cold and heat, summer and winter, day and night shall not cease. (Gen 8:22)

God's promise that He will never again destroy every living being as He did during the flood is followed by a guarantee of continuity. The form that this guarantee takes is as reassuring as its content: four pairs of opposites that evoke symmetry, totality, and endless progression. Of particular interest is the order in which these pairs are listed; food comes first. To the extent that the three environment-related pairs are pre-conditions for the first pair, we might have expected them to precede it. On reflection, it does make sense that the pair equated with food comes at the beginning. First, the order may reflect the priorities of Noah and his family; fears about what they would find to eat may well have been uppermost in their minds as they got off the ark. Second, seedtime and harvest are the most fragile of these four pairs, the first to be affected by natural disaster, and probably the only one affected by the flood. As far as we know, there were no climatic changes other than heavy rain for a long duration. At any rate, it's hard to read God's promise of continuity today without thinking about climate change and wondering how far we can go before we present it with a serious challenge.

DIANA LIPTON

Lekh Lekha

Genesis 12:1–17:27

Scarcity and Abundance

Alexander Kaye

The book of Genesis is framed by famine. Each of the patriarchs contended with famine and their experiences highlight its consequences – dislocation, conflict and exploitation – which continue to resonate with us today. Shortly after their arrival in the Promised Land, famine forced Abram and Sarai (their names had not yet been changed) to relocate to Egypt where, away from the safety of their home, Abram's life was endangered and Sarai was threatened with sexual violence (Genesis 12). Famine recurred in Isaac's time (Genesis 26). In its aftermath, conflict erupted between Isaac's shepherds and those of Abimelech over rights to water, whose scarcity was presumably associated with the famine. During the next famine (Genesis 41), Jacob had to relocate his entire family to Egypt in search of food. Egypt had food only because, under Joseph's guidance, Pharaoh had stored surplus grain during the years of plenty. This policy no doubt saved many from starvation but it also had the effect of centralizing all land ownership into Pharaoh's hands. Scarcity, coupled with the lack of regulation of the most powerful, made the rich richer and the poor poorer.

Famine and its consequences are with us still. About one in seven people do not have enough to eat. As in the time of Abram, famine displaces millions. As in the time of Isaac, food and water shortages are linked to violent conflict all over the world. As in the time of

Jacob, scarce resources are increasingly concentrated into the hands of a small elite. What is more, these factors – scarcity, poverty, migration, conflict and corruption, all exacerbated by climate change – reinforce each other, contributing to a perpetual systemic global crisis.

The Bible's accounts of famine are even more striking because the first chapters of Genesis depict the abundance of creation. The earth gives forth its fruit for human beings to eat. Even with the exile of Adam and Eve, Noah's flood and the dispersion of Babel, there is no hint that there was ever a shortage of food. The first famine in the Bible, in the time of Abram and Sarai, presents a terrible contrast to the abundance of the first generations. This juxtaposition of abundance and scarcity is very familiar to us. Even when the earth produces enough, too much food ends up in some places and too little in others. Today, about a third of the food produced annually is lost or wasted and almost all undernourished people live in the developing world. There is no easy resolution to the absurd and ghastly contrast between the earth's fecundity and the malnourishment of millions. Perhaps, at least, the Bible's stark presentation of this state of affairs encourages us to do all we can to alleviate it.

ALEXANDER KAYE is an Assistant Professor of history and the Saul and Sonia Schottenstein Chair in Israel Studies Designate at the Ohio State University. He received a Doctorate from the History department of Columbia University, rabbinical ordination from Yeshivat Chovevei Torah Rabbinical School and a B.A. and M.Phil. from the University of Cambridge. His current research engages with the religion, law and politics in the thinking of religious Zionist thinkers of the twentieth century.

> *Lot, who went with Abram, also had flocks and herds and tents, so that the land could not support them staying together; for their possessions were so great that they could not remain together. And there was quarreling between the herdsmen of Abram's cattle and those of Lot's cattle . . . (Gen 13:5–7)*

The notion of territory and property disputes is all too familiar. Today, governments and individuals fight over territory for reasons including the need for space for expanding populations; a desire to capitalize on natural assets such as minerals or oil; an ambition to develop a region for tourism and other industries; and security concerns. We hear less often about farming and agriculture as a cause of land disputes, but in the ancient world, as still in some parts of the world today, the land's capacity to generate produce or support animals would have been a major factor. In the case of Lot and Abram, the land's inability to support all their cattle once Abram returned from Egypt with a much larger herd has long-term consequences. Disputes between their herdsmen eventually lead Lot and Abram to separate and live independently in different regions.

> *Lot looked about him and saw how well watered was the whole plain of Jordan, all of it – this was before the LORD had destroyed Sodom and Gomorrah – all the way to Zoar, like the garden of the LORD, like the land of Egypt. (Gen 13:10)*

Not surprisingly, given the reason for his separation from Abram, Lot's choice of the Jordan plain was determined by his assessment of its agricultural potential. A prime consideration is water. The region is so well irrigated that it merits two evocative parallels: Eden (which is presumably what is meant by "the garden of the LORD") and Egypt. In recent years, ecologically-minded gardeners, spurred on perhaps by water rationing or taxing, have created gardens using plants that can survive without much water. Traditionally, though, gardens have tended to depend on constant watering, and their lushness has been viewed as a particular prize. There is little doubt that the Garden of Eden was lush and green. Similarly, the land of Egypt was renowned for the produce that grew in the Nile's flood plain. As things turn out, all that glistens is not wet; Lot would have been better off staying in Canaan and letting Abram go east.

> *[The invaders] seized all the wealth of Sodom and Gomorrah and all their provisions, and went their way. (Gen 14:11)*

The catastrophe forever associated with the names Sodom and Gomorrah is reported a few chapters later: God rains sulfurous fire from heaven and annihilates the cities, their inhabitants and the surrounding countryside (Gen 19:23–24). Here in Genesis 14 the context is the war between the kings, and the catastrophe in question is the disaster of war. For reasons ranging from siege through obstructed travel and closed borders to crops damaged unintentionally or deliberately in battle, war almost always affects the food supply.

DIANA LIPTON

Va-Yera

Genesis 18:1–22:24

Mothers' Milk

Hanne Løland Levinson

Barrenness and the struggle for children are well-known themes in the ancestor stories in the Bible. Sarah, Rebecca, Rachel, and Leah all experienced periods of infertility, but in the end they all conceived and gave birth. In the story of Sarah we hear not only that she gave birth, but also that she breastfed. "Who would have said to Abraham that Sarah would nurse children! . . ." (Gen 21:7) What Sarah asks here resembles her rhetorical question earlier in the parasha, "Now that I am withered, am I to have enjoyment - with my husband so old?" (Gen 18:12) The idea of having pleasure, giving birth, and suckling a child was really foreign to Sarah because of her old age and her elderly body. Still, here she is breast feeding her own son, Isaac. "The child grew up and was weaned, and Abraham held a great feast on the day that Isaac was weaned" (Gen 21:8).

Women in ancient Israel nursed their children for two to three years and mothers generally nursed their own children. We do hear of some wet-nurses in the Bible (Gen 24:59; 35:8; Exod 2:7, 9), but wet-nursing is not thought to have been a widespread practice. Sarah nursed Isaac (Gen 21:7–8), Moses was nursed by his mother, though she did it as his wet-nurse (Ex 2:7 and 9), Hannah nursed Samuel (1 Sam 1:23), and one (or both) of the mothers judged by king Solomon nursed her child (1 Kgs 3:21). Breastfeeding has primarily a nourishing purpose; it provides the baby with its first food. But none of the stories in the Bible emphasizes the nourishing aspect of breastfeeding. Sarah is astonished that she gets the opportunity to breastfeed. Moses' own mother gets to breastfeed him because Miriam suggests to Pharaoh's daughter that she could find a wet-nurse for baby Moses among the Hebrew women (Exod 2:7–9). As long as Hannah breastfeeds Samuel she can keep her little boy at home (1 Sam 1:22–24); once she has weaned him, she gives him (back) to God. These stories emphasize the (emotional) connection between mother and child, a connection established and maintained through breastfeeding.

In addition to the narratives about breastfeeding in the Bible, we also find texts where breastfeeding is understood metaphorically. In Isaiah, the image of breastfeeding is used to portray fulfillment: "That you may suck from her breast consolation to the full, that you may draw from her bosom glory to your delight. For thus said the LORD: I will extend to her prosperity like a stream, the wealth of nations like a wadi in flood; and you shall drink of it. You shall be carried on shoulders and dandled upon knees" (Isa 66:11–12).

In contrast, refraining from breastfeeding a child, not giving the infant food, is seen as the uttermost cruelty: "Even jackals offer the breast and suckle their young; but my poor people has turned cruel, like ostriches of the desert. The tongue of the suckling cleaves to its palate for thirst. Little children beg for bread; none gives them a morsel" (Lam 4:3–4).

Two striking metaphorical uses of breastfeeding in the Bible are the images of Moses as the nurse of the people and God as a nursing mother. In Numbers 11:12, Moses is speaking in anger to God: "Did I conceive all this people, did I bear them, that You should say to me, 'Carry them in your bosom, as a nurse carries an infant . . . ?'" Moses does not want the responsibility for the people, a responsibility that includes nursing them. Being the wet-nurse is here explicitly connected to the responsibility of providing food, but this time the responsibility is not to provide milk for the infant, but meat for the people. Moses asks: "Where am I to get meat to give to all this people?" (Num 11:13).

Finally, in the book of Isaiah, God is compared to a mother who breastfeeds her child. Again, it is the intimate connection between the mother and the child that is emphasized: "Can a woman forget her baby, or disown the child of her womb? Though she might forget, I never could forget you" (Isa 49:15). Why can a mother not forget her suckling child? In addition to the emotional bond between a mother and her child, there is also a bodily bond between them that this text draws on. Longer intervals between lactations cause physical pain in a mother's breasts and that pain eases only with the emptying of the breast. Breastfeeding women can also experience milk ejection (let-down) when hearing a baby cry or seeing an infant. Sometimes the mere thought of her child will lead to milk ejection. The body itself is thus a strong reminder to the mother of her child. This image of the mother who cannot forget her child because of the bodily connection between them is the image applied to God, to assert that God cannot forget Zion.

Sarah became a mother, the mother of Isaac, the matriarch of Israel, and the mother of everyone who chooses to become a Jew. Her elderly body gets to experience giving birth, breastfeeding, giving life and sustaining life. She affirms, "*God has brought me laughter; everyone who hears will laugh with me*" (Gen 21:6). I smile at the image of the old Sarah nursing the little boy at her breast. I smile at Isaiah's bold image of God not being able to forget God's people due to breast pain.

HANNE LØLAND LEVINSON is an Assistant Professor in the Department of Classical and Near Eastern Studies at the University of Minnesota. She is also a faculty member in Jewish Studies and Religious Studies. She taught formerly at MF Norwegian School of Theology in Oslo, where she received her Ph.D. Hanne's commentary here draws on her book, *Silent or Salient Gender? The Interpretation of Gendered God-Language in the Hebrew Bible*, (Tübingen: Mohr Siebeck, 2008) which was awarded the John Templeton Award for Theological Promise in 2008.

Looking up, he [Abraham] saw three men standing near him. As soon as he saw them, he ran from the entrance of the tent to greet them and, bowing to the ground, he said, "My lords, if it please you, do not go on past your servant. Let a little water be brought; bathe your feet and recline under the tree. And let me fetch a morsel of bread that you may refresh yourselves . . ." (Gen 18:2–5)

These verses are the main sources of Abraham's reputation for hospitality. Commentators often emphasize speed: Abraham did not simply offer hospitality to strangers, but *ran* to greet them (v. 2); he did not merely organize a meal, but *hurried* to do it (v. 6 below), telling Sarah to make cakes *quickly*, *running* to select a calf from the herd, and inspiring his servant to prepare it *fast* (v. 7).

Abraham's haste could have been motivated by practical concerns. The three men were not dinner guests anticipating a leisurely evening of companionable dining, but travelers on a journey, almost certainly keen to reach their destination. It could also reflect his enthusiasm for giving hospitality, and still more important perhaps, a desire to convince his guests that he was enthusiastic, even if he wasn't. But haste is not the only lesson to be learned from Abraham's example. Perhaps his decision to address the angels "lords" and call himself "your servant" was based on their fine appearance. More plausibly, it corresponds to cultural norms prevalent at the time. An important part of being hospitable involves making guests feel that, far from being a burden, their presence is an honor for their hosts. By addressing the men as lords, Abraham demonstrated that he, their servant, was honored by this opportunity to feed them.

Along similar lines, it is striking that he offered them a drop of water and a morsel of bread, only to serve them a feast that included meat – surely a luxury. Had he mentioned the meat upfront, the men might well have refused, embarrassed by the time, energy, and expense Abraham would have to spend on their account. By minimizing what he was offering them, Abraham minimized the extent to which they might feel that they were imposing upon his hospitality.

Abraham hastened into the tent to Sarah, and said, "Quick, three seahs of choice flour! Knead and make cakes!" Then Abraham ran to the herd, took a calf, tender and choice, and gave it to a servant-boy who hastened to prepare it. (Gen 18:6 7)

When it comes to gender, there is rarely a simple account of who cooks what and where. Even in those present day societies in which women are mainly responsible for the food preparation at home, restaurant cooking is frequently the provenance of men. Indeed, it is often the case that the finer the restaurant, the more likely it is that that the chef is male. These verses suggest another kind of gender divide that remains recognizable, if only on occasions when a barbecue is involved – women bake bread and cakes, and men take care of the meat. Along with the continued emphasis on haste, the verses contain a new indication of Abraham's hospitality: he serves only the best. Unlike the rich man in Nathan's parable who avoids serving a visitor with a sheep from his own flock (2 Sam 12:4), Abraham takes not just an animal of his own, but among the best of his herd.

> *He took curds and milk and the calf that had been prepared and set these before them; and he waited on them under the tree as they ate. (Gen18:8)*

It is difficult to know what to make of this verse in the light of Jewish dietary laws prohibiting the mixing of milk and meat. On the one hand, Abraham lived before the Torah was given on Sinai, so the laws of kashrut had not yet been codified. On the other hand, tradition has it that Abraham kept all the Sinai laws and was perhaps even a model for them, so he would have known about milk and meat. One answer to this puzzle is that time has been conflated in this verse; Abraham set the meat before the men only after they had digested their soft curds and milk. Alternatively, perhaps Abraham knew all along that they were angels, and assumed that the laws of kashrut do not apply to them.

No matter what, the discussion of kashrut here brings us back to another important aspect of hospitality: it is a two way street. The host requires a guest. Anyone who keeps the laws of kashrut will guess what is coming. There is little more uncomfortable than having to explain to a would-be generous host that you can't eat their food. It seems that the angels had no concerns on this matter; they agreed to eat without asking questions. But on the other hand, the two angels who go from Abraham's tent to Lot's home in Sodom and Gomorrah may be exercising due caution when they insist at first that they prefer to spend the night in the town square (Gen 19:2).

> *... He [Lot] prepared a feast for them and baked unleavened bread, and they ate. (Gen 19:3)*

Lot convinces his two visitors, now identified explicitly as "angels" rather than "men" as in the previous episode, to accept his hospitality. Seeking to contrast Abraham and Lot, some commentators point out that, unlike Abraham, Lot did not hurry to take care of his visitors and was therefore less hospitable. This seems unfair. Lot does after all beg them to sleep in his home, and on top of that prepares a feast (that word is not mentioned in connection with Abraham) and unleavened bread which, strictly kosher or otherwise, the angels eat.

> *And the older one said to the younger, "Our father is old, and there is not a man to consort with us in the way of all the world. Come, let us make our father drink wine, and let us lie with him, that we may maintain life through our father." That night they made their father drink wine, and the older one went in and lay with her father; he did not know when she lay down or when she rose. (Gen 19:31–33)*

It's hard to overlook the parallel between these verses and Gen 9:18–28, the culmination of another disaster. In both cases, a father gets blind drunk on wine in the presence of his children; something vaguely or explicitly sexual and definitely inappropriate ensues; and future hostile neighbors of Israel enter the scene. As far as food is concerned, the message seems to be clear. Wine can transform a regular meal into a feast worthy of a celebration, but there's nothing celebratory about drinking wine without food. Indeed, to judge from the experiences of Noah and Lot, wine drunk alone in situations like these is more likely to signal an attempt to come to terms with catastrophe (survivor guilt, perhaps?) than to celebrate its end.

> *Early next morning Abraham took some bread and a skin of water, and gave them to Hagar. He placed them over her shoulder, together with the child, and sent her away. (Gen 21:14)*

We don't know where Abraham thought Hagar would go when he sent her away, but he might have guessed that she would head towards home: Egypt. Even if she had chosen a different location, their starting point in the Negev meant that before long Hagar and Ishmael were likely to find themselves in the desert, as indeed was the case (v. 14). Given the likelihood of this outcome, it's worth asking why Abraham prepared food and water for the journey. Surely he knew that it wouldn't get them far in this kind of environment, and in the meantime would be just another burden for Hagar to shoulder. A devastating answer to the difficult question of why a parent might pack food for a journey with no return is suggested by Primo Levi's account of transports to death camps in his memoir *If This is a Man* (1959, pp 5–7):

> *All took leave from life in the manner which most suited them. Some praying, some deliberately drunk, others lustfully intoxicated for the last time. But the mothers stayed up to prepare the food for the journey with tender care, and washed their children and packed the luggage; and at dawn the barbed wire was full of children's washing hung out in the wind to dry. Nor did they forget the diapers, the toys, the cushions and the hundred other small things which mothers remember and which children always need. Would you not do the same? If you and your child were going to be killed tomorrow, would you not give him to eat today?*

Diana Lipton

Hayyei Sarah

Genesis 23:1–25:18

Kindness to Strangers

Malke Bina

In parshat Hayyei Sarah, Abraham sends his servant, traditionally identified as Eliezer, on a mission to find a wife for Abraham's son Isaac. As Eliezer assembled ten camels and headed towards Abraham's birthplace, he surely wondered how he would choose the right wife for his master's son.

When Eliezer arrived at Aram Naharayim, he prayed to God: "Let the maiden to whom I say, 'Please, lower your jug that I may drink,' and who replies, 'Drink, and I will also water your camels' – let her be the one whom You have decreed for Your servant Isaac . . ." (Gen 24:14).

The medieval French Jewish commentator Rashi says that offering water will be a sign that the young woman is worthy of Isaac because she is charitable and fit to enter the house of Abraham. Rabbi Samson Raphael Hirsch (Germany, 1808–1888) adds that this trait of *Gemilut Chassadim*, loving-kindness, was developed and brought into the world by Abraham and his family and it became their unique and identifying characteristic.

Abraham and Sarah are known for their unparalleled hospitality. By offering wayfarers sustenance they were – metaphorically – sustaining and nourishing humankind: strangers and those in need as well as family and friends. This quality is exemplified when Abraham sits at the entrance to his tent in the heat of the day and three strangers pass by (Gen 18:1–8). He urges them to rest, eat, and drink. He doesn't know they are angels. What matters is that they are wayfarers in need of hospitality, and he wants to provide it. *Gemilut Chassadim* permeated and defined Isaac's childhood home – part of his lifeblood. He needed a wife who would become part of the house of Abraham and embrace all its traditions.

After Rebekah passed the test, Isaac brought her into his mother Sarah's tent; he married her and loved her and he was comforted for the loss of his mother. Rashi explains that Rebekah became the image of Sarah. All the time that Sarah was alive, the candles in her tent burned from the eve of Sabbath to the eve of Sabbath; there was a blessing found in the dough which miraculously increased so there was always sufficient bread for the household and guests; and a cloud of Divine presence attached to the tent. When Sarah died, all this disappeared, and when Rebekah arrived, it all returned.

The story of Rebekah offering water to Eliezer and his camels reminds us that man is created in God's image and that respecting our fellow human beings by offering hospitality and sustenance is a profoundly Jewish way of serving God. This is a fundamental principle of our faith; a tradition learned from our matriarchs and patriarchs, passed down through the generations. This forms the foundation of the Jewish home.

RABBANIT MALKE BINA is the founder and Chancellor of MaTaN: The Sadie Rennert Women's Institute for Torah Studies in Jerusalem. She is the recipient of an Honorary Doctorate from Yeshiva University for her work in teaching Torah to women, aliyah, education and social services.

> *. . . She [Rebekah] went down to the spring, filled her jar, and came up. The servant ran toward her and said, "Please, let me sip a little water from your jar." "Drink, my lord," she said, and she quickly lowered her jar upon her hand and let him drink. When she had let him drink his fill, she said, "I will also draw for your camels, until they finish drinking." Quickly emptying her jar into the trough, she ran back to the well to draw, and she drew for all his camels. (Gen 24:16–20)*

As noted above in relation to Genesis 18:2, commentators often cite the speed with which Abraham offers rest and refreshment to the three angels as evidence of his exceptional hospitality. But even if speed was to an extent an established trope of Middle Eastern hospitality, there can be no doubt that Rebekah, exactly like her future father in law, exemplifies this virtue in spades. Perhaps Abraham's servant, "Eliezer," shows even more foresight than is usually credited to him when he devises his test to find Rebekah. She is not only a good fit for the family in general, but, like Abraham, capable of going the extra mile when it comes to hospitality. Sarah stays in the tent when the angels come (Gen 18:6), and does not go out to greet them. Abraham hurries at every step of the game, running to greet the strangers (Gen 18:2), rushing to issue instructions to Sarah and the servant boy, and telling them to be quick with the food (Gen 18.6). The boy for his part hastens to prepare the meal (Gen 18.7). Only Sarah, so far as we can tell, does not rush (though she presumably prepares the cakes in a timely fashion). Is there a hint here that the servant is not merely selecting a wife for Isaac, but also someone capable of taking on Abraham's mantle when the time comes and maintaining the family tradition of "over-the-top" hospitality to which we should all strive?

> *. . . He [Laban] went up to the man, who was still standing beside the camels at the spring. "Come in, O Blessed of the Lord," he said, "why do you remain outside, when I have made ready the house and a place for the camels?" So the man entered the house, and the camels were unloaded. The camels were given straw and feed, and water was brought to bathe his feet and the feet of the men with him. (Gen 24:30–32)*

The emphasis on camels in relation to Rebekah and Isaac begins when Abraham's servant includes them in his test for Rebekah's hospitality – she must take care of his animals as well as him – and climaxes when Rebekah falls off her camel as she sees her future husband (Gen 24:64, "alighted" in the NJPS translation; usually "fell" in Hebrew). Rebekah's brother Laban also contributes, taking care of the camels before Eliezer and his men. Anyone who has experience with camels will guess that he was motivated by more than concern for animal welfare. Tired, hungry, thirsty camels are not known for their patience and good tempers; it made sense to attend to them first. Each camel represents in addition significant wealth for its owner and an invaluable asset on a journey through the desert. Laban surely knew that Eliezer would prioritize his camels over himself and his men when it came to gratifying their need for food and drink.

> *But when food was set before him [Abraham's servant], he said, "I will not eat until I have told my tale." (Gen 24:33)*

It's easy to overlook the extent to which meals – formal and informal – serve to structure and punctuate our time. Just as many societies organize their days around prayer times (*shaḥarit, minḥa, maariv*), so they also organize their days around meals (breakfast, lunch, dinner). And if meals structure ordinary days, they play an even more important role on festival days (the three *seudot,* halakhically stipulated meals, of Shabbat and *ḥagim*).

In a different but, I think, related way, people use food to accent and punctuate events and activities that have no inherent connection to eating. Eating a special meal lends significance to an event, and refusing to eat until something has been accomplished highlights its importance. Eliezer could reasonably have said, "I'm starving – let me eat something and then I'll tell you why I've come." Instead, even though the food has been set temptingly in front of him, Eliezer insists that he won't eat until he's told his tale. By this means he demonstrates the seriousness of his mission and his utter commitment to it.

DIANA LIPTON

Toledot

Genesis 25:19–28:9

A Taste for Game

Jack M. Sasson

Does blind Isaac know what is happening as he readies to bless his son? This fundamental question arises from close reading of Genesis 27, a chapter that chronicles the spectacular deception that Rebekah and her preferred son Jacob perpetrate on the blind Isaac. As a character, Isaac has little of the adventurous spirit of his father Abraham – in fact most everything about his life is pre-ordained: his conception, his choice of bride, and his area of activity. He does not question his father's sanity when trussed for sacrifice, and his wife skirts his authority by questioning God directly. He also displays none of the chutzpah that his son Jacob had in abundance.

In fact, Isaac shows individuality just once: wishing to confer his blessing on his favored son, he charges Esau, a hunter, with preparing for the solemn occasion a meal, "such as I like" (Gen 27:4). Given the indiscriminate palate that has led him to give up his birthright (Gen 25:32–34), could Esau be trusted to satisfy Isaac's whim? Esau would have brought back quail, antelope, or deer (to list only what's kosher). After aiming his arrow so perfectly as to emulate proper *sheḥiṭah*, Esau would have skinned or feathered his catch before setting it on hot ashes or roasting it on a spit. Not bad, but hardly likely to satisfy a taste sharpened by home cooking.

For, as we know from Mesopotamian recipes dating to the early Second Millennium, good cooks had by then learned to let meat simmer in liquids, enriched with spices and herbs, and allowed to absorb flavors from fats and oils, seeds, vegetables, and legumes. When the scene in Genesis 27 opens, Rebekah has had years of married life in which to cultivate Isaac's taste. When she hears her husband give instruction to their oldest son, Rebekah knows what must be done to steer him away from a grievous error. God's will, as it had been imparted to her, had to be done.

As it happens, all of Isaac's operating senses are deployed the moment Jacob enters the room. He cannot see, so he touches the sheep-clad hands. He listens to Jacob's distinctive voice. He utters pointed questions to ferret out the truth, hardly fooled by what is unfurling. He asks for the food, tastes it, and recognizes it for being exactly the sort he loves. Its aroma betrays Rebekah's involvement. The wine he drinks is another sign of her expertise at pleasing him. So Isaac leans over to smell his son's clothing. It is Esau's best garment that Rebekah had forced on Jacob. Letting himself seem fooled, Isaac blesses that son whose garment it was ("Ah, the smell of my son . . ." Gen 27.27). In the process, however, he bestows his best hope on the son Rebekah had clothed.

Esau comes back, whines, and receives a lesser blessing. Isaac never touches the food Esau had prepared. Why would he? Isaac, it turns out, had a taste for game of another sort. It was he, after all, who gave Jacob his name, hence also determining his character.

JACK M. SASSON was Mary Jane Werthan Professor of Judaic and Biblical Studies Emeritus at Vanderbilt University. He retired to Chapel Hill, North Carolina. He researches the Bible and the Ancient Near East and has lectured internationally. Jack was born in Aleppo, Syria (1941), and became a US citizen in 1961. Alongside extensive scholarly work in Assyriology, he has published commentaries on the books of Ruth, Jonah, and Judges (1–12).

Isaac favored Esau because he had a taste for game; but Rebekah favored Jacob. (Gen 25:28)

Continuing now with the traditional interpretation of Isaac's role in the narrative, in an ideal world parents would not have "favorite" children, but in the real world they sometimes do. Reasons for the preference of one child over another, when that occurs, are varied and complex. For example, it seems that Jacob prefers Joseph because he was the first child (after a long wait) of Rachel, the beloved wife who died giving birth to her second son, Benjamin. In the case of the twins Jacob and Esau, one is preferred by his mother and one by his father. Both have pros and cons.

On the one hand, in a patriarchal society such as ancient Israel, it was arguably more advantageous to be a father's favorite child than a mother's. Yet the Bible is not short of stories in which the mother triumphs over the father when it comes to promoting offspring; think of Sarah and Isaac, and Bathsheba and Solomon. This turns out to be an example of the power of mother love: Rebekah's preference for Jacob outweighs Isaac's for Esau. A clue that this will be the case emerges from the verse that reports their different preferences. No justification is given for Rebekah's choice, as if Jacob is self-evidently more impressive than his brother and thus no comment is required. Isaac's choice of Esau, however, is undermined by its justification: "*because he had a taste for game.*" Isaac, it seems, is motivated not by a serious consideration of which of his sons is nobler in character, but by a slightly distasteful (in the context) taste for hunted meat.

> *Once when Jacob was cooking a stew, Esau came in from the open, famished. And Esau said to Jacob, "Give me some of that red stuff to gulp down, for I am famished" – which is why he was named Edom. (Gen 25:29–30)*

If Esau as an individual is undermined by his association with hunting and preparing game, so are his descendants doubly undermined by being associated with lentil soup. As reported here, their name is derived from the "red stuff" for which Esau was willing to sell his birthright. The bargain suggests a poor sense of priority on Esau's part, as well as a tendency to exaggerate – he can't really have been close to death. Yet Esau's hyperbolic language is not completely unfamiliar. It's not unusual to hear children claiming to be "famished" when they come home from school, or adults "dying" for a glass of water or a cup of coffee. Such are the physical and psychological effects of hunger that there is a sense in which this is not hyperbole – they really mean it.

Jacob then gave Esau bread and lentil stew; he ate and drank, and he rose and went away. (Gen 25:34)

This is one of several cases in which someone asks for or is offered a particular dish which, when served, turns out to come with bread on the side. One explanation for this is that bread takes the place of cutlery in many cuisines, including those typical of the Middle East. Another explanation is that a meal was no more likely to be served without bread than without water. Both are thus taken for granted, as in this verse, which reports that Esau drank without reporting that he was served water.

There was a famine in the land – aside from the previous famine that had occurred in the days of Abraham – and Isaac went to Abimelech, king of the Philistines, in Gerar. (Gen 26:1)

The reference in this verse to a famine in the days of Abraham links this episode in the life of Isaac to one of two similar episodes in the life of his father. It was famine that drove Abraham to Egypt, where he too claimed that his wife was his sister and subsequently experienced a problematic engagement with a foreign ruler (Genesis 12). History repeats itself and children repeat the mistakes of their parents. But references to famine function as historical markers as well as a family ones. Certain catastrophic events survive in the collective consciousness as points around which to organize other events in the history of a people. They include earthquakes (Amos 1), battles and attacks (September 11, 2001), and famines (Ireland's Great Potato Famine).

And he [Isaac] said, "I am old now, and I do not know how soon I may die. Take your gear, your quiver and bow, and go out into the open and hunt me some game. Then prepare a dish for me such as I like, and bring it to me to eat, so that I may give you my innermost blessing before I die. (Gen 27:2–5)

In *The Omnivore's Dilemma*, a powerful book about the way we eat today, Michael Pollan sets out to prepare a meal consisting entirely of ingredients with which he has been intimately involved. For a year, he grows, forages and, eventually, hunts. Kashrut is not a concern for Pollan; his meat course is a wild boar that he shot himself. There were some rocky moments along the way – gutting the boar turned out to be more challenging than shooting it, not least because of its intense "gamey" aroma – but at the end he feels a sense of connection with, and gratitude for, the food he's eating: something approximating a blessing. The detailed instructions that Isaac issued to Esau ensured that Isaac would eat a meal in which his son was involved at every stage, from taking up weapons, through the hunting expedition, to preparing and serving the meal. Is it possible that the intimate connection between Esau and the dish was a crucial element in Isaac's ability to give him his blessing?

> *Rebekah said to her son Jacob, "I overheard your father speaking to your brother Esau, saying, 'Bring me some game and prepare a dish for me to eat, that I may bless you, with the* Lord*'s approval, before I die.' Now, my son, listen carefully as I instruct you. Go to the flock and fetch me two choice kids, and I will make of them a dish for your father, such as he likes. Then take it to your father to eat, in order that he may bless you before he dies." (Gen 27:6–10)*

Rebekah's deception in passing off Jacob as Esau by wrapping his arms in goat skin is mirrored in her cooking: she tries to pass off baby goat (the source of the aforementioned hairy skin) as game. Perhaps Rebekah had no choice – Jacob was no hunter. Or perhaps there was no time – Jacob had to get to Isaac before Esau came home. Either way, she must have trusted her culinary ability to disguise one kind of meat as another. Disguise is not a term that usually springs to when it comes to food preparation, and yet there is a sense in which most cooking can be described by the similar, though less loaded, term: transformation. Raw ingredients are skinned and gutted, peeled and de-seeded, cut, chopped, sliced, sauced and spiced, exposed to high temperatures, and served to diners who often cannot tell what they are eating. But this raises a crucial difference between disguise and transformation. Most cooks do not intend to deceive but rather to create a new whole that is more than the sum of its parts. And perhaps this is precisely what Rebekah intended for Jacob . . .

> *He [Jacob] got them and brought them to his mother, and his mother prepared a dish such as his father liked . . . Then she put in the hands of her son Jacob the dish and the bread that she had prepared. (Gen 27:14, 17)*

The interaction between Jacob and Rebekah over food follows a pattern that is familiar in many societies, ancient, and modern: males procure and females prepare. An added factor in this particular equation could have been that Rebekah was most likely to know how to prepare what her husband liked to eat, at least when it came to non-hunted meat. Their joint responsibility for the meal also mirrors their joint participation in the deception. It's worth noting that once again, bread is not mentioned in advance but is nevertheless served as part of the meal.

> *Jacob said to his father, "I am Esau, your first-born; I have done as you told me. Pray sit up and eat of my game, that you may give me your innermost blessing." (Gen 27:19)*

Jacob misleads his father on two counts: his own identity, and the identity of the food he has brought with him. In the context of these deceptions, Jacob's gentle request that his father should "sit up" is uncomfortable. It serves as a reminder that Isaac is lying, blind and weak, on his deathbed, waiting for his last taste of earthly pleasure.

> *He [Isaac] asked, "Are you really my son Esau?" And when he said, "I am," he said, "Serve me and let me eat of my son's game that I may give you my innermost blessing." So he served him and he ate, and he brought him wine and he drank. (Gen 27:24–25)*

This verse reveals the extent to which meals and blessing are inextricably connected. It's not merely that Isaac wants a last taste of game before he dies – thought surely he does. The blessing is contractual, and requires reciprocity, an element of exchange. Isaac literally could not confer this blessing on his son – either son – without first eating the meal he has served him. This explains the presence of the word "[so] that" in the sentence: "Let me eat of my son's game [so] that I may give you my innermost blessing." It's easy to make the mistake of seeing food as the icing on the cake of a ritual. It's not. The meal is one of the cake's essential ingredients.

> *No sooner had Jacob left . . . than his brother Esau came back from his hunt. He too prepared a dish and brought it to his father. And he said to his father, "Let my father sit up and eat of his son's game, so that you may give me your innermost blessing." (Gen 27:30–31)*

Whereas Jacob procures the food and Rebekah prepares it, Esau is responsible for both components of the meal. Cooking has historically been a highly gendered activity, but the divisions of labor can be unpredictable. For example, even in societies in which food in a domestic setting is most likely to be prepared by women, "professional cooks" are most likely to be men. For different reasons, men are more likely than women to undertake "outdoor" cooking such as barbecuing. A possible reason for this is that barbecues seem more intimately connected than other cooking methods to the animals being prepared. Perhaps they evoke past worlds where men like Esau went out and hunted animals they brought home and cooked over fire. Or perhaps the entire process is seen as too visceral and unrefined for women – flames, skewers, sizzling flesh, dripping fat, the heady aroma of dead animals.

> *Isaac was seized with very violent trembling. "Who was it then," he demanded, "that hunted game and brought it to me? Moreover, I ate of it before you came, and I blessed him; now he must remain blessed!" (Gen 27:33)*

Isaac, it seems, had not internalized Jacob's deception, even if he was suspicious enough to question him about the sound of his voice and the surprising speed with which he hunted and prepared his game. Even now, he still believes he ate game not goat – Rebekah must have been a skillful cook. Isaac's words confirm the inextricable link between the meal and the blessing. Even if he could theoretically have retracted or cancelled the words of his blessing, he is bound to it by having eaten the meal prepared by his wife and served to him by his younger son.

DIANA LIPTON

Va-Yetse'

Genesis 28:10–32:3

Bargaining for Bread

Alicia Ostriker

Waking from an extraordinary and beautiful dream of angels ascending and descending a ladder to heaven, and God promising him land, and seed "as the dust of the earth" that will spread in every direction and in whom "all the families of the earth shall bless themselves" (Gen 28:14), Jacob is afraid, or awed. He recognizes immediately that "the Lord is present in this place and I did not know it" (Gen 28:16). Is it fear, or awe, that prompts the deceptively simple vow that Jacob proceeds to utter?

> *Jacob then made a vow, saying, "If God remains with me, if He protects me on this journey that I am making, and gives me bread to eat and clothing to wear, and if I return safe to my father's house - the Lord shall be my God. And this stone, which I have set for a pillar, shall be God's abode; and of all that You give me, I will set aside a tithe for You." (Gen 28:20–22)*

After the unconditional and immense magnitude of God's promise, Jacob asks for only the most basic necessities: food, clothing, survival, safe return. "Bread" is mentioned for the first time in Genesis at this moment, and is clearly to be understood here as meaning "enough to eat." The request is a humble one, and seems at first glance to exemplify Jacob's humility. But does he recall, in the back of his mind, that incidents involving food and clothing – cheating his brother – are what got him where he is this morning? Does he perhaps fear that he does not deserve what he is asking for? Is this why his vow takes a conditional form, the form of a virtual bargain, promising to worship God in exchange for being allowed to survive?

Or perhaps the vow is not quite as humble as it seems. The proposal "If God will be with me. . . . then the LORD will be my God" uses both the generic name for a deity and the name by which Jacob's ancestors Abraham and Isaac knew their God. This tacitly presumes that Jacob has the option of worshiping other gods – and the form of the bargain recalls the bargain Jacob made with Esau: I'll give you the pottage if you give me your birthright. It is as if he is putting himself in the role of Esau the beseecher. But if so, then God is in the role of Jacob . . . receiving a birthright. Is this humility, or is it chutzpah? Jacob's further promise, that the place will be named Beth-El and be (literally and spiritually) God's house, links him to Abraham, who named the mountain on which he almost sacrificed his son (Gen 22:14). The final aspect of his promise, to offer a tenth of whatever God gives him beyond mere survival, implies the expectation of prosperity. He hopes for more than just enough "bread."

Jacob in his vow, as throughout his story, is deeply human and deeply ambiguous. He is both a cheat and an honest man. He is both humble and ambitious. He is both frightened and bold. Overwhelmed by his visionary dream, he draws from his inner being the knowledge that life itself – clothing, safety and food – can never be guaranteed by one's own efforts, but are the gift of God. For this we may honor him.

ALICIA OSTRIKER is a poet and critic, recipient of Guggenheim and Rockefeller Foundation fellowships, and twice a finalist for a National Book Award. Her work appears in many journals and anthologies of Jewish poetry, and her collection, *The Book of Seventy*, received a 2010 National Jewish Book Award. As a critic she has written several books on the Bible, including *Feminist Revision and the Bible: the Bucknell Lectures on Literary Theory* and *For the Love of God: the Bible as an Open Book*, a set of essays on Song of Songs, Ruth, Psalms, Ecclesiastes, Jonah, and Job. She is Professor Emerita of English Literature, Rutgers University.

He [Jacob] said, "It is still broad daylight, too early to round up the animals; water the flock and take them to pasture." But they said, "We cannot, until all the flocks are rounded up; then the stone is rolled off the mouth of the well and we water the sheep." (Gen 29:7–8)

Jacob doesn't know it yet, but he is about to meet for the first time his beloved wife, Rachel. The circumstances of their encounter bode well. Springs and wells, signifying fertility, were popular meeting places for couples in the ancient world (Moses too meets his wife by a well, Exod 2:15–22), and as we will see below, animals also mated when they came to drink (Gen 30:38). It was particularly auspicious that Jacob used his strength to remove the stone from the well, opening up a source of life-giving fluid – water in this case.

From now on, sheep and shepherding will play a prominent role in the lives of Jacob and Rachel, but the meeting at the well turns out to be predictive in more explicit ways: after a seven year wait, Jacob and Rachel get married, and Laban "gathers" (from the Hebrew verb *asaf*) the people for a feast (Gen 29:22). After another long wait, "Rachel" (a noun meaning "ewe" in Hebrew), gives birth to their first-born son, Joseph (Yosef, again from the Hebrew verb *asaf*). "God has 'removed' [again *asaf*] my shame" (Gen 30:23), Rachel exclaims when Joseph is born. "May the Lord 'add' [again *asaf*] another son for me" (v. 24). The verb *asaf* also occurs twice in Jacob's first conversation with the shepherds, which takes place immediately after Rachel's arrival at the well with her father's sheep. ". . . It is too early to 'round up' [*asaf*] the animals, water the flock, and take them to pasture," Jacob says (v. 7). "We can't," reply the shepherds, "until all the flocks are 'rounded up' [*asaf*]; then the stone is rolled off and we water the sheep" (v. 8). How differently Jacob's life would have turned out had he not stopped to speak to a group of shepherds preparing to give food and drink to their sheep.

And Laban gathered all the people of the place and made a feast. (Gen 29:22)

The feast that Laban makes in honor of Jacob's marriage to Rachel is more than a means to celebrate; it's part of the contract. Jacob has fulfilled his prior obligations, working for seven years for his bride (v. 20), and is ready to fulfill his next role in the marriage contract: "Give me my wife [literally, "my woman"] . . . that I may cohabit with her [literally, "go into her"]" (v.21). Before this can take place, there must be a feast (v. 22), the sign of Laban's commitment to the marriage. Just one problem remained. Laban was indeed committed to Jacob's marriage to his daughter, but he had in mind a different daughter.

> *Once, at the time of the wheat harvest, Reuben came upon some mandrakes in the field and brought them to his mother Leah. Rachel said to Leah, "Please give me some of your son's mandrakes." But she said to her, "Was it not enough for you to take away my husband, that you would also take away my son's mandrakes?" Rachel replied, "I promise, he shall lie with you tonight, in exchange for your son's mandrakes." (Gen 30:14–15)*

The Hebrew word translated here as "mandrakes" is *dudaim*. Elsewhere in the Bible words with the same root letters are associated with love, as in "My beloved [*dodi*] is mine and I am his" (Song 2:16). It therefore makes sense to understand them as some sort of aphrodisiac or aid to conception. This raises several difficulties, however, not least that it's odd for a son to give his mother a love potion. It's worth noting too that, without the help of the mandrakes, Leah gets pregnant that night with her fifth son. At the same time, Rachel does not seem to have benefitted from them. Her pregnancy is announced a few verses later (v. 22), but since Leah has given birth to her sixth son and a daughter in the meantime, there's no reason to link it with the mandrakes and every reason to attribute it to God, "Now God remembered Rachel . . ."

> *Jacob then got fresh shoots of poplar, and of almond and plane, and peeled white stripes in them, laying bare the white of the shoots. The rods that he had peeled he set up in front of the goats in the troughs, the water receptacles, that the goats came to drink from. Their mating occurred when they came to drink . . . (Gen 30:37–38)*

Drinking is a lot more than just a solution for thirst. In this case, it provides an opportunity for animals to mate. This will come as no surprise to anyone familiar with Israel's parched summers, when flocks can walk all day with no glimpse of green grass, still less water. It makes sense that they would converge at a water source as the sun begins to set, and that, as temperatures drop and their energy levels rise, they would take the opportunity to be fruitful and multiply.

> *Then Laban spoke up and said to Jacob, ". . . Come, then, let us make a pact, you and I, that there may be a witness between you and me." Thereupon Jacob took a stone and set it up as a pillar. And Jacob said to his kinsmen, "Gather stones." So they took stones and made a mound; and they partook of a meal there by the mound. (Gen 31:43–46)*

A lot of water has passed under the bridge since Jacob removed the stone from the well and met Rachel, his future wife. Once again he moves a heavy stone, this time setting it up as pillar to mark a pact of mutual non-intervention with his father-in-law, Laban. As with Jacob and Rachel's wedding feast, the meal they eat by the mound has a symbolic or ritual function, sealing the pact. This time, there are no tricks, and Laban exits stage.

DIANA LIPTON

Va-Yishlah

Genesis 32:4–36:43

Food, Sex, and Life

Jonathan Price

The prohibition against eating the *gid hanasheh*, understood today as the sciatic nerve in the hind quarters of four-legged mammals, is included in the standard 613 mitzvot. The only place in the Torah where it is related is in parashat Va-Yishlah, as an explanation for the origin of an existing practice (Gen 32:33). The prohibition is never given in the form "Thou shalt not eat . . ." – either here or, significantly, after Sinai. This led the rabbis to wonder whether it was taught at Sinai, or whether its avoidance had begun already previously. That interesting question, discussed in Mishnah Hullin 7:6, the corresponding Gemara (Babylonian Talmud Hullin 101b) and later sources (e.g. Rambam, commentary on that Mishnah), is not our preoccupation here.

The *gid hanasheh* is one of three parts of kosher animals which may not be eaten. The other two are blood and a certain kind of fat around vital organs, called *ḥelev*. The prohibition of eating blood is repeated several times in the Torah, with a clear reason: "the blood is the life; you must not consume the life with the flesh" (Deut 12:23). The heart, kidneys, liver and other blood-rich organs may be eaten after the blood is drained. No such specific reason is given by the Torah for *ḥelev*.

The reason for the prohibition of the sciatic nerve *is* given, but the explanation offered by the Torah is at first glance more confusing than clarifying. Jacob had just wrestled with "a man" – whether with a man or angel, named or unknown, an actual physical presence or himself "alone," on earth or in a higher spiritual realm – these classic questions comprise the mystery which each generation of readers must confront on its own terms. What is not thought as mysterious, but rather perplexing, is the sequel to the wrestling match. As Jacob was prevailing, his opponent injured "the socket of his hip," so that after he prevailed and became Israel, "he was limping on his hip – that is why the children of Israel to this day do not eat the thigh-muscle [*gid hanasheh*] that is on the socket of the hip."

What does this "that is why" really explain? Do we avoid eating that nerve for symbolic reasons or an inherent quality? While Jacob had the kind of blemish which would disqualify an animal from kosher slaughter, a healthy animal with an intact nerve would not be disqualified on those grounds. If the reason is symbolic, is it commemoration of the wound, i.e., Jacob's escape from near-defeat (how close we came to destruction!), or celebration of his victory, a sign of Israel's future redemption?

It is possible to understand the disqualification as relating to an inherent quality in the nerve (the following is offered as a line of inquiry rather than a definitive conclusion). The "that is why" can be read as the end of a logical sequence: Jacob was limping from an injury on the sciatic nerve, *thus* the nerve has a vital function, *that is why* this vital function forbids its consumption. This would make the forbidden nerve comparable to blood: it contains a life force, but the parts of the body it serves may be consumed after its removal.

But what life-force? Some exegetes (see *Da'at Mikra* on Gen 32:6 and 33) have taught that the injury to Jacob's thigh muscle, in his wrestling match, was in fact an injury to his sexual organ. The association of a man's thigh with his reproductive powers is well established in the Torah; Jacob's offspring are in fact called 'those who come forth from his thigh' (Gen 46:26). It is also taught that when Abraham had his servant take an oath and said "put your hand under my thigh," and when Jacob had Joseph do the same, that the "thigh" was really their sexual organ (Gen 24:2–3, 37:29, cf. Rashi on Gen 24:2).

The connection between the sexual organ and truthful testimony is prevalent in other ancient cultures; in fact the word "testimony" comes from the same Latin root as "testicle." Oaths were confirmed by a man's most vital power. Moreover, *gid* in rabbinic Hebrew can mean the male sexual organ (e.g. Mishnah Yebamot 8:2). Finally, according to another tradition in Tosafot (cited in *Da'at Mikra* 437 n. 95), the *gid hanasheh*, a nerve diffused throughout the thigh, was the source of a man's seed.

Thus the nerve in Jacob's thigh represents his reproductive powers, his life. He limped because his *gid hanasheh* – his thigh-muscle, his sexual power, and his identity – was impaired. Just as the blood, which carries the life-force, may not be eaten, but the organs to which it brings life (and which themselves are essential for life) may be, so the thigh-muscle (and testicles) may be eaten, but only after the source and vehicle of their vitality, the sciatic nerve, has been removed. (Testicles appear on the menu of Israeli steak joints which tourists do not often visit; the delicacy should not contain semen, see Babylonian Talmud, Hullin 93b).

We are thus permitted to eat filet mignon and other hind-quarter cuts only if this vital nerve is removed. It is a difficult process requiring precise knowledge and great dexterity, so that outside Israel the hindquarters are generally sold to non-kosher butchers. That is why brisket, from the breast, is far more common in Jewish cuisine than round roast.

When we do eat a leg of lamb, filet mignon, sirloin steak, or other delicate cuts of hind-quarter meat, we should be even more appreciative of the mindfulness, the attentiveness, the awe and respect, which are embedded in the laws and practices of kashrut. It is meat from which a life-force, like blood, has been removed. The sanctification of food is the sanctification of life.

JONATHAN J. PRICE teaches in the Classics Department at Tel Aviv University, Israel. He received his Ph.D. in Classics from Princeton University, USA, and has published two books: *Jerusalem Under Siege: The Collapse of the Jewish State, 66-70 C.E* (1992), and *Thucydides and Internal Conflict* (2001). He was the general editor and the author of the introduction for a translation into Hebrew (by Lisa Ullmann) of *Josephus, Jewish Wars* (2010), and he was the co-editor of three volumes (so far) of inscriptions from the Hellenistic and Roman periods in Israel.

His academic interests include ancient historiography, rhetoric and the writing of history, internal war as an unsolved historical problem, and ancient imperialism.

> *After spending the night there, he selected from what was at hand these presents for his brother Esau: 200 she-goats and 20 he-goats; 200 ewes and 20 rams; 30 milch camels with their colts; 40 cows and 10 bulls; 20 she-asses and 10 he-asses. (Gen 32:14–16)*

The idea of giving food is familiar – from wine and chocolates for dinner parties, through fruit platters for holidays, to chicken soup for the sick – but Jacob takes food as gift to a whole new level. When he sets out to meet his brother Esau, Jacob takes his worldly goods with him. He has accumulated a lot in his many years of working for Laban: cattle, asses, sheep, and male and female slaves. Food, or rather the means of producing food, like slaves, represents property and wealth. When, after a long separation that began in tense circumstances (Genesis 27), Jacob wants to appease and impress Esau, he sends a generous gift ahead.

This list of animals (above) is interesting both because it indicates Jacob's considerable wealth – he could afford to give all this away – and because it is suggestive about the relationship between living animals and food on the table, or the blanket, in the nomadic world. Goats and sheep must have been primarily a source of milk, which is why there are so many females in relation to males. Eventually, however, the females grow old and stop producing milk, at which time they could be eaten or sacrificed. It was therefore necessary to keep a number of male goats and sheep on hand, to replenish the female flock. If male kids and lambs were born, they could replace an older male, or be eaten or sacrificed. Jacob must have seen 20 male goats and sheep to 200 females as a viable ratio for these purposes.

According to the dietary laws, camels could not have been eaten or sacrificed, and their milk could not have been drunk. This may explain why Jacob sends no males other than the dependent offspring of the 30 females. The absence of males indicates that a small number of male camels is sufficient to maintain a large number of females. Jacob must have assumed that Esau would have his own stud. It may also hint at the relative difficulty of travelling with adult male camels versus females

(males are more temperamental and aggressive, especially when females are around) and that female camels are better suited than males for carrying loads and people. The list suggests that this is not the case for asses, hence the 10 males for 20 females. This may also reflect the fact that asses live shorter lives than camels and need to be replaced more often; that male asses are easier to control than male camels, so there was less of a down-side to bringing them; and perhaps that they perform better than females as beasts of burden and that therefore there was even an advantage to bringing them.

It is tempting to skim biblical lists, but this one is as informative as modern-day supermarket shopping lists, recipe books, and restaurant and take-out bills about what Jacob and his family ate, and the extent to which their lives revolved around food.

> *That is why the children of Israel to this day do not eat the thigh muscle that is on the socket of the hip, since Jacob's hip-socket was wrenched at the thigh muscle. (Gen 32:33)*

Most of the Bible's dietary laws occur in legally and ritually oriented passages of the books of Leviticus (especially ch 11) and Deuteronomy (especially 14:3–21). In the main, they take the form of rules, positive and negative, about the living creatures that are permitted or prohibited as food for the people of Israel. When it comes to their eligibility to be eaten, animals, birds, and fish are categorized according to various combinations of physical attributes such as cloven hooves, fins and scales, and wings, habits such as chewing the cud and "swarming," and habitats such as dwelling on land or in water. In short, animals are deemed edible or inedible by legal taxonomies concerning dead meat, not by stories in which they feature as living beings.

That may sound self-evident; even if we do not presume to be able to explain or justify all the laws of kashrut, we do not generally think of them as anecdotal. But it could easily have been otherwise. Our assessment of the qualities and characteristics of many biblical peoples originates in part in episodes from their own lives or those of their ancestors. The Canaanites are destined to be slaves to their brothers (Gen 9:25) because their ancestor Ham saw his father Noah naked in his tent (Gen 9:22). Ammonites and Moabites are excluded from joining the congregation of Israel because they acted inhospitably towards Israel in the desert and hired the prophet

Balaam to curse Israel (Deut 23:4-7). Their own problems began when their ancestors were conceived from the incestuous unions of Lot and his daughters after Sodom and Gomorrah (Gen 19:36–38).

Yet the Eden story contains no postscript explaining that snakes are forbidden as food, let alone etrogs or apples or whatever kind of fruit it was that grew on the tree of knowledge of good and evil. The story of Balaam is not rounded off with a reminder that Israelites do not eat donkeys out of respect for the ass who tried to prevent her master from cursing Israel (Num 22:22–30), and nowhere among the lists of prohibited animals is there a warning against eating creatures, such as snakes and asses, that have been known to mimic humans and speak. Veal is not forever off-limits because of the Golden Calf (Exod 32:4), and the virtues of roast lamb are not extolled following the Akedah (Gen 22:13). More than this, it is hard to think of biblical narratives that showcase, even in passing, the food laws in action. Setting aside the decision of Daniel and his friends to be vegetarian in Babylon (Dan 1:8–16), we would search almost in vain for allusions to the laws of kashrut in biblical narratives. Where is it recorded that Rebekah went out to buy fish, but all that was remained were the types of fish that the Philistines eat? Or that Jacob was careful to drain the blood from the deer he slaughtered to make his father's favorite soup?

The account of Jacob's wrestling with the angel concludes with a fascinating exception to the general rule that the biblical laws of kashrut are neither explained nor exemplified in biblical narratives (even though it concerns food, I am not counting the instruction to eat matzah as a dietary law). Here we find the Bible's only reference to the prohibition against eating not a certain type of animal, but a specific body part, and it is derived from a story – not about an animal, but about an illustrious ancestor. Following the injury to Jacob's thigh-muscle in his wrestling match with the angel, the sciatic nerve in the hind quarters of four-legged mammals is forever off-limits.

> *But he said to him, "My lord knows that the children are frail and that the flocks and herds, which are nursing, are a care to me; if they are driven hard in a single day, all the flocks will die." (Gen 33:13)*

Once Jacob and Esau have been reunited and Jacob has convinced his brother to accept his generous gift (Gen 33:9–11), we catch a rare glimpse of what must have been a dominant concern among nomadic peoples:

Jacob must account for the needs of his children and his animals when he plans his itinerary. Concerned, for different reasons, with the welfare of both groups, Jacob sends his brother ahead and travels slowly behind.

> *But Jacob journeyed on to Succoth, and built a house for himself and stalls for his cattle; that is why the place was called Succoth. (Gen 33:17)*

On route to Shechem, Jacob arrives at a place called Succoth, where he builds a house (*bayit*) for himself and stalls (*succoth*) for his animals. Succoth are best known as the temporary shelters in which the Israelites lived during their wilderness wanderings, but on this occasion, the structures that gave their name to the place were intended for animals, not people. Not for the first time, we see the extent to which animal and human welfare were intertwined.

> *For their possessions were too many for them to dwell together, and the land where they sojourned could not support them because of their livestock. (Gen 36:7–8)*

Here we see, not for the first time, another consequence of owning animals. According to Esau's genealogy, Esau separates from Jacob and leaves the land of Canaan, taking his family and all his possessions with him, because the grazing land was not sufficient for their many cattle. On this view, Esau's decision to make his home in the hill country of Seir, that is Edom, was motivated by the demands of owning animals, the source of his economic security and sustenance. Precisely the same concerns motivated Lot's decision to move to the Jordan plains, leaving Abraham in the land of Canaan (Gen 13:1–12).

DIANA LIPTON

Va-Yeshev

Genesis 37:1–40:23

Bread With Another Meaning

Stefan C. Reif

Faced with the enticing invitation to have an affair with his boss' mature wife, young Joseph tries to avoid the temptation by convincing her that this would be a terrible betrayal of the trust placed in him. ". . . Look, with me here, my master gives no thought to anything in this house, and all that he owns he has placed in my hands. He wields no more authority in this house than I, and he has withheld nothing from me except yourself, since you are his wife" (Gen 39:8). When, a few verses earlier, the narrative introduces this state of affairs, it describes it in almost exactly the same terms as Joseph does in his moralizing speech: "He [Potiphar] left all that he had in Joseph's hands and, with him there, he paid attention to nothing save the food that he ate. Now Joseph was well built and handsome" (Gen 39:6). It mentions that there was no interference from the master and total control by Joseph. Only one thing was forbidden to him, that is, his master's food. Not his wife, just access to the contents of his freezer?

King Ahab tries desperately to persuade Naboth to sell him his vineyard but his stubborn subject withstands the king's overtures. No sale, no exchange. Being a Jewish king, he sees no solution to this and goes home thoroughly miserable. He lies down on his bed, depressed and bad-tempered, refusing to take what is being offered by his wife Jezebel, *Why are you so distant? Why won't you have some-*

thing? I shall get you Naboth's vineyard. Now come on and have a bit. According to the text, Ahab would *eat no bread*. Really? Was Jezebel offering a freshly delivered pizza? (1 Kgs 21:1–7).

The adulterous woman described in the book of Proverbs thoroughly enjoys what she does and thinks that she has done absolutely nothing wrong. The young man who participates with her risks everything. To the extent of a "loaf of bread," says the proverb of him. "Eating and wiping her mouth afterwards" says the proverb of her. So they each had a splendid meal of shwarma and pita bread, did they? (Prov 6:24–29, 30:20).

Jethro has seven daughters. He sends them to the well, the shopping mall of the day, perhaps hoping that, while they are drawing water, some wandering Egyptian prince might sweep one (or more?) of them off their feet and relieve him of at least some financial worries. His dream comes true but they don't see the potential and let Prince Moses off the hook. "Summon him immediately," he tells them, "he might have a meal." And then he gives him his daughter Zipporah. Exactly which kind of meal did Jethro (Exod 2:16–21) have in mind?

The Israelites of Jeremiah's day, immigrants to Egypt with him, are not very loyal to the religious ideals that motivated the prophet. The men and the women take pride in the fact that they offer incense to the goddess of heaven, pour out idolatrous libations and engage in disgusting activities. They themselves say that they have had a great time and "eaten their fill of bread." Now what exactly was it that always accompanied such idolatrous behavior in the ancient world (Jer 34:15–24) – a tuna sandwich?

Eating as metaphor for sex is a common element in literature and in popular parlance. Might we also find it in these biblical stories?

STEFAN C. REIF is Professor Emeritus of Medieval Hebrew Studies, University of Cambridge, England; Fellow of St John's College Cambridge; and former Director of Cambridge University's Taylor-Schechter Genizah Research Unit, where – though residing also in Israel – he now serves as a consultant. His many publications include *Judaism and Hebrew Prayer*, *A Jewish Archive from Old Cairo*, *Problems with Prayers*, and *Jewish Prayer Texts from the Cairo Genizah*.

> *When Joseph came up to his brothers, they stripped Joseph of his tunic, the ornamented tunic that he was wearing, and took him and cast him into the pit. The pit was empty; there was no water in it. Then they sat down to a meal." (Gen 37:23–25)*

Joseph's brothers abandon him to almost certain death in a pit without water in the middle of nowhere . . . and have a picnic. What explains this shocking juxtaposition? One possibility is that its purpose is to underline the sheer callousness of Joseph's brothers. What kind of people can eat a meal, rewarding themselves with pleasure and life-giving sustenance, minutes after effectively killing their own brother? Another possibility that the meal they eat together has a legal-ritual function. It seals the agreement between them and confirms that, just as they are eating together now, they acted together with a single intent when they left Joseph for dead in the pit, and will act together again when they confront their father with the news that his favorite son is dead.

> *Then the chief cupbearer told his dream to Joseph . . . Pharaoh's cup was in my hand, and I took the grapes, pressed them into Pharaoh's cup, and placed the cup in Pharaoh's hand. (Gen 40:9, 11)*

People routinely dream of themselves living their own lives, but with a twist. The twist here is that in "real life," the cupbearer would not have *made* the wine he served to Pharaoh. What explains this unexpected feature of his dream? First, it highlights the responsibility and the power that came with the cupbearer's job. Had he wanted to kill Pharaoh, as Ahasuerus' servants later plotted to overthrow their king (Esth 2:21–23), the cupbearer was in a perfect position to poison him. (There are intriguing verbal parallels between this episode in the Joseph narrative and the account of threats to the king described in Esther, for example, the perpetrators in both are impaled on stakes.) Second, the potentially sinister image of squeezing grape juice – possibly red and therefore blood-like – into a cup suggests that the idea of killing Pharaoh, or being accused of killing him, may indeed have been present in the cup bearer's dreaming unconscious. Had he been imprisoned as a suspect in a plot against the king? Topping it all, the cupbearer's squeezing the grapes into the cup himself attests to his innocence. He knows exactly what Pharaoh is drinking because in his dream he oversees the entire process of production, from the blossoming of the vines to the pouring of the wine.

> *When the chief baker saw how favorably he had interpreted, he said to Joseph, "In my dream, similarly, there were three openwork baskets on my head. In the uppermost basket were all kinds of food for Pharaoh that a baker prepares; and the birds were eating it out of the basket above my head." (Gen 40:16–17)*

The baker too dreams of himself carrying out his professional duties, but this time the twist works in the opposite direction. Whereas a cupbearer in Pharaoh's court could have been expected to serve wine but not make it, a court baker could have been expected to prepare bread and cakes, but not deliver them. Like the cupbearer, the baker made an obvious target for anyone seeking to harm Pharaoh. Had he been paid to deliver baked goods prepared by someone else in another kitchen with the intention of poisoning Egypt's ruler? Did he in fact bake the bread himself and then have a wish-fulfillment dream in which he didn't? Either way, the fact that he dreamed of taking bread to Pharaoh but not of making it may hint that he was in prison accused of plotting to poison the king. The image of the birds eating bread from a basket on his head, foreshadowing birds that would swoop down to eat his flesh after he has been impaled on a stake, suggests that the baker was guilty as charged.

> *On the third day – his birthday – Pharaoh made a banquet for all his officials, and he singled out his chief cupbearer and his chief baker from among his officials. (Gen 40:20)*

The notion of a birthday party is so familiar as to pass unremarked. But why do people routinely serve and eat special food, if only a symbolic cake, on their birthdays? An explanation that springs to mind is that birthdays celebrate another year of life, and eating and drinking are among the most life-affirming of all human activities. Food represents life. The same logic may explain a more obvious question that emerges from this verse. Why did Pharaoh single out the cupbearer and the chief baker from among all his officials? They are the two most closely connected with life-affirming food. Much more intriguingly, Pharaoh is celebrating another year of his own life by using two court prisoners to dramatize the choice between life and death. The cupbearer – innocent if his dream, as interpreted above, is a reliable guide – gets to live; the baker – guilty according to his dream as interpreted here – is sentenced to death.

DIANA LIPTON

Mikkets

Genesis 41:1–44:17

One could not tell that they had consumed them

Meira Polliack

Parashat Mikkets opens with a striking panorama: Pharaoh dreams that he is standing by the Nile when he sees seven "handsome," "sturdy" cows ascend from the river and graze nearby. Seconds later, the idyllic pastoral scene is shattered, and Pharaoh's dream turns into a nightmare: seven "ugly" gaunt cows ascend after the handsome, sturdy cows. But instead of grazing on the plentiful reed grass by the Nile, the gaunt cows turn on the sturdy cows and "eat them up": later, as Pharaoh tells his disturbing dream to Joseph, he adds a previously unmentioned detail that serves as a crucial clue for Joseph's interpretation: "When they [the gaunt cows] had *consumed them* [the sturdy cows], one could not tell that they [the gaunt cows] had consumed them, for they [the gaunt cows] looked just as bad as before. And I awoke" (Gen 41:21). Pharaoh is woken by the sheer shock of his nightmare. Not only are the handsome, sturdy cows devoured by the ugly, gaunt ones, but the sturdy cows are utterly erased, as if they never existed. The consumption leaves no trace in those who consume – they remain as thin and empty as before.

Pharaoh's dream exemplifies a theme that pervades the Joseph story, namely, the deceptive nature of outward appearance and its complex relationship to what lies hidden within. Food, bounty and stability, that which is "handsome," whether expressed in a "healthy" physique, social status or national strength, can evaporate into nothing when it encounters hunger and destitution. The disaster of famine destroys even the best memory of food and destroys the very fabric of a stable and orderly society. Moreover, it does so without leaving a trace of that old goodness which has now been literally eaten up by hunger. We must therefore learn to see differently, as Joseph does, that which appears good to us and that which appears bad.

Pharaoh's dreams represent a *reversal* of sorts of an episode in Joseph's own life. Joseph's lean years in exile and in prison will soon be erased, wiped out overnight by his new position as second to Pharaoh and ruler over Egypt. Joseph's success when he emerges from prison is as astounding as the consumption of the sturdy cows by the gaunt ones. The hungry and alienated boy, now well-fed and at the center of the universe, has swallowed up the good life of gourmet food and court luxury reserved for men of his station (Gen 43:16; 32-34), far from the simple meals of honey and almonds typical of his homeland and people (Gen 43:11), and further still from prison food. Yet, has he really digested this new food he's swallowed? Or, like the gaunt cows, has he remained the same as he was – a rejected brother, carted off to Egypt like an animal, abandoned and forgotten? Will the apparent "fullness" he has reached after years of undeserved abuse, slavery and imprisonment be sucked away without trace, if his past is revealed – a past he keeps carefully hidden from Egyptian eyes? The gaunt cows must have lingered on in Joseph's consciousness long after he put Pharaoh's mind to rest, a potent image of the insecurity that persists even after his meteoric rise to success and his subsequent hard-earned tranquility on the banks of the Nile.

So Pharaoh's dream comes to highlight a more sinister aspect of the tension between outward appearance and inner reality that emerges as our parasha unfolds. The dream and Joseph's interpretation of it spotlight the contrast between fullness and hunger. When it comes to his own psychological well-being, Joseph is hard-pressed to practice the restraint and self-control that he preached to Pharaoh. Refraining from the "over consumption" of his own emotions remains far from his grasp as he enters a painful emotional struggle with his brothers, his flesh and blood, who have come to Egypt to buy grain, "that we may live and not die" (Gen 42:2). Pharaoh's dream of the skinny and hungry cows held significance for Joseph himself which he had yet to decipher. His brothers, now hungry and a shadow of their former threatening selves, have "descended" from the land of Canaan to stand by him upon the banks of the Nile and feed off its plenty – a reversal of the cows "ascending" from the Nile. Is their weak appearance deceptive, like the gaunt cows? Will they devour Joseph in their quest for sustenance, or will he be able to hold his own?

The formal "eating of bread" (Gen 43:25) with his brothers in Pharaoh's court, together yet apart (v. 32), throws us back to his brothers' "eating of bread" while Joseph lay dying in the empty "waterless" pit (Gen 37:25–26). This time Joseph's belly is full but his heart is empty and dry. And so we come back full circle to the image of fullness and hunger, the dream of the handsome and ugly cows that opened our parasha. Now we can ask ourselves this: Will the "seller of grain": (*ha'mashbir*, literally "the hunger-breaker") to the whole of Egypt and "the people of the land" (Gen 42:6) be able to break (*lishbor*) his own hunger? Will his past "eat up" his present, and "break" him, or will he find ways to practice that very same restraint and control he was so quick to recommend to Pharaoh? Will his hungry brothers consume him? Will he consume himself in an attempt to efface his former identity? Or will he find a way to live with his past, to contain the bad years within the good ones, so that "one could not tell that they had consumed them"?

MEIRA POLLIACK is Professor of Bible at Tel-Aviv University. In recent years she has been a Visiting Professor of Judaic Studies at Yale University, and a member of the research group on early Jewish, Christian, and Muslim Strategies of reading and their implications at the Institute of Advanced Studies, Hebrew University of Jerusalem. She has published on literary approaches to the Bible and the development of medieval Jewish Bible interpretation, especially in the Islamic world, and on Medieval Arabic Bible translations, and Judeo-Arabic literature. Among her books: *Karaite Judaism: A Guide to its History and Literary Sources (2003);* C. Adang, M. Polliack, S. Schmidke (eds.), *The Bible in Arabic among Jews, Christians Muslims*, 2013; M. Polliack & A. Brenner (eds.), *Jewish Bible Exegesis from Islamic Lands in the Middle Ages: An Anthology* [forthcoming].

After two years' time, Pharaoh dreamed that he was standing by the Nile, when out of the Nile there came up seven cows, handsome and sturdy, and they grazed in the reed grass. (Gen 41:1–2)

Dreams frequently take place in the real world of the dreamer, involving places and people important to him or her. Such was the case for the cupbearer and the baker, who dreamed of their professional lives. At first glance, then, it seems surprising that Pharaoh dreams of cows, so far removed, we imagine, from his life in the palace. But of course almost no-one in the ancient world, not to mention many parts of the world today, could be as alienated from their food supply as are most readers of this volume. We can go for months, even years, without encountering in nature the source of the food – animal or vegetable – that we see in packages on supermarket shelves. With the possible exception of the Minister of Agriculture or an equivalent, a member of our ruling elites is more likely to dream of steak and fries than a field of cows. In ancient Egypt, by contrast, cattle would have been as prominent as "chuck" even in the life of the king.

And the ugly gaunt cows ate up the seven handsome sturdy cows. And Pharaoh awoke. (Gen 41:4)

As dreams often do, Pharaoh's dream shifts between reassuring, everyday scenes, such as cows grazing on a river bank, and unsettling, surreal images, such as cows emerging from the watery depths of the Nile and eating each other. The idea of cows eating each other is thoroughly disturbing. Since cows are herbivores, they are going against their nature in more ways than one. Cows are very large; it's not easy to visualize the consumption of an entire cow, even by another cow. Since there is no mention of death, it seems that the cows were eaten alive. In the normal course of events, we would expect the fat cows to eat the thin ones, and not the other way around. Not to mince words, this is a form of cannibalism. The idea of kind eating kind is unsettling in most contexts, and in this one – the prediction of a famine – it recalls the Israelite mothers who will eat their babies when starvation sets in in the land of Israel (Lam 2:20).

In the US today, the vast majority of cows are fed against their nature. They are forced to eat corn, which they cannot digest, instead of grass, which they can (Michael Pollan, *The Omnivore's Dilemma*). They are kept alive by a steady dose of antibiotics for long enough to justify their existence as a source of meat. The medication passes into the bodies of the humans who consume the cows. Pharaoh's dream for our times? Perhaps. It's reassuring to see that, in America at least, Jewish kashrut organizations are at the forefront of resistance to the cruel and dangerous exploitation of animals and people by greedy agricultural mega-corporations.

> *Immediately ahead are seven years of great abundance in all the land of Egypt. After them will come seven years of famine, and all the abundance in the land of Egypt will be forgotten. As the land is ravaged by famine, no trace of the abundance will be left in the land because of the famine thereafter, for it will be very severe. (Gen 41:29–31)*

Even in those parts of the affluent western world where the risk of starvation is very low, the idea of running out of food is universally terrifying. A predicted snow storm, or even a one day public holiday, drives people to the supermarket in droves, stock-piling whatever they can store in their pantries, refrigerators, and freezers. We cannot survive without eating, and for that reason alone we know that we cannot hold on indefinitely to food. Even with strict rationing, it will eventually run out. It is this phenomenon that Joseph draws out so powerfully from Pharaoh's dream. At some point during the years of famine, there will be absolutely no material evidence that the years of plenty had ever occurred.

> *Let all the food of these good years that are coming be gathered, and let the grain be collected under Pharaoh's authority as food to be stored in the cities. Let that food be a reserve for the land for the seven years of famine which will come upon the land of Egypt, so that the land may not perish in the famine. (Gen 41:35–36)*

Joseph's interpretation of Pharaoh's dream leads him to conceive a plan to save Egypt's population from starvation when the famine finally hits. It entails central management of the grain supply upon which the people depend for their main staple, bread. It's clear why Pharaoh's authority is required; without it, corruption, theft, and unequal distribution would inevitably occur. But along with the proper management that Joseph intended comes control, and with control comes wealth and power. Pharaoh was already Egypt's richest and powerful man, but to say that Joseph's intervention consolidates his position is the understatement of the century. What begins here as an economic measure to protect Egypt's entire population, rich and poor alike, ends with Pharaoh owning most of Egypt and most Egyptians.

> *There was famine in all lands, but throughout the land of Egypt there was bread. (Gen 41:54)*

There is arguably no differentiator starker than having versus not having. It's easy to imagine the range of complex responses that arose among the famine-struck lands of the ancient Near East when they learned that Egypt alone had grain: envy, resentment, admiration, respect, anger, a sense of injustice, suspicion. This is not the story the Bible chooses to tell, but we have enough experience from the global politics of our own time to fill in the gaps.

> *And when all the land of Egypt felt the hunger, the people cried out to Pharaoh for bread; and Pharaoh said to all the Egyptians, "Go to Joseph; whatever he tells you, you shall do." (Gen 41:55)*

Ultimately, even Egypt is not immune from the effects of the famine, and Pharaoh instructs his people to go to Joseph and do whatever he tells them. It might have been sufficiently motivating for the Egyptians that this instruction to obey Joseph came from Pharaoh, the leader they saw as semi-divine and all-powerful. But if any additional incentive was required to do "*whatever he says*," hunger was surely it. It is a rare starving person who would resist a leader whose commands were backed by the promise of regular meals.

> *When Jacob saw that there were food rations to be had in Egypt, he said to his sons, "Why do you keep looking at one another? Now I hear," he went on, "that there are food rations to be had in Egypt. Go down and procure rations for us there, that we may live and not die?" (Gen 42:1–2)*

Two grand themes of the Joseph story meet in these verses; surviving famine and – at once more and less challenging – surviving as a family. At their father's instruction, the brothers go back and forth from Egypt, procuring grain so that they as individuals may "live and not die" of starvation. With each journey they come ever closer to achieving the family reunion that will ensure in the long run that Israel as a people will "live and not die" through schism and separation.

> *Now Joseph was the vizier of the land; it was he who dispensed rations to all the people of the land. (Gen 42:6)*

It would have been physically impossible for Joseph to dole out food to all Egypt *himself*, but that is the image depicted here. In reality, Joseph must have been sitting atop a pyramid of administrators and laborers, far removed from the food itself, and yet the directness and immediacy of he "dispensed rations" is not misleading. It emphasizes that the seven years of famine transformed the Egyptians into helpless children, totally dependent on the inevitably problematic father figure who handed them their daily crust of bread.

> *Then Joseph gave orders to fill their bags with grain, return each one's money in his sack, and give them provisions for the journey; and this was done for them. So they loaded their asses with the rations and departed from there. (Gen 42:25–26)*

Joseph gave his brothers two kinds of sustenance: grain to be consumed back in the land of Canaan, and provisions for the journey that took them there. The latter was not an after-thought, the icing on the cake. Without it, the sacks of grain that must have formed the bulk of their cargo would have been worthless to them.

> *As one of them was opening his sack to give feed to his ass at the night encampment, he saw his money right there at the mouth of his bag. (Gen 42:27)*

This must have been the first time that one of the brothers opened his sack, otherwise the money that Joseph returned to each one would have been discovered earlier. Clearly they did not stop to feed their animals during the day, but waited to reach the night encampment.

> *Then their father Israel said to them, "If it must be so, do this: take some of the choice products of the land in your baggage, and carry them down*

as a gift for the man – some balm and some honey, gum, laudanum, pistachio nuts, and almonds. (Gen 43:11)

At first glance, this verse seems jarring. Jacob is sending his sons to *bring* food from Egypt, so why does he *send* food from Canaan? And how does Jacob have access to all this food when there is a famine in the land? Jacob's decision to send choice products of the land reflects the crucial role of exchange in transactions like this. He is not anticipating a hand-out in Egypt, but expects to "purchase" the staple that Canaan lacks (grain) with luxury items whose supplies have not yet been depleted (honey, nuts). The non-edible items in Jacob's list are the very same products carried down to Egypt by the travelling Ishmaelites to whom the brothers sell Joseph. This suggests either that Egypt did not produce these items at all or, more likely, that their demand for them exceeded their supply. That honey and nuts were still available in Canaan during a famine reflects the fact that they were typically stored for longer periods than grain. If the blessing of abundance in Lev 26:5 is anything to go by, grain was not usually stored for more than a year; in normal circumstances, a granary would be empty by the time the new crop was harvested.

When Joseph saw Benjamin with them, he said to his house steward, "Take the men into the house; slaughter and prepare an animal, for the men will dine with me at noon." (Gen 43:16)

Joseph's closing words to his steward suggest that the meal he plans is far more than sustenance for the brothers at the end of a long journey. Had that been the case, they would have eaten alone as soon as the animal had been prepared. It's the additional information that Joseph will dine with them, and at a specified time – noon – that makes this meal portentous.

Then the man brought the men into Joseph's house; he gave them water to bathe their feet, and he provided feed for their asses. (Gen 43:24)

Once again, the asses are highlighted. In this society, pack animals were both valuable in monetary terms and invaluable for their capacity to transport supplies from place to place. Feeding them first went far beyond kindness to animals.

They laid out their gifts to await Joseph's arrival at noon, for they had heard that they were to dine there. (Gen 43:25)

Although the special products they brought with them from Canaan were intended as an exchange, if only symbolic, for the grain they hoped to receive, the brothers present it to Joseph at the meal, as though it was in anticipation of the food they are about to eat. Either way, the food they bring is conceptually related to the food they expect to get. At first glance, this seems odd. Why give a small amount of food to someone about to give a much larger quantity of food to you? One possible answer is that it represents a kind of participation in the meal, much as when a guest presents her host with cake or chocolates, even though she's well aware that there'll be no shortage of food on the table.

Then he [Joseph] washed his face, reappeared, and – now in control of himself – gave the order, "Serve the meal." They served him by himself, and them by themselves, and the Egyptians who ate with him by themselves; for the Egyptians could not dine with the Hebrews, since that would be abhorrent to the Egyptians. (Gen 43:31–32)

These verses raise a fascinating question. Did the Egyptians usually eat with Joseph, or, as a Hebrew with whom eating was abhorrent for Egyptians, was he always forced to eat alone? Many readers of this volume will be familiar with this situation from the perspective of Jews whose capacity to share meals is constrained by the laws of kashrut. It's worth noting, though, that there's usually a way to enable Jews to eat in mixed company without breaking the laws of kashrut, even if it entails inedible airline food, plastic plates and cutlery and so forth. None of that would have satisfied the Egyptians, as they are described here. It's not the food that was a problem, but the notion of eating together.

As they were seated by his direction, from the oldest in the order of his seniority to the youngest in the order of his youth, the men looked at one another in astonishment. Portions were served them from his table; but Benjamin's portion was several times that of anyone else. And they drank their fill with him. (Gen 43:33–34)

Joseph's father used special clothing, a commonly used way of showing status, to distinguish Joseph from his brothers. Now Joseph used meals, another familiar way to show status – think of airline food in business class versus economy and who gets to sit on the head table at banquets – to distinguish Benjamin.

Diana Lipton

Va-Yiggash

Genesis 44:18–46:27

Bread Corrupts

DIANA LIPTON

As the famine in Egypt continued to rage, the people ran out of money to buy bread. For a time they exchanged their livestock instead, but eventually that resource too was exhausted:

> *Now there was no bread in all the world, for the famine was very severe; both the land of Egypt and the land of Canaan languished because of the famine. Joseph gathered in all the money that was to be found in the land of Egypt and in the land of Canaan, as payment for the rations that were being procured, and Joseph brought the money into Pharaoh's palace. And when the money gave out in the land of Egypt and in the land of Canaan, all the Egyptians came to Joseph and said, "Give us bread, lest we die before your very eyes, for the money is gone!" (Gen 47:13–15)*

The Egyptians returned to Joseph:

> *"We cannot hide from my lord that, with all the money and animal stocks consigned to my lord, nothing is left at my lord's disposal save our persons and our farmland. Let us not perish before your eyes, both we and our land. Take us and our land in exchange for bread, and we with our land will be serfs [Hebrew avadim, the same word as slaves] to Pharaoh . . ." (Gen 47:18–19)*

As Erich Auerbach observed in his opening chapter of *Mimesis*, the history of the representation of reality in Western literature he wrote in Istanbul in 1935 after fleeing from Nazi Germany, biblical narrative is short on background details. For example (Auerbach's case study), it reports only the bare bones of what went on between Abraham and Isaac as they ascended Mount Moriah. Its account of Joseph's distribution of the grain he had amassed during the seven years of plenty is similarly skeletal. It is up to us, the readers, to flesh out the story, but where do we start?

Ancient Egypt is not modern Egypt, and even modern Egypt has changed dramatically in the past few years, but my starting point is a New York Times article called *Egypt's Problem and Its Challenge: Bread Corrupts* (January 17, 2008, Michael Slackman):

> *CAIRO — "Get out! Get back! Get back! I am not selling to you!" Ibrahim Ali Muhammad, a bread seller, is shouting at his customers. His teeth are brown and misshapen from decay, and he says the stress of his 20 years on the job has given him diabetes. He is standing behind bars, jail-like bars, shouting into a crowd that is pushing, punching, thrusting money at him. "I already sold to you," he screams, again, this time distracted by a young man in a blue windbreaker who swiveled on his heels and punched the man behind.*

There was no famine in Egypt in 2008, and plenty of bread shops without lines at all, let alone violent hoards. What made Muhammad the bread seller's life so hard was that he sold subsidized bread (bread subsidies began in Egypt after the Second World War), essential for the 45% of Egypt's population at the time who survived on less than $2 a day, and a business opportunity for those, like the man in the blue windbreaker, who would immediately resell it at a massive profit.

Let's return to Genesis. First, to the potent cocktail of poverty, frustration and greed that fueled the aggression of the people lining up outside Muhammad's shop, we must add the real fear of imminent starvation. In Joseph's time, in contrast to 2008, there was a famine. There is a hint of this desperation in the people's words "give us bread lest we die," but that is easily dismissed as a rhetorical flourish. We the readers must supply the images of angry farmers about to lose their land, depressed working men about to lose their independence, distraught mothers unable to feed their families, children weakened by a long journey in search of bread, and crying babies. It seems unlikely that they formed an orderly queue. Second, in 2008 the Egyptian government did not sell directly to the people, but used intermediaries; Muhammad was one of many authorized sellers of subsidized bread in Cairo. When the Bible reports that all Egypt came to Joseph to buy bread, it must have been speaking figuratively. Surely Joseph too appointed agents to deal with the huge demand, and with those agents there surely came the openings for corruption described in the 2008 New York Times article:

> *"The most corrupt sector in the country is the provisions sector," said a government inspector who asked not to be identified for fear of punishment. His job is to go to bakeries to ensure they are actually using the cheap government flour to produce cheap bread that is sold at the proper price. The inspector explained why the system was so open to abuse. The government sells bakeries 25-pound bags of flour for 8 Egyptian pounds, the equivalent of about $1.50. The bakeries are then supposed to sell the flatbread at the subsidized rate, which gives them a profit of about $10 from each sack. Or the baker can simply sell the flour on the black market for $15 a bag.*

In parashat Va-yeshev we read about the massive store houses that Joseph filled with grain during the seven years of plenty following his successful interpretation of Pharaoh's dreams. When famine set in, Joseph began to sell the surplus grain for money, and later he traded it for animals. When those resources were exhausted, the people exchanged their land and ultimately themselves for bread. In the process of saving the Egyptian people from starvation, Joseph created a system that made them dependent upon their rulers for the foreseeable future. The New York Times article describes a similar state of dependence in 2008:

Much of what ails Egypt seems to converge in the story of subsidized bread. It speaks to a state that is in many ways stuck in the past, struggling to pull itself into the future, unable, or unwilling, to conquer corruption or even to persuade people to care about one another. How do you take a broken system that somehow helps feed 80 million people and fix it without causing social disorder?

If we stopped last week to think about how the grain that Joseph amassed in Egypt's seven years of plenty would be distributed during the years of famine, we probably did not envisage bondage. More likely, we half-imagined a scene like that evoked by the Passover Haggadah's expansive invitation about *leḥem oni*, the bread of affliction: "Let all who are hungry come and eat." Unintentionally perhaps, the New York Times piece recalls another part of the Haggadah:

Bread, in Egyptian Arabic, is called "aish," which literally means life, rather than "khobz," the word that other Arab speakers use. "The word, applied to bread, gives this everyday element an almost mystical quality . . . Egypt's relationship to bread is not one of freedom, but of necessity."

For the Israelites who left Egypt, matzah, unleavened bread, signified freedom from slavery. The Egyptian word for bread suggests that for Egyptians bread symbolizes not freedom, a luxury in the ancient world, but the most basic life force without which there is death. The New York Times piece may explain why the Egyptians were so ready to enslave themselves to Pharaoh, even offering their land and bodies to Joseph before he demanded them. In Egypt, bread equals life, and Egyptians were willing quite literally to sell their souls for it, measure for measure. But should Joseph – whose descendants would come to equate Egyptian bread with freedom – have accepted so readily their offer, or was there a better, more socially responsible way to feed Egypt during its lean years?

DIANA LIPTON read English Literature at Oxford and, after a period of investment banking and full-time motherhood, she completed a

Ph.D. in Hebrew Bible at Cambridge. From 1997 to 2006 she was a Fellow of Newnham College, Cambridge. In 2007 she moved to the Department of Theology and Religious Studies, King's College, London as Lecturer and later Reader in Hebrew Bible and Jewish Studies. In 2011 she went to Israel, where she teaches Bible at Rothberg, Hebrew University's International School. Her books include *Revisions of the Night: Politics and Promises in the Patriarchal Dreams of Genesis*; *Longing for Egypt and Other Unexpected Biblical Tales*; *Lamentations Through the Centuries* (with Paul Joyce), and several edited collections.

> *And to his father he sent the following: ten he-asses laden with the best things of Egypt, and ten she-asses laden with grain, bread and provisions for his father on the journey. (Gen 45:23)*

Joseph scales new heights of hospitality when he sends his brothers home with extensive provisions, not only for their journey to Canaan, but for Jacob's journey to Egypt. His generosity could have been motivated by fear that his elderly father would suffer during the arduous trip, especially given the food shortage in Canaan. Perhaps alongside that, Joseph wanted to make a big impression from the moment Jacob set out for Egypt to meet the son who left home and made good. The wagons that raised Jacob's spirit when he saw them (v. 27) were the equivalent of a seat in the first-class cabin, and the provisions were the equivalent of complementary champagne and smoked salmon. Joseph's message was clear: the luxury starts here.

> *So Joseph settled his father and his brothers, giving them holdings in the choicest part of the land of Egypt, in the region of Rameses, as Pharaoh had commanded. Joseph sustained his father, and his brothers, and all his father's household with bread, down to the little ones. (Gen 47:11–12)*

It's hard to know if "bread" is the best translation for *leḥem* here, or whether "food" would be better. On the one hand, it's unlikely that Joseph sustained his family with bread alone, to the exclusion of other staples. From that perspective, "food" seems preferable. On the other hand, it's not unusual for one particular staple to become the focus of food shortages that are more far-reaching. Ireland's great potato famine is one example, and Egypt's bread riots are another. Even if Joseph's family lacked all kinds of food, and even if Joseph sustained them with more than bread, the concentration of all that into one basic provision makes sense.

> *Then Joseph said to the people, "Whereas I have this day acquired you and your land for Pharaoh, here is seed for you to sow the land. And when the harvest comes, you shall give one-fifth to Pharaoh, and four-fifths shall be yours as seed for the fields and food for you and those in your households, and as nourishment for your children."* (Gen 47:23–24)

With these words, Joseph introduces the feudal system to Egypt. All the land of Egypt belongs to Pharaoh and all the Egyptians are his serfs. What made Joseph think it was a good idea to do precisely the opposite of what God planned for the land of Israel?

Diana Lipton

Va-Yehi

Genesis 47:28–50:26

Ask a Frenchman

Albert Baumgarten

One of the blessings Jacob conferred on Judah was that he would enjoy a territory rich in grapes and wine: "He tethers his ass to a vine, his ass' foal to a choice vine; he washes his garment in wine, his robe in blood of grapes. His eyes are darker than wine; his teeth are whiter than milk" (Gen 49:11–12). Verse 12 is perplexing: what sense does it make to wash one's clothes in wine, unless one is completely drunk? Next, are the "eyes darker than wine" meant as a criticism of someone who has over-indulged? If so, that would contradict the favorable implications of the "teeth whiter than milk" in the second half of the same verse. Furthermore, if Jacob intended to foretell that Judah would be a drunken sot, so out of touch with reality as to wash his clothes in wine and bleary-eyed from too much drinking, this would be a very awkward blessing for the son who was promised that "the scepter shall not depart from Judah, nor the ruler's staff from between his feet" just a verse earlier (Gen 49:10).

I suggest that if we want to better understand these verses we should ask a Frenchman, preferably someone who grew grapes himself, Rabbi Samuel ben Meir of Troyes (Rashbam), who was born around 1085 and died in about 1158.

Rashbam understood these verses as a three-part description of wine-making. In verse 11 the abundant grape are harvested. Next they are crushed, their juice staining the workers' garments. In verse

12 the wine is drunk. The point of the blessing, according to Rashbam, is to emphasize the plentiful harvest and the rich yield. None of this is pejorative or critical of drunkenness. It is pure enjoyment of a bountiful blessing. I cite from Rashbam's comments, according to the translation of Martin Lockshin, *Rabbi Samuel ben Meir's Commentary to Genesis: An Annotated Translation* (1989, pp 363–366):

> *49:11: "He tethers his ass to a vine." One ass . . . has to be tied up and loaded down with [just] one vine, for there are so many grapes.*
> *"He washes his garment in wine." After gathering the grapes and treading on them in the winepress, their clothes become dirty from treading the wine, as it is written (Isa 63:2), "Why is your clothing so red, your garments like his who treads grapes?"*
> *49:12: "His eyes are red from wine". As it is written (Prov 23:29-30), "Who has red eyes? Those whom wine keeps till the small hours." . . . ḥachlili that is how redness of the eyes is referred to.*

Concerning our first puzzle, as Lockshin notes, for Rashbam, it is more sensible to understand "*washing garments in wine*" for the treading process, not washing clothes.

Concerning the second puzzle, the verse in Proverbs in its original context is a warning against drinking too much wine, but Rashbam took *ḥachlili* from that verse in its pure linguistic sense, with no pejorative connotations, to be used in perfect favorable parallelism with the teeth white from drinking milk in the second clause.

To summarize, Rashbam understood Jacob's blessing as outlining three steps connected with wine: harvest, crushing, drinking. Rashbam's Judah was encouraged to drink and enjoy the piece of good fortune afforded by the land he would inhabit. I conclude as I began: if you want to know about wine, ask a Frenchman. *L'Haim*!

ALBERT BAUMGARTEN is Professor Emeritus in the Department of Jewish History at Bar Ilan University, Israel. His research focuses on the history of Second Temple Judaism, and he is also interested in the history of the scholars who worked on ancient Judaism. His 2010 book, *Elias Bickerman as a Historian of the Jews: A Twentieth Century Tale*, reflects this latter interest.

Asher's bread shall be rich, and he shall yield royal dainties. (Gen 49:20)

Leḥem, the Hebrew word translated here as "bread" can also be rendered simply as "food." In the context of Jacob's blessing of his son Asher, "food" seems more appropriate. First, the word translated in this verse as "rich" comes from the Hebrew root *shemen*, which usually signifies fat, an ingredient seldom used in Middle Eastern bread. Second, though open to interpretation, "royal dainties" is arguably more suited to fine baked goods than luxury meat items. A term such as the king's "delicatessen" or even "charcuterie" might better capture the sense of the Hebrew *me'adnei-melekh*, and translating *leḥem* as "food" instead of "bread" allows for this. But what difference does it make?

One difference concerns the image of Asher and his tribe that emerges from Jacob's blessing. Baking is a domestic activity that takes place in the confines of the home; bakers are not typically involved in the agricultural process that produces the ingredients they bake. Perhaps this is why baking is identified with women in many cultures. Meat preparation, on the other hand, is a more holistic activity; the person who cooks the meat is often the one who procures it, and procuring it involves killing it. For example, Esau himself hunted the game he prepared for his father Isaac (Gen 27:3). Did Jacob see Asher and his descendants as bakers or butchers? That is the question that hangs on the interpretation of the word *leḥem*.

Benjamin is a ravenous wolf; in the morning he consumes the foes, and in the evening he divides the spoil. (Gen 49:27)

Why does Jacob identify Benjamin – the son of his old age, the one he tried to protect from danger by keeping him at home when his brothers went to Egypt to procure food during the famine – as a dangerous, hungry wild animal? There is nothing obvious in the life of Benjamin or the unfolding history of his eponymous tribe that justifies this unflattering metaphor, so why does Jacob use it? A possible answer to this question emerges from an earlier reference that Jacob makes to a wild animal that tears and eats its prey. Not wanting to admit that they sold Joseph into slavery, the brothers kill a goat, dip Joseph's coat in its blood, and present the torn, bloody garment to their father. Just as they intended, their father jumps to the obvious conclusion: "My son's tunic! A savage beast devoured him! Joseph was torn by a beast!" (Gen 37:33). The Hebrew grammar makes it clear that the savage beast that Jacob assumes to have eaten and torn Joseph, though unidentified as to species, was female in gender. It is not surprising that Jacob identifies Benjamin as a male; the metaphor works better that way. Is it possible that Jacob's choice of this metaphor conceals a disturbing reversal?

In Jacob's blessing, Benjamin is not just a generic beast of prey but a wolf. All seven biblical references to wolves portray them explicitly or implicitly as aggressive killers, but only two mention their prey by name. Isaiah's two oft-(mis)quoted scenes of utopia depict the wolf dwelling alongside the lamb (Hebrew *keves*) instead of preying on it (Isa 11:6), and grazing *with* the lamb (Hebrew *taleh*) instead of *upon* it (Isa 65:25). The stereotypical prey of a wolf is a sheep. As well as being the proper name of Jacob's beloved wife and Benjamin's mother, *rachel* is the Hebrew for "ewe." Did Jacob transform on his deathbed the female beast he once imagined to have devoured Joseph, into a male wolf? Is this male wolf Benjamin, who, in Jacob's deepest subconscious, tore and devoured Rachel, the female sheep, who died giving birth to him?

DIANA LIPTON

Shemot

Exodus 1:1–6:1

Kindness to Animals

Robert Brody

Parashat Shemot describes the first steps in Moses' career as the leader of the Jewish nation. In a straightforward reading, it describes two episodes which preceded God's self-revelation to him: his killing of an Egyptian who struck "a Hebrew, one of his kinsmen," and his rescue of Jethro's daughters from the shepherds.

On the one hand, these episodes serve as narrative links in his biography and explain how he came to leave Egypt, arrived in Midian and met his future wife. On the other hand, it seems clear that these stories are also intended to display aspects of Moses' personality which justified his selection as the messenger who would lead the nation through its critical hours. The first story showcases, among other things, his sensitivity to the suffering of others. The second story goes even further: not only did Moses step forward to protect someone similar to himself – "a Hebrew, one of his kinsmen" – who was attacked and whose life may have been in danger; he also hurried to the defense of others who were very different from him from another nation– even though it appears that the only danger they faced was that of having to wait in order to water their father's flock.

Some sages, however, were not content with this, and found hints in our parasha that Moses' compassion crossed even the boundaries of the human species and extended to animals as well. A modest expression of this approach is found in the Targum of Onqelos to

Exodus 3:1, "Now Moses, tending the flock . . . drove the flock into the wilderness. . . ." One might perhaps think that a shepherd who takes his flock "into the wilderness" is failing in his duty. In order to prevent any such suspicion from falling on Moses, the Targum explains that he led the flock "after the best grazing, to the wilderness." It seems probable that the biblical Hebrew word *midbar,* translated as "wilderness" or "desert" did not have the meaning usually assigned to it in modern Hebrew – that of a parched and desolate place – but rather referred to a place outside the limits of human settlement and suitable for grazing, in keeping with the meaning of the root D-B-R, which is most familiar from the Aramaic, meaning "to lead."

Several late *midrashim* went even farther in this interpretive direction and claimed that working as a shepherd served as a test of Moses' suitability as a leader, and that his selection as the shepherd of Israel followed on his successful completion of this test, since "the Holy One blessed be He does not grant greatness to a man until He has tested him in something small, and afterwards He elevates him to greatness." True, it is difficult to find a hint of this idea in our weekly portion, but the midrashim compare Moses in this respect to King David, with regard to whom Scripture does seem to hint at such a connection (Ps 78: 70–71): "He chose David, His servant, and took him from the sheepfolds. He brought him from minding the nursing ewes to tend His people Jacob, Israel, His very own." One midrash even adds Jacob, Amos and Ezekiel to the list of leaders who were tested in this fashion.

Sensitivity to the needs of animals is expressed first and foremost through the provision of food, and the demand that one should provide nourishment to one's dependent animals is not restricted to outstanding individuals. The responsibility to supply the needs of these animals is expressed, for example, in Mishnah Shabbat 24:4, which permits the preparation of their food on the Sabbath: "One may cut up gourds before domestic animals and a carcass before dogs." But the most striking expression of this sense of responsibility is probably to be found in the law which the amora Rav derived from Deut 11:15. His interpretation is cited twice, with slight variations, in the Talmud: "A man may not eat before giving food to his animal, for it is said 'I will also provide grass in the fields for your cattle' and (only) then 'and thus you shall eat your fill.'" May our sensitivity to the needs of others help us to merit a bounty which will suffice for us all.

ROBERT BRODY did his first Ph.D. in Mathematics at Harvard University, and his second Ph.D. in Talmud at the Hebrew University in Jerusalem. Professor Brody teaches in Hebrew University's Talmud Department and is a world expert on the works of the Geonim (6th to 11th century Babylonia). His published books include *Teshuvot Rav Natronai bar Hilai Ga'on, Tsohar Le-Sifrut ha-Ge'onim, Rav Se'adyah Ga'on, Otsar Ha-Ge'onim He-Ḥadash* (in Hebrew), as well as *The Geonim of Babylonia and the Shaping of Medieval Jewish Culture* (Yale, 1998).

Then his sister said to Pharaoh's daughter, "Shall I go and get you a Hebrew nurse to suckle the child for you?" And Pharaoh's daughter answered, "Yes." So the girl went and called the child's mother. And Pharaoh's daughter said to her, "Take this child and nurse it for me, and I will pay your wages." So the woman took the child and nursed it. (Exod 2:7-9)

A woman breastfeeding a baby in the west today – and probably in most parts of the world – is most likely to be the baby's mother. Regardless of social status, women who are unable or prefer not to breastfeed their babies do not usually pay other women to do it for them, but give the baby a bottle instead. Until recent times, though, a woman breastfeeding a baby could well have been its wet nurse, especially if the baby's mother belonged to a social elite in which breastfeeding – even in private – was considered unbecoming.

For modern readers, then, this episode has a sense of a happy ending, at least for the time-being, that it perhaps once lacked. We find it fitting and pleasing that the real mother ends up nursing her son. In the ancient world, however, the connection between breastfeeding and motherhood was more fluid than now, and audiences might not have experienced the satisfaction we feel. Even if Pharaoh's daughter had been the real mother of Moses, she would probably have passed him to a wet nurse, likely a slave. And had Moses' mother not been a slave, she would probably have found someone else to nurse her baby, possibly – had the tables been turned – an Egyptian.

> *Now the priest of Midian had seven daughters. They came to draw water, and filled the troughs to water their father's flock; but the shepherds came and drove them off. Moses rose to their defense, and he watered their flock. (Exod 2:16–17)*

At the public level, the reference to Moses' shepherding activities links him to King David. David too worked as a shepherd (1 Sam 16:11), and is identified metaphorically as the shepherd of his people (Ezek 34:23), in keeping with an ancient Near Eastern tradition of calling kings "shepherds." Being or being like a shepherd is an important leadership credential. At the private level, this episode links Moses to Jacob, who also competes with shepherds at a well to water the flocks of the woman he will end up marrying. The episode at the well is the equivalent of those movie scenes in which the stranger from out-of-town out-maneuvers the unworthy local competition to get the girl. It's striking, then, that Moses impresses his future wife not by beating up the neighborhood bully (though there would have been scope for that in this story), but by enabling her animals to drink.

> *He [Reuel] said to his daughters, "Where is he then? Why did you leave the man? Ask him in to break bread." (Exod 2:20)*

Reuel knows exactly how to interpret his daughters' account of what just happened at the well: the stranger is a potential husband for one of them. He wastes no time inviting Moses in, ostensibly for a meal, but probably to check him out, much as Laban does with the servant of Abraham who came in search of a wife for Isaac (Gen 24:31). The above translation implies a formal agreement of some kind. "Breaking bread" sounds almost contractual, as is fitting in the context of a marriage. In Hebrew, however, Reuel speaks of eating not breaking, which has another connotation altogether (though also connected with marriage). In rabbinic Hebrew, and arguably also in biblical Hebrew (see S.C. Reif on Va-yeshev), "bread" is a euphemism for "woman," used most often in a sexual context. With or without his daughters' understanding, Reuel is hinting that Moses will get more than a meal if he accepts his hospitality. And that's exactly what happens. It is not mentioned if Reuel and Moses eat bread together, but Reuel does give Moses "his daughter Zipporah" (Exod 2:21).

> *I have come down to rescue them from the Egyptians and to bring them out of that land to a good and spacious land, a land flowing with milk and honey, the region of the Canaanites, the Hittites, the Amorites, the Perizzites, the Hivites, and the Jebusites. (Exod 3:8)*

God has just appeared to Moses at the burning bush and proceeds to tell him what will happen next. First the good news: He will rescue his people from slavery in Egypt and bring them to a good and spacious land, flowing with milk and honey. Now the bad news: they might not get a warm reception. In the order of information presented here – out of Egypt, into the good land, flowing with milk and honey, the territory of the Canaanites – the milk and honey functions as pre-battle fortification, strengthening the Israelites for the ordeal ahead of them.

> *Go and assemble the elders of Israel and say to them: the LORD, the God of your fathers, the God of Abraham, Isaac, and Jacob, has appeared to me and said . . . "I will take you out of the misery of Egypt to the land of the Canaanites, the Hittites, the Amorites, the Perizzites, the Hivites, and the Jebusites, to a land flowing with milk and honey." (Exod 3:16–17)*

The words are almost the same as those quoted just above, but now God is telling Moses what he needs to say to the Israelites. The information is ordered differently this time: out of Egypt, into the land of the Canaanites, flowing with milk and honey. In this order, the milk and honey functions not as pre-battle fortification, as was the case in just above, but as a reward to which the Israelites can look forward once the Canaanites have been appropriately dealt with.

DIANA LIPTON

Va-'era'

Exodus 6:2–9:35

Water World

Rachel Havrelock

The divine acts recounted in parashat Va-'era' are commonly called in English "plagues," yet the equivalent Hebrew term is used only rarely in the Exodus narrative (Exod 9:14). In fact, the disruptions that devastate the land and attack the routine affairs of ordinary Egyptians are most commonly called "signs." This biblical terminology for the plagues challenges contemporary interpretations of unusual weather patterns, super storms, and declining species by suggesting that such "plagues" of weather might be best understood as "signs" that something is wrong. In the present case, current levels of human consumption are having a deleterious effect on the health and stability of our environment.

Blood frames the series of "ten signs." They begin with the transformation of life-giving waters into deadly aquifers (Exod 7:17), and they end with blood smudged on Israelite doorposts to deflect the macabre visit of the Angel of Death (Exod 12:23). The image of blood connects the death of a water system, however temporary, with large-scale loss of human life. As both source of abundance and site of Egyptian divinity, the Nile is God's first target. The stench of dying fish and despoiled water must have accompanied his destruction of Egypt's mighty river.

After the river itself turns to blood, God afflicts every last drop of Egyptian water contained in tributaries, ponds, and springs

(Exod 7:19). The two stages of this destruction unfold in the very way that water systems really do collapse: a central river is diverted or polluted to the point of depletion, then the supporting water sources begin to dry out. Unfettered use of rivers by industries and individuals alike tends to leave those dependent on their water, like the Egyptians in the Exodus story, "dig[ging] round about the Nile for drinking water" (Exod 7:24).

The magicians of Egypt, Moses and Aaron's opponents, respond to the crisis by showing their power to match the destruction. Such a race to destroy water sources as a means of displaying political power has rendered mighty biblical rivers like the Nile, the Euphrates, and the Jordan close to collapse. Flowing as they do across borders and connecting different populations, rivers challenge the notion of terrestrial control and territorial sovereignty. This is as true today as it was in the ancient world. Just as God, Moses, and Aaron begin their assault on Pharaoh by compromising the Nile, contemporary riparians (owners of land or property next to a water source), often assert political power by diverting rivers.

The Jordan River provides the perfect case in point. Since the 1950s, Israel has diverted water from the upper Jordan River and Kinneret (Galilee) in order to support the development of Jewish communities. Syria, Lebanon, and Jordan have responded in kind, rerouting tributaries from the Jordan River basin to serve their populations alone. Although the Johnston Plan – an American sponsored water sharing agreement proposed in the 1960s – tried to foster a transnational culture of stewardship, the transboundary nature of water has proven to be a challenge to both Middle Eastern nationalisms and global commerce imperatives.

Currently, the Jordan River conveys only 3% of its historical flow. The lower Jordan River (from the Kinneret to the Dead Sea) carries wastewater and agricultural runoff as a result of unfettered dumping. With so little water reaching its shores, the Dead Sea is sinking at a rate of approximately one meter per year. No one benefits from the destruction of a freshwater system. But perhaps these conditions can operate as "signs" of a situation in urgent need of transformation. Just as a Nile running with blood was a catalyst for the process of liberating Egypt's slaves, perhaps a desiccated Jordan Valley can move stakeholders to restore fresh water to the Jordan, share this vital resource, and appraise water use and abuse. A significant step in this direction is the reallocation of 30 MCM of fresh water from the Kinneret to the lower Jordan River that the Israeli Water Authority began in spring 2013. While this falls short of the 220 MCM needed to maintain the health of the water system, it gestures toward the possibility of change.

The image of the bloody Nile reminds us that our life giving waters can become deadly. That God's assault on the Nile begins a process that ends with the miraculous splitting of the Red Sea reminds us that warning signs can motivate great political transformations as well as deadly destruction. A change in our relationship to water can usher in a change in our relationships with our immediate neighbors, as well as with those who draw from the same river.

Rachel Havrelock is Associate Professor of Jewish Studies and English at the University of Illinois at Chicago. Trained in Hebrew Bible, Rabbinics, Folklore, and Middle East Studies at the University of California, Berkeley, Rachel's research concerns three distinct areas and the overlap among them. Her work on gender and the Bible began with a co-authored book, *Women on the Biblical Road* (1996), that introduced the idea of a female hero pattern. *River Jordan: The Mythology of a Dividing Line* (2011) examines the long history of the Jordan as a border, as well as a river. Her work on the Israeli-Palestinian conflict and modern Middle East has been published in the journal *National Identities and in Understanding Life in the Borderlands: Boundaries in Depth and in Motion* (2010). Her current research in this area focuses on the oil pipeline that once ran from Kirkuk to Haifa. She is involved with efforts on the part of Ecopeace Middle East (FoEME) to develop a trans-border ecological peace park at the Jordan River. Rachel wrote this piece in memory of Ruth Rapoport, who brought food to the hungry of Israel before each Shabbat.

> *Thus says the* LORD, *"By this you shall know that I am the* LORD.*" See, I shall strike the water in the Nile with the rod that is in my hand, and it will be turned into blood; and the fish in the Nile will die. The Nile will stink so that the Egyptians will find it impossible to drink the water of the Nile. (Exod 7:17–18)*

There is no food without water. The second paragraph of the *Shema*, citing verses from Deuteronomy, makes precisely this point:

> *If, then, you obey the commandments that I enjoin upon you this day, loving the* LORD *your God and serving Him with all your heart and soul, I will grant the rain for your land in season, the early rain and the late. You shall gather in your new grain and wine and oil – I will also provide grass in the fields for your cattle – and thus you shall eat your fill. Take care not to be lured away to serve other gods and bow to them. For the* LORD'S *anger will flare up against you, and He will shut up the skies so that there will be no rain and the ground will not yield its produce; and you will soon perish from the good land that the* LORD *is assigning to you. (Deut 11:13–17)*

From a biblical point of view, as reflected in this passage from Deuteronomy, the water that irrigates the land of Israel comes from the heavens, but the picture is more complex when it comes to the rest of the earth. God created the world by dividing a body of water that covers the earth and assigning it to different locations: above the heavens, below the earth, and in rivers and seas (Gen 1:9–10). The flood is much more than torrential rain. It is the threat of a reverse creation when water breaks out from the safe places where God allocated it on the first day and it covers the earth as it once did (Gen 7:11–12). In normal weather conditions, just as water can fall as rain from the heavens to water the earth and enable plants to grow, so it can come from below the earth, as with a well, and from natural bodies of water, such as rivers that burst their banks on a seasonal basis. This latter case describes the situation in Egypt. Whereas Israel's agriculture depends on rain, Egypt's fields are fertile because the Nile floods. This fundamental difference between Israel and Egypt is noted in an agricultural context in Deut 11:10–11. It also plays a crucial role in Israel's history, explaining why people head for Egypt when famine strikes the land of Canaan (Abraham in Gen 12:10 and Jacob's sons in Gen 43).

Since Egypt, unlike Israel, does not rely on rainfall but rather upon water from a river, they can be confident that there will be food in Egypt even when there is a drought in Israel. It's not surprising, then, that God's first target in his power struggle with Pharaoh is the river Nile. At a single blow God threatens Pharaoh himself, whose claim to divinity rests partly on his association with the Nile, and the entire Egyptian population, who rely on the Nile for almost every aspect of their lives.

One reason it can be challenging to apply the Bible's lessons to our own times is that in the intervening centuries we have sometimes changed sides. If the Exodus story were to replay today, most of readers of this volume – educated, employed home-owners with pensions and health insurance – would have more in common with Pharaoh and the Egyptian overlords than with the Israelite slaves whom God liberated, the uneducated, unemployed, homeless, uninsured, often incarcerated ethnic minorities of today. It is hard to accept that, structurally speaking, at least, we are the bad guys in the Exodus story. Even more challenging is the case when, viewed from a present-day perspective, God seems to be on the wrong side in a biblical narrative. Such is arguably the situation when God turns the Nile to blood. Who pollutes rivers today? Greedy corporations, heedlessly pouring toxic waste into the rivers of the foreign countries in which they have built their factories for the purpose of exploiting cheap labor and natural resources? Dangerous political dictators, mindlessly killing innocent civilians and destroying the environment with chemical weapons? Terrorists, threatening to poison civilian water supplies in order to coerce enemy governments into making concessions? Irresponsible local governments, unwilling to invest the resources required for safe waste disposal? To be sure, God does not poison the Nile with inorganic substances, as in these cases, but turns it into an organic substance, blood. Viewed in its ancient Israelite context, however, blood was the equivalent of chemicals. Not only was there a strong prohibition against drinking blood (Deut 12:23) that robbed the river of its life-giving role, but blood spilled through violence, as this in a sense was, polluted the earth into which it seeped (Gen 4:10–12). Applying the messages of the ten plagues to our own times is challenging. We need to see the Nile as if it were the Jordan, as Rachel Havrelock did just above; we need to see ourselves as the Egyptians, suffering the economic and ecological consequences of our devastated natural environment; and we need to see the pollution of a river as something to be resisted and reversed at all costs.

> *When seven days had passed after the LORD struck the Nile, the LORD said to Moses, "Go to Pharaoh and say to him, 'Thus says the LORD: Let my people go so that they may worship Me. If you refuse to let them go, then I will plague your whole country with frogs. The Nile shall swarm with frogs, and they shall come up and enter your palace, your bedchamber and your bed, the houses of your courtiers and your people, and your ovens and your kneading bowls. The frogs shall come up on you and on your people and on all your courtiers.'" (Exod 7:25–29)*

Given that the ten plagues and are recited annually at the Passover Seder by groups of family and friends who are already smelling the matzah ball soup or its equivalent, we should be more sensitive than we are to the extent to which the plagues are bound up with food. Two specific aspects of the plague of frogs seem calculated to disturb: the frogs will enter Pharaoh's bed-chambers, and his ovens and kneading bowls (Exod 7:28). A live frog, even many frogs, in a lily pond can be picturesque; out of place they provoke something between squeamishness and revulsion. Frogs are nowhere more out of place than in the bedroom and the kitchen, and the rare biblical allusion here to actual cooking implements – ovens and kneading-bowls – only intensifies our visceral reaction to this plague.

> *For if you refuse to let them go, and continue to hold them, then the hand of the LORD will strike your livestock in the fields – the horses, the asses, the camels, the cattle, and the sheep – with a very severe pestilence. (Exod 9:2–5)*

This plague is deeply intimidating. First, the hand of God must have been visible to all. Frogs, hail, dust, darkness and so forth could have been natural disasters, but here all the affected animals die at once (v. 5), and it is only Egyptian animals that die (v. 6). The Egyptians could have been in no doubt that this was a punishment intended for them or, worse still, a sign of more to come. The second reason that this plague is particularly threatening is that its consequences must have included poverty and eventual starvation for many Egyptians. Animals represented wealth and food-supply, directly from milk and meat, and indirectly from their role in agriculture and trading. Since all the Egyptian animals were killed, the only options for replacement were from Israelite animals that survived.

For an Egyptian, witnessing this plague must have been like logging in to your on-line banking account and watching the money flow out. For an Israelite, it could have represented a business opportunity; Egyptians with other resources to trade would soon be coming in search of new stock to rebuild their flocks and herds.

> *Then the LORD said to Moses and Aaron, "Each of you shall take handfuls of soot from the kiln, and let Moses throw it toward the sky in the sight of Pharaoh. It shall become a fine dust over all the land of Egypt, and cause an inflammation breaking out in boils on man and beast throughout the land of Egypt." (Exod 9:8–9)*

The plague of dust threatens another source of sustenance for the Egyptians. Whichever creatures survived the cattle disease – presumably wild animals, some of which, whether routinely or in extremis, could have been eaten – got boils along with the people and were rendered inedible.

> *Throughout the land of Egypt the hail struck down all that were in the open, both man and beast; the hail also struck down the grasses of the field and shattered all the trees of the field. (Exod 9:25)*

Anyone who has experienced an extreme hail or snow storm out of season will know the havoc it wreaks, even in anticipation. For several reasons, the damage to trees can be among the most distressing consequences of a severe storm. Buildings can be repaired, crops will grow again next year, but trees felled by the weather are gone forever. And if they are fruit trees, as could well have been the case here, gone with them is part of the annual food supply.

> *Now the flax and barley were ruined, for the barley was in the ear and the flax was in bud; but the wheat and emmer were not hurt, for they ripen late. (Exod 9:31–32)*

It's hard to know precisely when the loss of crops would be most devastating for the farmer who planted them and the community that depended on them. On another occasion in the Bible when severe weather conditions are used as a punishment, the crops are destroyed at harvest time:

> *It is the season of the wheat harvest [says Samuel]. I will pray to the* Lord *and He will send thunder and rain; then you will take thought and realize what a wicked thing you did in the sight of the* Lord *when you asked for a king. (1 Sam 12:17)*

It must be painful in the extreme to witness the destruction of crops with the knowledge that, in just a few more days, they would have been safely in the granary. But on the other hand, it's extremely painful to see crops literally nipped in the bud – to know that there's nothing to be done now but to wait for the next planting season in almost another year. Either way, the reference to the season intensifies the sense of intentionality; this was not an arbitrary natural disaster, but a carefully timed attack.

Diana Lipton

Bo'

Exodus 10:1–13:16

Slow Cooking versus Fast Food

Jennie Rosenfeld

Parashat Bo' is rife with food references; from the locusts that caused famine and depletion for the Egyptians, to the animal sacrifices requested for the Israelites to worship God in the desert. My interest here is the *Korban Pesaḥ*, the Paschal Lamb taken by all Israelites and slaughtered the night before the exodus from Egypt. The emphasis on the preparation of the *Korban Pesaḥ* is striking. The Israelites are commanded to take the lamb into their homes and to guard it for four days before slaughtering it (Exod 12:3,6); they must account for everyone who will eat from the sacrifice before slaughtering it (Exod 12:4), preventing any last minute guests (see Babylonian Talmud, Pesahim 61a, which states the law that the *Korban Pesaḥ* can be eaten only by those who have affirmed participation in advance); and they are given precise details about how the lamb should be cooked (only grilled), what side dishes should accompany it (*matzah* and *maror*), what should be done with its blood (smeared on the doorposts and lintel) and when it may be eaten (only that night). The preparation surrounding the *Korban Pesaḥ* seems almost to serve as an end in itself. It sanctifies the ritual from start to finish as one directed towards God, by following precisely His detailed instructions.

It is strange, then, that the very next morning, when the Israelites wake up and leave Egypt, we see almost the opposite attitude towards food and food preparation. On their way out of Egypt, the

Israelites are so rushed that they are forced to bake their bread before it rises (thereby ending up with *matzah*), and they were unable to prepare any snacks for their travels (Exod 12:39). The sages see the lack of preparation here as evidence of the Israelites' faith and reliance upon God to sustain them through the journey.

The days of preparation preceding the *Korban Pesaḥ* stand in stark contrast to the lack of preparation for the departure from Egypt. Sometimes worshiping God requires meticulous food preparation and sometimes it requires stepping back in faith and trusting in God's sustenance. Be it through meticulous food preparation or through refraining from preparing and planning for food, food emerges as a critical theme surrounding the Exodus – both as a part of the Exodus itself and, later on, as a source of ritual memory of the Exodus. Towards the end of the parasha, the verse states, ". . . in order that the Teaching of the LORD may be in your mouth" (Exod 13:9). This theme is felt throughout the Exodus. What better way to show tangibly that we have incorporated God's teachings than by expressing it through the food we eat and how we prepare it!

JENNIE ROSENFELD serves as *Manhiga Ruchanit*, Spiritual Leader, in Efrat, appointed by Rabbi Shlomo Riskin, as she completes her studies at the Susi Bradfield Women's Institute for Halakhic Leadership at Midreshet Lindenbaum. She also teaches Talmud and Halakhah at the Pelech High School for Girls in Jerusalem. She holds a Ph.D. in English from the CUNY Graduate Center, where she wrote her dissertation, *Talmudic Re-readings: Toward a Modern Orthodox Sexual Ethic*, as a Wexner Graduate Fellow. A graduate of Stern College, Jennie completed the Yeshiva University Graduate Program in Advanced Talmudic Studies for Women. She lectures in Israel and abroad on topics relating to Judaism and sexuality, as well as Talmud and Hasidism, and was named one of the "36 under 36" by the Jewish Week in 2008. She co-authored *Et Le'ehov: The Newlywed's Guide to Physical Intimacy* (2011; Hebrew translation 2013). Jennie wrote this piece in memory of her father, Dr. Norman Rosenfeld (Nata Shmuel ben Yosef Chaim) *z"l*, on his fourth yahrzeit.

For if you refuse to let My people go, tomorrow I will bring locusts on your territory. They shall cover the surface of the land so that no one will be able to see the land. They shall devour the surviving remnant that was left to you after the hail; and they shall eat away all your trees that grow in the field. (Exod 10:4–5)

According to a story told in Babylonian Talmud, Gittin 55b, the destruction of the second Temple began with a man who felt slighted by being uninvited from a feast. The host's name was Kamtza and his unwanted guest was called Bar Kamtza; some sources associate "kamtza" with "locust." Locusts are doubly threatening. Like other swarms of winged creatures, they invade from the skies and cover the earth; unlike other winged creatures, they eat absolutely everything. The extent of their voracious appetite is captured in the words "surviving remnant." Elsewhere in the Tanakh, this phrase is used to distinguish between Israel's punishment for extreme immoral or unethical conduct, and the punishment meted out to the nations. In Israel's case, God will show compassion and allow a remnant to survive; the nations, however, will be utterly destroyed (Ezek 14:12–23).

Locusts invaded all the land of Egypt and settled within all the territory of Egypt in a thick mass; never before had there been so many, nor will there ever be so many again. They hid all the land from view, and the land was darkened; and they ate up all the grasses of the field and all the fruit of the trees which the hail had left, so that nothing green was left, of tree or grass of the field, in all the land of Egypt. (Exod 10:14–15)

In two ways, these verses take the measure of the catastrophe that this plague represents. First, the locusts are given a mythological status: "never before had there been so many, nor will there ever be so many again." Second, the words used to describe what they ate – "all the grasses of the field and all the fruit of the trees" and "nothing green was left," – evokes the creation of the world. Genesis 1:29 relays God's endowment for people: "See, I give you every seed-bearing plant that is upon all the earth, and every tree that has seed-bearing fruit; they shall be yours for food." Genesis 1:30 adds His provision for animals: "all the green plants for food." Once the locusts have finished with it, Egypt will look like the earth before creation, *tohu va'vohu*, with sustenance for neither man nor beast.

> *Pharaoh then summoned Moses and said, "Go, worship the Lord! Only your flocks and your herds shall be left behind; even your children may go with you." But Moses said, "You yourself must provide us with sacrifices and burnt offerings to offer up to the Lord our God; our own livestock, too, shall go along with us – not a hoof shall remain behind: for we must select from it for the worship of the Lord our God; and we shall not know with what we are to worship the Lord until we arrive there." (Exod 10:24–26)*

Pharaoh and Moses are negotiating over what the Israelites will take and what they'll leave behind when they go out of Egypt. There is one bone of contention – the Israelites' flocks and herds. As presented here, as so often in negotiations, they mean different things for the two negotiating parties. For Pharaoh, the animals represent the food supply for his people, and a means of rebuilding the flocks and herd decimated by the plagues. For Moses, they represent the means of offering sacrifices to God.

> *Moses said, "Thus says the Lord: Toward midnight I will go forth among the Egyptians, and every first-born in the land of Egypt shall die, from the first-born of Pharaoh who sits on his throne to the first-born of the slave girl who is behind the millstones; and all the first-born of the cattle." (Exod 11:4–5)*

Many food-related activities are gendered. In the west, even today, the family member primarily responsible for food preparation is most likely to be a woman, while the chef in an expensive restaurant is most likely to be a man. These verses (and others in the Tanakh, such as Job 31:10) suggest that grinding was a woman's activity. They also indicate that it was an occupation with very low social status. The intention here is to demonstrate that the death of the first-born affected every single Egyptian, from the highest, a male king, to the lowest, a female slave. It's worth noting that the female slave in question is Egyptian; even if all Israelites were slaves, not all Egyptians were masters.

> *This day shall be to you one of remembrance: you shall celebrate it as a festival to the LORD throughout the ages; you shall celebrate it as an institution for all time. Seven days you shall eat unleavened bread; on the very first day you shall remove leaven from your houses, for whoever eats leavened bread from the first day to the seventh day, that person shall be cut off from Israel. (Exod 12:14–15; see also Exod 12:17–20 and Exod 13:6–8)*

Even before they left Egypt, *Pesaḥ*, memory, and food comprised a holy trinity in the consciousness of the Israelites. Over time, it was not just eating matzah that would remind their descendants of the days of slavery in Egypt and their glorious escape, but a host of other edible mnemonics – lettuce, potatoes, parsley, grated apple and chopped nuts, and salt water.

> *You shall celebrate a sacred occasion on the first day, and as sacred occasion on the seventh day; no work at all shall be done on them; only what every person is to eat, that alone may be prepared for you. (Exod 12:16)*

The prohibition of work on the festival day excludes the work needed to prepare food to be consumed on the day itself. By focusing on the work rather than the workers, this verse elides an important point. Who will be working on the festival when "you" are resting? As things have turned out, the division of labor has been heavily gendered: women, the main food preparers in most Jewish homes, work; men rest. Perhaps that was always the case.

> *The Egyptians urged the people on, impatient to have them leave the country, for they said, "We shall all be dead." So the people took their dough before it was leavened, their kneading bowls wrapped in their cloaks upon their shoulders. (Exod 12:33)*

The *Pesaḥ* Haggadah gives the impression that it was because they feared for their lives that the Israelites didn't have time to let the dough rise. Here, however, it's clear that the rush was because the Egyptians feared for *their* lives. From a modern Western perspective, it's easy to assume that carrying kneading bowls on their shoulders was a reflection of extraordinary times. But the kneading bowl in question was not a Kitchen Aid. In the ancient world, as in the many parts of the world today, it was normal, and indeed essential, to travel with a means of preparing a simple, basic meal.

> *And they baked unleavened cakes of the dough that they had taken out of Egypt, for it was not leavened, since they had been driven out of Egypt and could not delay; nor had they prepared any provisions for themselves. (Exod 12:39)*

The reference to provisions, or the lack of them, is strange. True, it makes the case slightly stronger for baking the dough they brought out of Egypt, but who would question that decision? They were hardly in an environment where wasting food could be justified, and in any case, unleavened bread was a familiar staple, not a meal in extremis. Perhaps they were depending on God to provide the snacks for the journey, or perhaps, right to the end, the Israelites did not in their hearts believe that that they were leaving Egypt.

> *The LORD said to Moses and Aaron: This is the law of the passover offering: No foreigner shall eat of it. But any slave a man has bought may eat of it once he has been circumcised. No bound or hired laborer shall eat of it. It shall be eaten in one house: you shall not take any of the flesh outside the house; nor shall you break a bone of it. The whole community of Israel shall offer it. If a stranger who dwells with you would offer the passover to the LORD, all his males must be circumcised; then he shall be admitted to offer it; he shall then be as a citizen of the country. But no uncircumcised person may eat of it. There shall be one law for the citizen and for the stranger who dwells among you. (Exod 12:43–49)*

Given the enormous effort that God has just made to separate Israel from Egypt, one might have expected a set of rules designating Israel and Israel alone as the celebrants of the *Pesaḥ* offering. It's not a free-for-all – neither foreigners nor hired laborers may eat of it, and all who partake must be circumcised. But resident aliens are emphatically included. From the very first moment, non-Israelites had a place at the table in that most Israelite and particularist of all activities: the commemoration of the exodus from Egypt.

DIANA LIPTON

Beshallah

Exodus 13:17–17:16

Experiences with Manna

Deena Garber

Parashat Beshallah (Exod 16:4–36) describes the miraculous daily nourishing of the Israelites in the wilderness for forty years by the remarkable "heavenly bread" which rained down each night except Shabbat in the form of a fine crystalline layer spread over the ground (see also Num 11:6–9). Sandwiched between layers of dew from above and below, it fell perfectly ready to be gathered in the early morning, six days each week, and then to be ground, cooked, or baked for consumption without further agricultural activities such as planting or threshing. The daily quantity was measured exactly as one *omer* per person, according to each household's needs, and on Friday mornings it descended as a doubled portion, sufficient for two days.

The account of the heaven-sent manna for the Israelites' desert journey from Egyptian slavery to the Promised Land is one of the primary root metaphors describing God's continued sustenance, care, and providence after the people finished the unleavened matzah of the Exodus. Conversely, receiving the manna is seen as a necessary precursor to receiving Torah at Sinai. The people are tested by their motivation and ability to absorb and appreciate the physical and spiritual qualities of the desert food. They are also sensitively healed from the traumatic wounds of slavery by the healing delicacy of the toil-free manna, so that they are ready for the refinement and challenges of Torah and its Revelation (*Midrash Shir Hashirim Rabbah* 2:5:2).

Why is this manna experience so crucial? What is entailed by this divinely prepared food? What may we learn about the elements and sensitivities involved in the process of providing and sharing food where there is lack? In interpreting the biblical narrative, both talmudic and later commentators describe the inherent intertwining of multiple physical and spiritual dimensions of the manna, combining physical and spiritual sustenance for the collective and the individual.

For example, depending on the spiritual standard and life-cycle stage of the individual, manna descended nearer or farther from home, making it easier or harder to collect (Hebrew root verb *leket*). The Babylonian Talmud, Yoma 75 suggests that like mother's milk, manna was experienced with a variety of possible tastes, colors and forms, and in general provided for individuals' differing needs and desires. The Torah teaches that "Man does not live on bread alone, but on anything that the Lord decrees" (Deut 8:3). Spiritual life and vitality accompany the manna, which incorporates spiritual food beyond the physical and is unlike other food since the blissful days of Eden. Psalm 78 calls manna *leḥem abirim*, "a hero's meal" (v. 25). *Midrash Tehillim* puns on this as *leḥem aivarim*, bread which can be absorbed entirely into the inner organs (Heb. *aivarim*) with no waste to filter or expel. The Zohar (*Va-yetse*) sees manna nourishing through the influx of heavenly light itself, thus providing the infrastructure for all experiences of spiritual life.

These concepts are developed by Rabbi Avraham Yehoshua Heschel of Apt (1748–1825). In *Ohev Yisrael* he cites the kabbalistic idea of three levels of nourishment, *hazana,* all as aspects of manna. The first is the purely physical level which gives the body nourishment essential to sustaining life. The second is manna as spiritual "heavenly bread," derived from the life-giving vitality of the Torah from above. The third most refined level, from hidden realms of the Unknown, is a day-by-day ongoing realization of the archetypal Days of Creation as a source for spiritual creativity in human life.

Rabbi Yehudah Aryeh Leib Alter (1847–1905), *Sefat Emet,* offers profound insights about nourishment by manna, including its relationship to the Tree of Life, as it refined the physical body, prepared one to receive Torah knowledge and integrated physical, psychosomatic and psycho-spiritual dimensions.

The idiosyncratic psychoanalytic writings of Wilfred Bion may suggest some clarification of these complex dimensions. Bion, who appreciates the significance of the whole household and its emotional inter-relationships expressed in the individual's feeding process, seeks to explain the weaving together of sensual, alimentary and psychological processes facilitated by a mother for an infant. These optimally result not only in physiological ingestion and digestion of presented food/milk, but also, he claims, a simultaneous psychological ingestion, absorption and transformation of psychological elements and raw undigested experiences (beta elements). These raw elements loaded with primordial fears and emotions could be transmuted in the context of the mother's protective psychological presence and "reverie" state, with love, wisdom, and other higher functions. They become psychologically available elements of thinking and being (alpha elements) that promote development, knowledge and experience, connection and emotional truth.

Otherwise, if physical feeding is disconnected from being and meaning, what may be a material "feeding" on one level may be experienced as a "starving" and "taking" rather than as a welcome gift of food, followed by splits between satisfying the physical lack and psychological fulfillment.

By extrapolation, in bringing food to a hungry household or person, the giver needs extreme sensitivity to minimize the possible negative subliminal interactions with the receiver and the fragmentation of self and other (as widely discussed in halakhic and other sources). In such careful giving, one makes a space to open the potential for healing, creativity, and knowledge of truth which such an encounter may bring, beyond the material food itself, whilst also being sensitive to the diversity of emotions generated in such an exchange and aware of the subtle complexity of human beings and their needs.

DEENA Z. GARBER studied psychology at University College London, and the Tavistock Institute, and was a fellow at Yale Psychiatric Institute. She has studied Talmud at Bruria, MaTaN and The Hebrew

University, and Hassidut in various settings. Deena has taught psychology at Bar Ilan University and Touro College, and Torah at Yakar and other Jerusalem venues. She worked extensively with Professor Eliane Amado Levi-Valensi, and established Bet Midrash LeTorat Hanefesh for interdisciplinary learning and research. Her teaching emphasises Hazal and pre-modern Jewish thought and Hassidut in relation to psychological issues.

> *They came to Marah, but they could not drink the water of Marah because it was bitter; that is why it was named Marah. And the people grumbled against Moses, saying, "What shall we drink?" So he cried out to the LORD, and the LORD showed him a piece of wood; he threw it into the water and the water became sweet. (Exod 15:23–25)*

This is the first of many occasions when the Israelites complain because of lack of sustenance. They start with water, not a lack of it in this case, but water that's not fit to drink. It's hard to know which would have more dispiriting: a parched desert landscape with not a drop of water to be seen, or a landscape dotted with natural wells and springs, none of which supply drinking water?

> *The Israelites said to them, "If only we had died by the hand of the LORD in the land of Egypt, when we sat by the fleshpots, when we ate our fill of bread! For you have brought us out into this wilderness to starve this whole congregation to death."(Exod 16:3)*

"Fleshpots" is an archaic term that today is used most often with comic undertones to signify excess, and more or less only when an allusion – direct or indirect – to the Bible is intended. It conjures up images of a sort of orgy – half-naked people lying around stuffing themselves. In Hebrew, however, the term gives a very different impression: a simple clay pot filled with a homely meat stew, the bread on hand to scoop it up, as is still common in the Middle East. Presumably "fleshpots" has been retained in modern translations because it allows the possibility of a value judgment. The Israelites are not simply yearning for the decent meal evoked by the pot of meat. They are longing for the almost perverse sexual gluttony evoked by "fleshpots."

> *And the Lord said to Moses, "I will rain down bread for you from the sky, and the people shall go out and gather each day that day's portion – that I may thus test them, to see whether they will follow My instructions or not. (Exod 16:4)*

These verses contain a sharp disjunction. The image of bread from heaven screams abundance and abandon: It's raining bread, hallelujah! All that is undermined by the assertion that it was a display designed by God to test the people. It's a bit like throwing sweets at a Bar Mitzvah and telling the children to stay in their seats.

> *The Lord spoke to Moses: "I have heard the grumbling of the Israelites. Speak to them and say: By evening you shall eat flesh, and in the morning you shall have your fill of bread; and you shall know that I the Lord am your God." (Exod 16:11)*

As "fleshpots" seems jarring in v. 3, so too does "flesh" in this context. Surely only cannibals ask if they're having "flesh" for dinner tonight. One explanation for the decision to translate the Hebrew *basar* as "flesh" is that God is about to feed the Israelites with quail; as when chicken is on the menu, "meat" sounds misleading. Another possible explanation is that, again like "fleshpots," "flesh" evokes perverse appetite and greed. It captures the sense that all this talking about food is distasteful to God (as to Moses). He'll give the people what they want, but not without letting them know that He's not happy about it.

> *In the evening quail appeared and covered the camp; in the morning there was a fall of dew about the camp. When the fall of dew lifted, there, over the surface of the wilderness, lay a fine and flaky substance, as fine as frost on the ground. (Exod 16:13–14)*

The image of the quail covering the camp continues the theme developed above. It hints at nauseating excess. A carpet of manna, like frost, could be quite beautiful. You'd have to be very hungry indeed to find a carpet of quails alluring.

> *The Israelites did so, some gathering much, some little. But when they measured it by the omer, he who had gathered much had no excess, and*

> *he who had gathered little had no deficiency: they had gathered as much as they needed to eat. And Moses said to them, "Let no one leave any of it over until morning." But they paid no attention to Moses; some of them left of it until morning, and it became infested with maggots and stank. And Moses was angry with them. (Exod 16:17–20)*

Depending on your perspective, and perhaps life experience, this account of the manna could sound like a utopian dream or a totalitarian nightmare. On the one hand, it outlines a system in which everyone gets exactly what he or she needs to eat, no less and no more. There can be no black market profiteering, exploiting the laziness of those who prefer to let someone else do the gathering for them. On the other hand, it could be reminiscent of Soviet-era supermarkets – no variety and therefore no choice.

> *"This is what the LORD meant: Tomorrow is a day of rest, a holy sabbath of the LORD. Bake what you would bake and boil what you would boil; and all that is left put aside to be kept until the morning." So they put it aside until morning, as Moses had ordered; and it did not turn foul, and there were no maggots in it. Then Moses said, "Eat it today, for today is a sabbath of the LORD; you will not find it today on the plain. Six days you will gather it; on the seventh day, the sabbath, there will be none." (Exod 16:23–26)*

This is one of the earliest examples of a discussion that became central in post-biblical Judaism: the intersection of food and Shabbat. Not surprisingly, time is a crucial element of food preparation: what can and cannot be done on Shabbat. But it also introduces the idea that Shabbat can be transformative when it comes to food. Manna kept overnight was inedible by the morning every day except for Shabbat. The cholent that will look so unappetizing on Sunday morning tastes delicious at the Shabbat morning kiddush.

> *The house of Israel named it manna; it was like coriander seed, white, and it tasted like wafers in honey. (Exod 16:31)*

Coriander seed is mentioned here not to give a sense of the taste of manna, but rather to convey its appearance – color, size and, perhaps, texture. Coriander seed is an interesting choice for this purpose, given that what stands out about coriander is its very strong (and, for those genetically disposed, soap-like) taste. It takes a mental effort to stop thinking about spicy Mexican or Indian food when you hear the word coriander, and think instead about the sweet and comforting taste of honey. Perhaps we are being asked to mimic the mind-games that must have been played by the Israelites themselves when they thought about their menu options for the day . . . manna, manna, and . . . manna.

> *They encamped at Rephidim, and there was no water for the people to drink. The people quarreled with Moses. "Give us water to drink," they said; . . . "Why did you bring us up from Egypt, to kill us and our children and livestock with thirst." (Exod 17:1–3)*

This is another example of a familiar conjunction: food or water deprivation reminds the people of Egypt. This is not, as one might have predicted, because it recalls another period in their lives when they suffered from lack of sustenance. Rather, they are contrasting the present, when they lack food and (in this case) water, with the past when, regardless of whatever else was wrong, they apparently did not go hungry or thirsty. Perhaps this is an indication of how primal is our fear of death by starvation or dehydration. Almost anything is tolerable if it enables us to fend off that.

DIANA LIPTON

Yitro

Exodus 18:1–20:23

Eating before God

Gilla Rosen

Parashat Yitro opens with the arrival of Moses' wife and his father-in-law, Jethro. Moses and Jethro are joined by the seventy elders and "eat before God" (Exod 18:12). We wonder what makes this a meal before God. Is it the hospitality to a newcomer and the fact that Moses, like Abraham, is serving rather than partaking of the feast? Is it the great sages involved, or Jethro's religious inspiration and his offering of sacrifices? After that initial meal, there is not even the scent of food as the people receive the Torah at Mount Sinai in the midst of thunder and lightning and a mountain on fire (Exod 19:16).

Nor do the Ten Commandments explicitly relate to any of the positive commandments or prohibitions regarding food that appear later in the Bible. Why not? That question is contingent upon another: that of the character of the Ten Commandments. Are they the most fundamental commandments? Or the best to start with? Or the heads of categories which include all the rest of the commandments like "ripples between the waves" (Palestinian Talmud, Shekalim 6 [49:4])? If so, where would kashrut, the dietary laws, for instance, fit into the Ten Commandments? (Philo suggested they belong with the last commandment: do not covet!)

But between the lines, in those ripples between the waves, questions about food surface. One of the most interesting relates to the Sabbath. Exodus 20:8 reads: "Remember the Sabbath day and keep it holy (*lekadsho*)." How does one keep the Sabbath holy? The answer to this question was by no means always obvious. At various periods in Jewish history there existed competing visions of the ideal Sabbath.

One vision was ascetic: one should remove oneself as much as possible from daily life, fast, study Jewish law or mysticism, meditate, speak as little as possible. . . . In such a way one could hope to sanctify the day.

The other vision called for eating fine meals and for making sure that the poor could do so as well, for lighting lamps or candles to create a beautiful Friday night, and expressing the meaning of the Sabbath in blessings over a cup of wine – that great delight and scourge of mankind. The latter vision won out and the Sabbath is a day which integrates prayer and Torah study and physical pleasure. Good food mingles with words of Torah and the singing of zemirot, and of course we say Kiddush over a cup of wine. This decision regarding the character of the Sabbath is the expression of a deeply challenging vision of life. How do we enjoy our food on Shabbat without being gluttonous? Join the rush of modern life and yet listen for quiet voices? Week after week, how do we get the balance right between the physical and spiritual? Or even better: loosen the boundaries between the two?

How do we prepare a holiday meal "before God," enjoy "the happiness of the mitzvah rather than of our stomachs?" Maimonides makes it clear: by inviting the poor and the less fortunate to join us at our tables (*Laws of the Holidays*, 6:18–19, see Deut 16:11–12).

GILLA ROSEN is Director of Yakar Jerusalem & Tel Aviv. She has a Master's Degree in Comparative Literature and has taught at Nishmat (Torah Education for Women), Pardes, Yakar, in addition to serving as the Head of Beit Midrash Lindenbaum, 2002–2003. Gilla also lectures at various institutions and for the past six years has served as a halakhic advisor for women on an open hot-line sponsored by Nishmat.

> *Make for Me an altar of earth and sacrifice on it your burnt offerings and your sacrifices of well-being, your sheep and your oxen; in every place where I cause My name to be mentioned I will come to you and bless you. (Exod 20:21)*

Many ancient cultures, including those surrounding ancient Israel, saw sacrifices as food for their gods. Whether to thank, praise, dispose favorably, or simply as a way of saying sorry, people took choice meat and offered it up on altars. These gods were typically highly anthropomorphized in the sacred texts of their worshipers. For example, they were often represented as hungry and even salivating. In the Mesopotamian Gilgamesh epic, which has striking similarities to the biblical flood narrative, the gods swarm around like flies, attracted by the smell of the sacrifice that was offered when the water subsided. At the end of the biblical flood narrative, by contrast, God remains remote. He smells the "pleasing odor" of Noah's sacrifice, but there's not the slightest suggestion that He's hungry. In the Bible, hunger is a way of differentiating human from divine. People want and need to eat; God does not. A great deal rides on that, not least that although food is so often a way to control people, it cannot be used to control God.

DIANA LIPTON

Mishpatim

Exodus 21:1–24:18

Feed Your Servant as You Would Feed Yourself

Ed Greenstein

When Joseph's Hebrew brothers went down to Egypt, they were free persons; and yet the Egyptians would not eat with them (Gen 43:32). The Egyptians held foreigners, even free persons engaged in trade, in low esteem. The Torah does not altogether do away with differentiations in status. But when it comes to the treatment of the Israelite who had to sell himself into servitude in order to pay off his debts (see Lev 25:39), the Torah instills a sense of social equality. In treating one's servants one must internalize the lessons of the exodus, in which God set an example of freeing a people from the domination of another people.

There are many laws in Parashat Mishpatim that have striking parallels in other collections of law from the ancient Near East, from Mesopotamia and Asia Minor. Virtually all of them deal with various aspects of slavery. Only our parasha, however, positions the laws of servitude at the beginning, front and center. It is hard to avoid the inference that the pride of place given to these laws is connected to the deliverance of the Israelites from servitude by the God who identifies himself at the beginning of the Ten Commandments, in the portion of the Torah immediately preceding ours, as the God, "who brought you out of the land of Egypt, the house of bondage" (Exod 20:2). As the commentator Umberto (Moshe David) Cassuto put it, the Israelites must learn to liberate their servants and provide for them as God had done for the Israelites.

The law of indentured service in parashat Mishpatim sets a limit of six years on the term that an Israelite must work for his master. In Deuteronomy 15 (parashat Re'eh) the law is expanded to include a provision for supplying the manumitted servant with flocks, grain, and wine (v. 14), and there the lesson of the exodus is made plain: "Bear in mind that you were slaves in the land of Egypt and the LORD your God redeemed you; therefore I enjoin this commandment upon you today" (v. 15). Servants must take with them the food that will sustain them in transitioning to the life of a freely earning person.

The trend to show special concern for the Israelite servant was developed very specifically by the rabbinic sages. Maimonides devotes an entire section of his encyclopedic code of Jewish law, the *Mishneh Torah* ("reiteration of the Torah"), to the rules concerning servants. In the first chapter of this section, law nine, he spells out the details of equal treatment that are to be accorded to the servant: "As for every Hebrew male or female servant, the master must treat them equally (to himself) in food and in drink, in clothing, and in lodging."

This rabbinic law is apparently based on a law in our parasha, according to which a woman who is sold by her father in order to pay a debt must not be denied the clothing, lodging, and food to which she had been accustomed, even if her husband later takes a wife he likes better (Exod 21:7–11). Maimonides goes on:

> *For the Torah says because it is good for him [the servant] with you (Deut 15.16), meaning, you should not be eating a fine bread while he is eating a coarse bread, you should not be drinking an aged wine while he is drinking new wine; you should not be sleeping on cushions while he is sleeping on straw; you should not be residing in town while he is residing in a village . . .*

Rabbinic law draws the tendencies of the Torah's rules to their logical conclusion. The servant is "your brother" (see the formulation in Deuteronomy). Even if he is down and out, he must be treated as your equal – same food, same housing, same comfort. Most if not all of us will find the implications of that law an imposing challenge. What can we do to see that all members of our people are eating, dressing, living as well as we are? How far are we willing to go to make that happen? That is the challenge posed by the Torah as understood by tradition. No wonder the rabbis said, "One who acquires a Hebrew servant acquires a master for oneself!"

ED GREENSTEIN is Professor of Biblical Studies and Head of the Institute of Jewish Biblical Interpretation at Bar Ilan University. Before Bar Ilan, Ed was a professor at Tel Aviv University and at the Jewish Theological Seminary in New York, where he taught for 20 years. He has also taught at Columbia, Yale, Princeton, and has lectured widely. He has edited the *Journal of the Ancient Near Eastern Society* since 1974 and published extensively in Biblical and ancient Semitic studies; his wide-ranging research interests span from the ancient Near East to post-modernism. Ed is engaged now in writing commentaries on Job and Lamentations.

> *When a man lets his livestock loose to graze in another's land, and so allows a field or vineyard to be grazed bare, he must make restitution for the impairment of that field or vineyard. When a fire is started and spreads to thorns, so that stacked, standing, or growing grain is consumed, he who started the fire must make restitution. (Exod 22:4–5)*

There's an interesting difference between the two examples of property damage mentioned here. In both cases, A's food source (a field, vineyard, grain) is consumed by B (livestock, fire) because of the actions of C (letting loose livestock or starting a fire). But in the first case, C benefits; his animals are sustained. Indeed, one could say that when he makes restitution he is also paying the bill for the grass and vines they grazed on. In the second case, by contrast, no-one benefits; the sense in which the fire "ate" the food was strictly metaphorical. From A's point of view, it doesn't make much difference, but from a more detached perspective, there's something distressing about wasting food that applies to ravenous fires but not to hungry animals.

> *You shall not put off the skimming of the first yield of your vats. You shall give me the first-born among your sons. You shall do the same with your cattle and with your flocks; seven days it shall remain with its mother; on the eighth day you shall give it to Me. (Exod 22:28–29)*

Why must the baby animal remain with its mother until it is eight days old? Is it structural – paralleling the eighth day on which a baby boy is circumcised? Or is it emotional – taking into account the baby animal, who would otherwise be deprived of a bond with its mother, and the mother, who would otherwise know the pain of losing her baby the moment it's born? The idea that Torah legislation responds to the feelings of animals will sound to some far-fetched. Yet surely it's not far-fetched to imagine that the Torah incorporates an economy in which the value of life cannot be reduced to the purely utilitarian. An animal cannot be born *only* to be sacrificed . . . or eaten.

> *You shall be holy people to Me: you must not eat flesh torn by beasts in the field; you shall cast it to the dogs. (Exod 22:30)*

Much has been said about what renders unfit for consumption the meat of an animal that was killed by another animal. Less often noted is the emphasis on not wasting it: it's perfectly good for the dog! Here again we glimpse the complex economy in which even dogs – of no value as food for humans in and of themselves – have a part to play: they can consume what humans cannot.

> *Six years you shall sow your land and gather in its yield; but in the seventh you shall let it rest and lie fallow. Let the needy among your people eat of it, and what they leave let the wild beasts eat. You shall do the same with your vineyards and your olive groves. (Exod 23:10 –11)*

Yet again, the theme of waste emerges. Allowing the land to rest during the sabbatical year does not entail the wasteful destruction of the crops and produce generated during that year. First, those in need are given carte blanche to eat their fill, and what remains can be consumed by wild animals.

Three times a year you shall hold a festival for Me: you shall observe the Feast of Unleavened Bread – eating unleavened bread for seven days as I have commanded you – at the set time in the month of Abib, for in it you went forth from Egypt . . . (Exod 23:14–15)

The laws of Passover as they developed in rabbinic literature emphasize the negative side of this commandment: for seven days you shall eat no leaven, as in Exod 13:7, which prohibits even possession of leaven during Passover. The commands to eat and not to eat affect in very different ways those who observe them. Removing all trace of leaven entails herculean labor before Passover begins. Once the festival starts – with the exception of Shabbat, when there's a gap on the table where the challah would usually be – it's possible to get through the week without missing leaven too much. Omissions are not always striking. By contrast, depending on how much you eat (which is of course a significant subject of rabbinic discussion), it's hard to forget that you *are* eating unleavened bread in the way that you might forget you're *not* eating leavened bread. When it comes to the association of food and the memory of the Exodus, it's not surprising that the positive commandment comes to the fore.

The choice first fruits of your soil you shall bring to the house of the Lord your God. You shall not boil a kid in its mother's milk. (Exod 23:19)

In Exod 22:28–29 above, laws about the first fruits were followed by the stipulation that a baby animal should remain with its mother for the first seven days of its life. In the present verse, the commandment to bring first fruits is followed by the extraordinarily influential ruling – it's the source of the many, many laws of kashrut dealing with the separation of milk and meat – that a kid cannot be boiled in its mother's milk. This parallel serves, perhaps, to reinforce the notion that, as usually read and as translated above, the verse has been misunderstood. Its interest is not how to cook a dead kid, but rather when it's appropriate to slaughter it. Exod 22:29 above expresses this in temporal terms: the kid can be removed from its mother and slaughtered at the age of eight days. According to our verse, perhaps, this is expressed in terms of an activity: it's not appropriate to slaughter a kid while it's still drinking milk at its mother's breast.

> *Yet He did not raise His hand against the leaders of the Israelites; they beheld God and they ate and drank. (Exod 24:11)*

It's not unusual to read in right-wing Jewish media criticisms of Muslim behavior on the Temple Mount that focus on picnics. As anyone who has been up there will know, the spacious platform includes an area where people, especially women, sit under shady trees in the summer and eat and drink. Cultural notions of holiness have developed differently, especially in the West (from where many of these critics originate) versus the East. In the West, the idea of eating and drinking in a holy place seems inappropriate. Yet, as we see in this verse, they were once a natural combination. Moses, Aaron, Nadab and Abihu and the seventy elders of Israel ascend *to heaven* and *see* the God of Israel . . . and they eat and drink.

DIANA LIPTON

Terumah

Exodus 25:1–27:19

Food Fit for Princes

Lynn Kaye

In specifying the permanent structure of the Tabernacle, the book of Exodus mentions not merely its frame of drapes and poles or its heavy furniture, such as the candelabrum and table. The final constitutive element of the Tabernacle was a particular kind of food, the *leḥem panim*, loaves of bread that were to be present at all times in the sanctuary: "And on the table you shall set the bread on display, to be before Me always" (Exod 25:30).

Leviticus 24:5–7 describes this bread in greater detail. There were twelve loaves divided equally into two stacks. Near each stack frankincense was placed, which was "a token offering for the bread, as an offering by fire to the Lord." The medieval commentator Rashi explains that that the bread needed the frankincense to be a "reminder" ("token offering" according to NJPS) before God because the bread was replaced weekly, and never burned on the altar. In explaining this point, Rashi compares the show bread and its seasoning of frankincense to the grain offering and its *qomets,* the handful of flour, oil, and frankincense scooped from it and burnt on the altar: "Through [the frankincense], [the bread] is remembered above, just as the handful (of flour) is a reminder (*azkarah*) for the grain offering."

Of all foods, why was bread, linked with the grain offering, the most modest sacrifice offered on the altar, chosen to be placed permanently on the LORD's table? True, bread does not spoil as quickly as meat, but perhaps this choice has a deeper significance. In rabbinic literature, the grain offering is frequently identified as the sacrifice of the poor. The final mishnah of tractate *Menahot* states that the burnt offerings of cattle, fowl, and grain are all described as "a burnt offering, an offering by fire of pleasing odor to the LORD" (Lev 1:9,1; 17,2:2) "in order to teach that it is all the same whether one gives a lot or a little, as long as he directs his intention to Heaven." In other words, the Mishnah asserts that the grain offering smells as good to God as the most expensive bull. In the Babylonian Talmud, Menahot 104b, Rabbi Yitzhak expands on this sentiment with a midrash:

> *What is distinctive about the grain offering that the Torah mentions five different methods of preparation? Consider a parable of a king of flesh and blood, whose subject made him a banquet. The king knew that the man was poor, so he said to him, "Bake five types of pastries for me, so that I will have delight from you."*

The midrash suggests that the grain offering has more variety than the other sacrifices in order to give expression to God's delight in the offerings of the poor, possibly in contrast to the potentially uncharitable assessment of bread offerings by other people.

Perhaps the reason that bread was the food chosen to remain perpetually on God's table, part of the fundamental structure of the Tabernacle, is precisely because it evokes the grain offering, the sacrifice that is accessible to all. Maybe this is what Rashbam, another medieval commentator, had in mind when he described the bread as "fit to be placed before princes." By being the sacrifice open to all people, the humble bread is ennobled, becoming a delight, the choicest food set before a king.

LYNN KAYE is Assistant Professor of Near Eastern Languages and Cultures at the Ohio State University, specializing in rabbinic literature. During her time in New York City, Dr. Kaye served as Assistant Congregational Leader at the Spanish and Portuguese Synagogue, the oldest Jewish congregation in North America.

> *Make its bowls, ladles, jars and jugs with which to offer libations; make them of pure gold. (Exod 25:29)*

When it comes to the furnishings of the Tabernacle, and later the Temple, a simple distinction can be made between objects and utensils – such as the cherubim and the menorah – that are unlikely ever to have had a role outside a sanctuary of some kind, and those – such as "bowls, ladles, jars and jugs" – that almost certainly originated in a domestic setting. What differentiates the latter from the vast majority of kitchen utensils is the nature of the materials of which they are made – here, pure gold. However, even this wouldn't set them apart from items typically found in ancient Near Eastern (and many other) royal palaces, which may explain why the interior decoration of Ahasuerus' palace (Esth 1:5–7) sounds so familiar. So how can we distinguish between everyday kitchen items, such as jugs, and vessels from the Tabernacle or Temple? The best answer is probably context. In other words, we already need to know that we're looking at a sacred structure (or its remains) before we can determine whether or not the artifacts within it are sacred. In the absence of an inscription, a bowl is a bowl and a jug is a jug.

DIANA LIPTON

Tetsavveh

Exodus 27:20–30:10

The Closer, the Finer

Ariel Kopilovitz

Parashat Tetsavveh opens with the instruction "Instruct the Israelites to bring you clear oil of beaten olives for lighting, for kindling lamps regularly" (Exod 27:20). Olive oil was one of the most important agricultural products of the biblical land of Israel. It was used as a food, for light, for baking, for anointing and even for the production of various cosmetics. The many olive presses found throughout Israel testify to its wide usage.

The place of oil in worship is likewise established: already in Genesis, Jacob anoints with oil the rock on which he has slept, thus marking its transformation into a monument (Gen 28:18), and oil is prevalent in the many parshiyot which deal with the Tabernacle and the sacrifices brought there. Parashat Tetsavveh commands that the oil brought to light the lamp be "clear oil of beaten olives," that is, pure and clean oil produced through delicate blows of a mortar, not through the heavy beams used in oil presses. Unlike this fine oil, the oils used for other ritual purposes – such as the oil brought together with the grain offerings (Lev 2:1) – were regular oils, of inferior quality.

The rabbis already queried this difference in quality, given that normal practice would dictate that the finer oil should be used for food, while the oil of inferior quality should be reserved for lighting. Some explained that the demand that the oil for the lamp be pure and superior was intended to ensure a brighter and clearer light, and to prevent soot that might form from debris in unclear oil and stain the ornamental curtains and fabrics in the Tabernacle.

It appears, however, that the solution to this question about superior and inferior oils lies in an understanding of the notion of holiness reflected in the parshiyot that describe the Tabernacle. A central aspiration in these chapters is to ensure that God reside permanently amongst his people: "Let them make Me a sanctuary that I may dwell among them" (Exod 25:8). The Tabernacle, especially the Holy of Holies at its center, is understood as the actual resting place of God. One of the physical expressions of this notion was the way in which the Tabernacle was built and arranged. The further inside a ritual object was placed – and thus the nearer it was to the actual place of God's residing, the Holy of Holies – the more expensive and precious the materials it was made from.

Accordingly, in the Holy of Holies itself everything was made of pure gold or gold-plated, whereas the courtyard of the Tabernacle contained objects made of silver or copper. The inner partitions of the Tabernacle and the garments of the High Priest were made of the most expensive materials – blue and purple yarns "worked into designs" (Exod 28:6). The outer partitions, on the other hand, were made of simple wool, prepared more simply – "made of woven work" (Exod 39:22) or "done in embroidery" (Exod 26:36). The incense which the High Priest used when entering the Holy of Holies on Yom Kippur was "finely ground aromatic incense" (Lev 16:12); the incense used on the incense altar inside the Tabernacle was "aromatic incense" (Exod 30:7), and the incense used outside the Tabernacle was just regular "incense."

Following this principle – the nearer, the finer – the Torah determined that the olive oil used in the inner sanctuary, that is, for the lighting of the lamp, should be of higher quality than the oil used for the sacrifices, made on the copper altar located outside in the Tabernacle courtyard.

The description of choice olive oil using the term "beaten olives" has been preserved throughout the ages, and even today the authorities in charge of ranking the various olive oils sold in Israel grade the oils according to whether or not they are "beaten."

Ariel Kopilovitz is a doctoral student in the Bible Department at the Hebrew University of Jerusalem. His Doctorate deals with the descriptions of Israel's future in the restoration prophecies in Ezekiel. Ariel is married and a father of four. He resides with his family in the mixed communal yishuv Haruv-Eliav, in east Hevel Lakhish in south Israel.

> *On its hem make pomegranates of blue, purple, and crimson yarns, all around the hem, with bells of gold between them all around: a golden bell and a pomegranate, a golden bell and a pomegranate, all around the hem of the robe. (Exod 28:33–34)*

The pomegranate is a fruit that cries out for interpretation. Its color commands attention. Its crown recalls royalty. Its juice looks like wine. Its seeds evoke fertility and multiplicity. Small wonder that it was chosen to decorate the priestly garments.

> *Then take the breast of Aaron's ram of ordination and offer it as an elevation offering before the* Lord*; it shall be your portion. You shall consecrate the breast that was offered as an elevation offering and the thigh that was offered as a gift offering from the ram of ordination – from that which was Aaron's and from that which was his sons' – and those parts shall be a due from all times from the Israelites to Aaron and his descendants . . . (Exod 29:26–28)*

In the midst of instructions about the offerings Israel must make to God, comes an instruction about the offerings due to Aaron and his sons. They are entitled, in perpetuity, to the breast and the thigh of the ram, beginning with the ram that was slaughtered during the ceremony in which they were ordained as priests. At one level, these gifts to Aaron and his sons must have been practical; they ensured that they would not go hungry. But the gifts also served as a constant reminder to a priest of who he was. Every breast and thigh he ate linked him both to the ram slaughtered at his own initiation as a priest, and to the ram slaughtered when the first priests were initiated.

> *You shall take the ram of ordination and boil its flesh in the sacred precinct; and Aaron and his sons shall eat the flesh of the ram, and the bread that is in the basket, at the entrance to the Tent of Meeting (Exod 29:31–32).*

The holiness of the ram of ordination demanded that it be prepared and eaten in sacred spaces. The explanation for this lies in the specific biblical laws of sacrifice, but more generally it resonates with an aspect of food preparation and eating that's evident in many cultures: both take on elements of the environment in which they take place. You can tie your shoes absolutely anywhere, but there are many locations in which you would not usually be tempted to make a sandwich or eat a bagel.

> *These things shall be eaten only by those for whom expiation was made for them when they were ordained and consecrated; they may not be eaten by a layman, for they are holy. (Exod 29:33)*

In modern society, most explanations for restrictions about who is and is not entitled to eat this or that particular food would appeal to status. For example, in staff dining rooms members of the senior management are often served food of a higher quality than that served to lower level workers. This difference helps observers to know who's who. With regard to the priests, signifying the status of the eater was not a primary motivation. Rather, the meat itself had acquired a status that would be compromised in an inappropriate vessel, that is, the belly of a layman.

> *And if any of the flesh of ordination, or any of the bread, is left until the morning, you shall put what is left to the fire; it shall not be eaten, for it is holy. (Exod 29:34)*

Eat-by dates are usually for the benefit of the eater, protecting her or him from the consequences of eating spoiled food. In this case, the food itself is protected from being degraded by being consumed after its designated time.

DIANA LIPTON

Ki Tissa'

Exodus 30:11–34:35

Consumers and Cannibals

Jeremy Rosen

While Moses is still up on Mount Sinai, God tells him about the image of a Golden Calf that the children of Israel have made in his absence. God goes on to say "Now leave me so that my anger will blaze forth against them and I may consume them [eat them up], and make you into a great nation" (Exod 32:10). This threat is followed by an impassioned plea by Moses which mirrors in its way Abraham's plea over the impending destruction of Sodom and Gomorrah. Unlike Abraham, however, Moses succeeds in changing God's mind, in part because he appeals to His relationship with Abraham, Isaac, and Jacob. It may also have helped that the majority, it seems, were good people; after all, when the Levites joined Moses in killing the perpetrators, the dead amounted to no more than around 3,000.

As in English, the Hebrew word with the *alef chaf lamed* root means both "to eat" and "to consume." Fire is said to eat up or consume those who have challenged God or who behaved in a manner seen as challenging the established order, as in the case of Nadab and Abihu (Lev 10:2), And of course fire is essential for cooking, most specifically in this context the Paschal Lamb, which must not be eaten raw (Exod 12:9). If it sounds inappropriate to think of God as eating people up, as in relation to the Golden Calf in Exod 32:10, we must remember that the Torah is not speaking literally. God does not have a digestive system; the word "consume" is associated with a heavenly fire that consumes sacrifices, as at the end of Elijah's tour de force on Mount Carmel (1 Kgs 18:38).

After Moses came down from Sinai he took hold of the Golden Calf and "ground it to powder and strewed it upon the water and so made the Israelites drink it" (Exod 32:20). This is a powerful image of the futility of the people's search for protection in Moses' absence. The image of what they once saw as a god is now being drunk by the very people who worshipped it. This idea reveals a yet deeper dimension of the language of eating and consuming we encountered above. Eating entails rejecting as well as ingesting. It involves taking something into ourselves, digesting the useful and discarding the rest in a manner that most of us find unattractive. If the excreta are unappealing, nevertheless with food there is a positive result through nourishment. What possible positive result can there be from God "eating" humans? Only perhaps the realization of how different spiritual food is from material food.

Unlike the children of Israel who were forced to eat the Golden Calf, I have eaten gold and silver only as coatings on sugared almonds. Once upon a time this gold or silver confectionary seemed positive and pleasurable, a good sign at weddings and other *semachot*. Now many of us understand how unhealthy it is for our constitutions. Perhaps the Golden Calf should have served as a warning! The message is clear: humanity does *not* necessarily thrive on everything edible that comes from God. It is our responsibility to distinguish good from bad and choose our food accordingly.

JEREMY ROSEN received his rabbinic ordination from Mir Yeshiva in Jerusalem. He studied philosophy as an undergraduate at Cambridge University, and went on to earn his Ph.D. in philosophy. For more than forty years he has worked in the rabbinate, Jewish education, and academia in Europe and the US, and he now lives in New York City, where he writes, teaches, lectures, and serves as rabbi of a small Persian community.

> *The LORD spoke to Moses, saying: Next take choice spices: five hundred weight of solidified myrrh, half as much – two hundred and fifty – of fragrant cinnamon, two hundred and fifty of aromatic cane, five hundred – by the sanctuary weight – of cassia, and a hin of olive oil. Make of this a sacred anointing oil, a compound of ingredients expertly blended, to serve as sacred anointing oil. (Exod 30:22–25)*

It's hard to think about food today without thinking about recipes. Bookstores and the internet are overflowing with cook books and food blogs, not least Jewish ones. There's no dearth of instructions in the Torah concerning which animals are permitted for food, and in some cases who may eat them, not to mention rules and regulations about when the fruit of trees and agricultural produce can be eaten. But there are no recipes – at least for food. Instead, the kind of instructions, and even ingredients, we would expect to find today in an Ottolenghi cook book are reserved for inedible blends of oil, as here, and incense (a few verses later).

> *And speak to the Israelite people, as follows: This shall be an anointing oil sacred to Me throughout the ages. It must not be rubbed on any person's body, and you must not make anything like it in the same proportions; it is sacred, to be held sacred by you. Whoever compounds its like, or puts any of it on a layman, shall be cut off from his kin. (Exod 30:31–33)*

Today, the legal protection of ingredients and processes is most familiar in the fast-food arena, notoriously with certain soft drinks. It's motivated, of course, by money. By contrast, the list of ingredients for anointing oil (and later incense) is published in the Torah for all to see. There is, however, a strict ban on using it inappropriately; the unlicensed producer will be removed from his community.

> *Then the LORD said to Moses, "Set out from here, you and the people you have brought up from the land of Egypt, to the land of which I swore to Abraham, Isaac, and Jacob . . . a land flowing with milk and honey." (Exod 33:1–2)*

At the end of this passage, following the Golden Calf episode, comes the bad news: God won't be travelling with them on their journey to the land, in case he destroys them in anger on the way (Exod 33:3). Until then, the news had been all good: God had brought them out of Egypt, led them towards the Promised Land, and sent an angel to deal with its previous residents. The "milk and honey" was the icing on that tempting cake, now jeopardized by Israel's bad behavior.

> *You must not make a covenant with the inhabitants of the land, for they will lust after their gods and sacrifice to their gods and invite you, and you will eat of their sacrifices. And when you take wives from among their daughters for your sons, their daughters will lust after their gods, and will cause your sons to lust after their gods. You must not make molten gods for yourselves. (Exod 34:15–17)*

These verses illustrate perfectly the interaction between food (eating their sacrifices), sex (taking their daughters for your sons), and idolatry (lusting after their gods and making idols) that is so prominent in post-biblical Jewish texts.

> *You shall observe the Feast of Unleavened Bread – eating unleavened bread for seven days, as I have commanded you – at the set time of the month of Abib, for in the month of Abib you went forth from Egypt. (Exod 34:18)*

Both by the name used to designated it here (*ḥag ha'matzot*) and the single commandment given here for its observance (eat matzah for seven days), the emphasis in this particular verse falls heavily on the positive (eating matzah), not the negative (avoiding leaven).

> *The choice first fruits of your soil you shall bring to the house of the Lord your God. You shall not boil a kid in its mother's milk. (Exod 34:26)*

In Mishpatim (Exod 22:29), the reminder about bringing the first fruits is followed by a warning that babies among the cattle or flocks must be permitted to stay with their mothers for seven days before being removed for sacrifice. This raises an interesting possibility for the extremely influential ruling, prohibiting cooking a kid in its mother's milk. Although this forms the basis of all the laws of kashrut having to do with the separation of milk and meat, in its original context it is rather obscure. A French culinary term, "veau de lait," refers to a particular delicacy in some circles – a calf exclusively milk-fed and still suckling at its mother's breast at the time when it's taken for slaughter. Among biblical scholars, at least, it's been tentatively discussed that our verse might once have prohibited not the cooking of a baby animal in its mother's milk, but rather the cooking of an animal so young that it's still dependent on its mother's milk.

DIANA LIPTON

Va-Yakhel

Exodus 35:1–38:20

Haroset and the transformation of memory

Susan Weingarten

Parashat Va-yakhel deals with building the Mishkan, the Tabernacle, the resting-place of the Shekhinah, the Divine Presence, amidst the Israelites in the desert. I will show how this building process has been related to the delicious Passover food haroset (see recipe below).

The Passover Haggadah is full of word-games and plays on words. So it is not surprising that a later rabbi should add yet another word-game, playing on the names of the ingredients of his haroset. This rabbi was the Ari, (from the Hebrew initials of ha-Elohi Rabbi Itzhaq, the divine Rabbi Isaac Luria), and he was both mystic and poet. In the sixteenth century, in the holy city of Safed in the Land of Israel, he became the leader of a group of kabbalists. His pupil Rabbi Hayim Vital wrote down his mystical explanations of the halakhah, Jewish law, in a book called *Pri Etz Ḥayim*, the *Fruit of the Tree of Life*.

The Ari's word-game with haroset is bilingual, using both the holy language, Hebrew, and secular German. He talks about "*ḥaroset even* and *ḥaroset etz*" (R. Hayim Vital, *Pri Etz Ḥayim: Sha'ar Ḥag Hamat-zot*, ch. 6). Haroset, according to him, is made mainly from three ingredients: apples, pears, and nuts, whose initial letters in German (or as he calls it, "the language of Ashkenaz") – ***A**pfel, **B**iren, **N**üsse* – spell the word *even*, which means stone in Hebrew. He then adds to them the German names of two traditional spices: ***I**ngbar* and

Tzimmerind (ginger and cinnamon), whose initial letters become the mnemonic *etz*, which means wood in Hebrew. We know from German illustrated Haggadot of that time that all these ingredients were indeed used then to make haroset.

But *ḥaroset even* and *ḥaroset etz*, literally "haroset of stone" and "haroset of wood," are not simply jokes about the ingredients using the initial letters as mnemonics of the real thing. There is a further, highly serious word-play here. *Ḥaroset even* and *ḥaroset etz* are lisping puns on the biblical phrases "*ḥaros**h**et even*" and "*ḥaros**h**et etz*," meaning "the cut[ting] of stone and carv[ing] of wood," (Exod 31:5; 35:33) from parashat Va-yakhel, where they are used to describe the work of building the Mishkan. The Ari has taken these words which refer to the work of building the Mishkan as a reference point for the ingredients of his haroset.

It seems to me clear that this has spiritual significance. Beginning with the Jerusalem Talmud and the Babylonian Talmud, haroset has been interpreted through the ages as a reminder of the clay and blood in the bricks which, according to the rabbis, were used to build the cities of ancient pagan Egypt. The Ari has transformed his haroset into a reminder of the building of the Mishkan, the holy Tabernacle. The clay and blood used to build idolatrous Egypt are now transformed by his word-play into the materials for the earthly home of the Shekhina, the seat of the Divine presence.

The very first real recipe (as opposed to a simple list of ingredients) for haroset comes from the Rambam in his commentary on the Mishnah, 10.3. He writes:

> *Haroset is a mixture which has in it acidity and something like straw in memory of the clay. We make it like this: soak figs or dates and cook them and pound them till they get soft, and knead them with vinegar and put in spikenard or thyme or hyssop without grinding them.*

This is not too difficult to make, although the result tastes very different from any *ḥaroset* nowadays, and more like a chutney.

250 gr stoned dry dates
½ cup vinegar
1–2 tsp of dried thyme or za'atar (*not* the za'atar mix sold ready made, which has added sumac, sesame seeds etc., just the dried leaves)

Put the dates in a saucepan and add water to cover. Cook until the dates are a thick mass, taking care to stir occasionally with a wooden spoon to break up the dates and ensure the mixture does not catch. Add half a cup (100ml) of vinegar and simmer a little longer, then add one to two teaspoons of the dried thyme or za'atar leaves before taking the pan off the heat. The spikey little leaves should be visible in the finished haroset – like the straw in the bricks the Israelites made in Egypt.

Susan Weingarten wrote her Doctorate at Tel Aviv University on the Church Fathers in the Holy Land. Having had her fill of Christian asceticism, she moved to the study of Jewish Food. She now specializes in Food in Talmudic Literature.

> *You shall kindle no fire throughout your settlements on the sabbath day. (Exod 35:3)*

The prohibition against lighting a fire on the Sabbath follows the familiar formula,

> *"On six days work may be done, but on the seventh day you shall have a sabbath of complete rest . . ." (Exod 35:2)*

In connection with other examples of this formula (Exod 20:9; 23:12, 34:21; Deut 5:13), the prohibitions implied by the benefits specified – so that you and your servants and your animals can rest – suggest agricultural labor and heavy housework. Lighting a fire in the ancient world was a lot harder than it is now, but still it's not exactly work as we might usually define it. More plausibly, it's an act that makes possible many other kinds of work, from those mentioned a few verses later in the construction of the Mishkan to the work most often associated with fire and its descendants: food preparation.

Diana Lipton

Pekudei

Exodus 38:21–40:38

Gazing with eyes of blessing

Nehemia Polen

Parashat Pekudei begins with a tally of materials that were donated by the Israelites for the construction of the Tabernacle: "These are the records of the Tabernacle, the Tabernacle of the Pact, which were drawn up at Moses' bidding . . ." (Exod 38:21). The accounting provides specific amounts in shekels for the gold, silver, and copper donations. On this, the great hasidic master Rabbi Levi Yitzhak of Berditchev (1740–1809) juxtaposes the following Talmudic passage:

> *On entering the barn to measure the new grain one should recite the benediction, "May it be Your will, O Lord, our God, that You may send blessing upon the work of our hands." Once he has begun to measure he says, "Blessed be God who sends blessing into this heap." If, however, he first measured the grain and then recited the benediction then his prayer is in vain, because blessing is not to be found in anything that has been already weighed or measured or numbered, but only in a thing hidden from sight. (Babylonian Talmud, Ta'anit 8b)*

This passage from the Babylonian Talmud suggests that the bounty of a harvest is open and uncertain before it is measured. The crop may actually increase – its growth continuing – until such time as it is actually inventoried. It follows that the farmer may pronounce a blessing, a berakhah, over his crop, inviting the flow of divine beneficence, shefa, only until such time as he measures it. The measuring has the effect of fixing it in place so that change is impossible. This is something like a Talmudic "principle of indeterminacy."

Rabbi Levi Yitzhak asks: If this is so, how is it that the materials for the Tabernacle were weighed and numbered, yet the Tabernacle was a place of blessing (see Exod 39:43; Ps 90:17)? He responds that there are two ways to look at an object: one way might be called "the possessive gaze;" the other way is the "appreciative gaze." The first seeks to control and has the effect of desiccating the object, emptying it of vitality and sweetness. The possessive gaze looks with desire, betrays the wish to grasp, to seize and incorporate into the self; it has the effect of visually pinching and constricting. As Levi Yitzhhak puts it, this gaze "separates the object from its supernal root in the wellspring of vitality." On the other hand, the appreciative gaze is one of blessing, seeing the object in its own intact fullness and integrity. Such a gaze imparts bounty; it enriches by strengthening the object's connection to its sources of vitality and allows for the flow of abundance, the shefa, to continue.

Moses' activity of inventory, even though it involved measuring, was done with the gaze of blessing. The hasidic master playfully engages in a Hebrew wordplay, reading Song of Songs 7:5, Eynayikh berekhot be-Heshbon, "your eyes [are] like pools in [the place] Heshbon," to yield, "Your eyes are pools of blessing even while measuring [Hebrew heshbon]." Moses was able to make an accounting of the materials in the Tabernacle in a way that did not stultify or constrict; to the contrary, he saw the divine potential in each object. By extension, we too are invited to see the objects in our world – most especially food – not as commodities to be hoarded and appropriated, but as divinely-rooted sources of blessing, to be appreciated, respected and shared in a spirit of benevolence and generosity of spirit.

NEHEMIA POLEN is Professor of Jewish Thought at Hebrew College, Boston, USA. He is a leading expert in Hasidism and Jewish thought, whose books include *The Holy Fire: The Teachings of Rabbi Kalonymus Kalman Shapira, the Rebbe of the Warsaw Ghetto* (1977); *The Rebbe's Daughter* (2002); and *Filling Words With Light: Hasidic and Mystical*

Reflections on Jewish Prayer (2004), written with Lawrence Kushner. Polen holds a Doctorate from Boston University, where he studied with and served as a teaching fellow for Nobel Laureate Elie Wiesel. Prior to his career in Jewish academia, Polen served for 23 years as a congregational rabbi.

> *At the entrance of the Tabernacle of the Tent of Meeting he placed the altar of burnt offering. On it he offered up the burnt offering and the meal offering – as the Lord had commanded Moses. He placed the laver between the Tent of Meeting and the altar, and put water in it for washing. From it Moses and Aaron and his sons would wash their hands and feet; they washed when they entered the Tent of Meeting and when they approached the altar – as the Lord had commanded Moses. (Exod 40:29–32, see also Exod 30:17–21)*

In post-biblical Jewish practice, the washing of hands is associated with the transition from profane to holy. This can apply to physical spaces – Jews might wash when entering a synagogue, or when leaving a place that defiles, such as a bathroom or a cemetery. It's also evident in connection with food, when, depending on levels of observance, Jews wash before eating meals that include bread – signifying a proper meal, not just a snack. Relating these developments back to the hand (and feet) washing mentioned in this verse, it's interesting to see the respect in which all meals have taken on the holiness that may once have been associated only with food sacrificed on the altar.

DIANA LIPTON

Va-Yikra'

Leviticus 1:1–5:26

Satisfying the Hungry

PINCHAS ROTH

Parashat Va-yikra', which opens Leviticus and its many discussions of animal sacrifices, splits quite neatly into two parts. The first half (chs. 1–4) discusses sacrifices brought voluntarily, while the second (chs. 4–5) deals with obligatory sacrifices to atone for sins.

Midrash *Va-yikra' Rabbah* on the opening verse of Leviticus 4 comments:

> *R Yehoshua of Sikhnin in the name of R Levi [said]: Six times, the word nefesh (soul) appears here, corresponding to the six days of creation. God says to the soul – Everything that I created in six days was created only for your sake. And you go out and sin, stealing and robbing?*

Taking what rightfully belongs to another person, according to this midrash, is a sin not only against a fellow human being, but against the entire universe. All of creation is offended by this violation. Bringing an animal sacrifice, killing another living thing, is an act of destruction that reflects that cosmic violation, and the sinner must shoulder the responsibility for the pain that he or she has brought into the world.

This same midrashic passage holds the key to a different approach to sacrifice. The verse which serves as the point of departure for this section in the midrash is Ecclesiastes 6:7: "All of man's earning is for the sake of his mouth, yet his gullet [*nefesh*] is not sated." According to Rabbi Levi, the world was created for the sake of man, or more specifically for the sake of his soul. According to this approach, it is legitimate for humans to avail themselves of the culinary possibilities in the natural world around them. Indeed, to some degree it is even their function in the world. However, following that command onto a path of self-indulgence leaves the soul, according to Ecclesiastes, with a gnawing sense of emptiness.

How can that emptiness be filled? How can the soul become satiated? Bringing a voluntary sacrifice, linking one's appetite and desire with the Creator who created that appetite – who placed desire in the world and the means to fulfill desire – might provide the solution. An animal slaughtered not out of displaced self-loathing but out of a desire to enjoy and celebrate the world and all its possibilities, is something that can satisfy the hunger of the soul.

PINCHAS ROTH is a lecturer in the Talmud Department at Bar Ilan University.

> *And the remainder of the meal offering shall be for Aaron and his sons, a most holy portion from the* LORD*'s offerings by fire. (Lev 2:3, 10)*

On one level, the instruction to reserve a portion of an offering for Aaron and his sons, that is, the Levites, has a practical explanation. Since the Levites are not permitted to own land, they cannot produce their own food. On a deeper level, it moves them further away from their fellow Israelites and closer to God on the holiness spectrum. Here we see that this is not simply a case of giving the Levites a percentage of the community's produce; their portion comes from "the LORD's offerings." Sharing food implies a certain degree of intimacy, and Aaron and his sons are more or less eating from God's plate.

> *All fat is the* LORD*'s. It is a law for all time throughout the ages, in all your settlements: you must not eat any fat or any blood. (Lev 3:16b–17, see also Lev 7:23–25)*

On many occasions, in a variety of different contexts, the Israelites are prohibited from consuming the blood of the animals they eat. Explanations often accompany the prohibition, such as that the blood is the "life-force" of the animal. The fat prohibition, by contrast, is not widely mentioned, and the closest thing to an explanation is that fat "is the LORD's" (v. 16b). Yet these words turn out to be crucial. Moreover, it's easy to define what blood is, but much less easy to define what constitutes fat. Exactly what kind of fat is off-limits? Just preceding the fat prohibition is a list of body parts and organs: "He shall then present, as an offering by fire to the LORD, the fat from the sacrifice of well-being: the whole broad tail, which shall be removed close to the backbone; the fat that covers the entrails and all the fat that is about the entrails; the two kidneys and the fat that is on them, that is at the loins; and the protuberance on the liver" (Lev 3:9–10). As we see, all these fall under the general heading of "fat." This fat is the LORD's, and for that very reason (though it happens to have significant health benefits) is prohibited for human consumption.

DIANA LIPTON

Tsav

Leviticus 6:1–8:36

Saying thank you with food

Harlan Wechsler

The Psalmist said it well: "Let them praise the Lord for His steadfast love, His wondrous deeds for mankind. Let them offer thanksgiving sacrifices . . ." (Ps 107:21–22).

Few concepts in faith, as in human relations, are as central to the development of virtue and piety as is the concept of gratitude. Think of the person who is convinced that everything good that comes his way is but a token of what he really deserves, and you will be thinking of someone who is crude and who sees others as his servant. How much more so the person who is convinced that all the gifts he receives from God are payback for what the Holy One owes him for the life he leads. Piety expects a refined sense of gratitude. Religion seeks to cultivate the character trait that leads to lips that frequently say thank-you to others and to God.

In parashat Tsav, we are introduced to the *shelamim*, offerings of well-being. Not brought to the Mishkan (or, later, the Temple) because of any obligation – neither to expiate sin nor to fulfill a requirement such as that associated with Passover or coming to the Temple not "empty handed" – the *shelamim* are an expression of a person's positive feelings. First among them is a special well-being offering: the *Todah*, the Thanksgiving Offering.

The *Todah* is not the only offering of well-being. The Torah also mentions a votive or a free will offering, but the Thanksgiving Offering is unique in two ways: First of all, it has to be brought accompanied by four types of bread, three unleavened and one leavened: unleavened cakes with oil mixed in as well as unleavened wafers spread with oil. Then unleavened cakes of choice flour with oil mixed in, well soaked (a precursor to our modern bagel, perhaps?) and, added to that, cakes of leavened bread. The second unique feature of the *Todah* offering is that it has to be eaten on the day it is brought; none of it can be set aside until morning. Other *shelamim* offerings are not brought with this immense amount of bread and they may be eaten on the morrow. Not so the Thanksgiving offering. The obvious questions are: why all the breads and what's the hurry?

The Babylonian Talmud, Menahot 77a notes the required quantities of these breads, quantities which further emphasize our question: ten loaves of each kind must be brought. In total, then, forty loaves of bread accompany the sacrifice of meat. Now think about it: who can eat that much bread and who can eat it in so short a time?

Rashi, in his commentary to the Torah (Lev 7:12), describes the person who is supposed to express his gratitude to God:

> *The matter of thanksgiving is applicable to a person who has experienced a miracle, such as having sailed the ocean (and come back safe), someone who has walked the desert (and come back safe), someone who was imprisoned and is now free, and someone who was ill and is now healed. These are people who need to give thanks for it is written in relation to them: "Let them give thanks to the* Lord *for His steadfast love, for His wondrous deeds to humankind. Let them offer thanksgiving sacrifices . . ."*

This is the source of our post-Temple custom of "blessing *gomel*" after having been delivered from a perilous situation. Even flying across an ocean will trigger the requirement to say the *gomel* prayer, expressing gratitude to the Lord for arriving safely.

The person delivered from danger should not take that deliverance for granted but rather should say thanks to He who is behind the mystery of all deliverance. The way it is done in the Torah is for an offering to be brought. Part of that would go to the priest who officiated but ninety percent would be left, still a very large amount of food to be consumed by one person. The obvious solution? If you *must* bring all that food and it *must* be eaten on that very day and there is too much for the grateful person to consume, he must, of course, share it with others.

The experience of gratitude therefore culminates with a shared meal. Others are brought into the orbit of the grateful person and that is how thanksgiving is experienced. As we might say today: you have been fortunate and been delivered from a risky and dangerous fate? Well, then: sponsor a kiddush! Share your joy with others, for gratefulness to God spreads if that gratitude is acknowledged publicly. Eating with others, sponsoring the food that will yield bread broken together, is the proper way to thank God for His steadfast kindness that we, the delivered, feel so deeply in our bones and in our souls. Sharing food with others is the proper format for giving thanks to God, and that we learn from the *Todah*.

HARLAN J. WECHSLER is an alumnus of Harvard College and received his ordination and Ph.D. degrees from the Jewish Theological Seminary of America. He is author of *What's So Bad About Guilt?* and the soon to be published *Old is Good: Ideas of Aging in Rabbinic Literature*, as well as articles on theology and ethics that have appeared in numerous journals. Rabbi Wechsler taught Jewish ethics and the history of Jewish thought for over thirty years in the Department of Philosophy at the Jewish Theological Seminary of America. Founding Rabbi of Congregation Or Zarua in New York City, he currently hosts *Rabbi Wechsler Teaches*, a weekly program of Jewish intellectual interest on SiriusXM Radio, broadcast from New York and Jerusalem.

> *What is left of it [the meal offering] shall be eaten by Aaron and his sons; it shall be eaten as unleavened cakes, in the sacred precinct; they shall eat it in the enclosure of the Tent of Meeting (Lev 6:9, see also 6:22, 7:6).*

Why were Aaron and his sons instructed to eat the meal offering as leavened cakes? Meal, unlike meat, cannot easily be eaten alone or unprocessed. It is usually transformed before being consumed. Yet if meal was simply used as an ingredient in a dish, it wouldn't be the meal offering any more. The priest's obligation to eat it would seem somewhat compromised. Unleavened cakes are about as close as it's possible to get to eating unprocessed meal. The only additional ingredient is oil (Lev 7:12), and although a transformation has occurred – from something loosely constituted like flour to something bound, like porridge or a pancake – the final product is one in which the significant ingredient, meal, remains visible and tangible. Whether by taste, texture or appearance, cooking can so often conceal or disguise ingredients, but here that's minimized.

> *Only the males among Aaron's descendants may eat of it, as their due for all time throughout the ages from the LORD's offerings by fire (Lev 6:11).*

The information that only Aaron's male descendants can eat the meal offering distinguishes it from some other offerings, which could be consumed by female family members. Reserving the remains of the meal offering for the priests was not, in this case, a means of sustaining the priests nutritionally without paying them a salary. Rather, they had to eat the leftover offerings because that was the most fitting way to dispose of them. I think about "fitting" disposal every Friday morning when I look at my sink full of beautiful, multicolored vegetable peelings and feel guilty that I still haven't found out where the nearest compost heap is.

> *The priest who offers it as a sin offering shall eat of it; it shall be eaten in the sacred precinct, in the enclosure of the Tent of Meeting (Lev 6:19).*

Regardless of the motivating force, these restrictions about where and by whom the meat of the sin offering may be eaten have the consequence that, in contrast to other kinds of sacrificial offerings and "holy food," it cannot be shared. A piece of meat that was touched or partly eaten by a priest cannot be divided up between a select group of followers or the highest bidders. In the case of the sin offering, eating is not a means of disseminating holiness abroad, but rather of concentrating it in one place.

> *But no sin offering may be eaten from which any blood is brought into the Tent of Meeting for expiation in the sanctuary; any such shall be consumed in fire (Lev 6:23).*

Sacrificial animals can serve multiple functions. A single cow can be divided into parts. Its fat can be thrown on the fire "for the LORD," its blood can dashed on the altar, and its flesh can be eaten by the priest. Some combinations, however, are not permitted. If the blood of an animal is brought into the sanctuary for expiation, to remove sin, its flesh cannot be eaten, but must be burned. Did this additional restriction protect a priest from internalizing meat "contaminated" by association with the sin its blood expiated? Or did it reflect the special status of the meat of an animal whose blood had been used to remove sin? In other words, are these instructions primarily about the eater or the eaten?

> *If, however, the sacrifice he offers is a votive or a freewill offering, it shall be eaten on the day that he offers his sacrifice, and what is left of it shall be eaten on the morrow. What is then left of the flesh of the sacrifice shall be consumed in fire on the third day. If any of the flesh of his sacrifice of well-being is eaten on the third day, it shall not be acceptable; it shall not count for him who offered it. It is an offensive thing, and the person who eats of it shall bear his guilt (Lev 7:16–18).*

This timetabled consumption underlines the inextricable link between eating and sacrifice. The meat of a votive or freewill offering can be eaten on the day the sacrifice is offered, or the next day. If, however, it is eaten the day after that, the sacrifice is retroactively nullified. The sacrificial animal may be divided up into parts destined for different functions but, in some conceptual respects, it remains whole. It could be instructive to extend this way of thinking to food in general.

> *As for other [clean] flesh, only he who is clean may eat such flesh. But the person who, in a state of uncleanness, eats flesh from the LORD's sacrifices of well-being, that person shall be cut off from his kin. When a person touches anything unclean, be it human uncleanness or an unclean animal or any unclean creature, and eats flesh from the LORD's sacrifices of well-being, that person shall be cut off from his kin (Lev 7:19b–21).*

We intuitively think about whether the food we eat is sufficiently "clean" – fresh, uncontaminated – to be ingested. The question of whether we are sufficiently "clean" to ingest the food we eat is less intuitive, though the practice, ritual or otherwise, of washing before eating certainly leads the mind in that direction.

> *Speak to the Israelite people thus: You shall eat no fat of ox or sheep or goat. Fat from animals that died or were torn by beasts may be put to any use, but you must not eat it. If anyone eats the fat of animals from which offerings of fire may be made to the* Lord, *the person who eats it shall be cut off from his kin. And you must not consume any blood, either of bird or of animal, in any of your settlements. Anyone who eats blood shall be cut off from his kin (Lev 7:23–27).*

These prohibitions underline an obvious point about animal products. It seems at first glance obvious that consuming the fat of an animal that died a natural death or was killed by other animals is prohibited; that category of animals is prohibited in its entirety (Lev 7:24). On second thought, however, it's clear how easy it is to convince ourselves that a particular animal product has been transformed – for example by drying – to the extent that it no longer "belongs" to the animal in question. The product takes on an identity of its own. The logic of the fat prohibition as expressed here discourages that way of thinking about the animals we eat.

> *Moses said to Aaron and his sons: Boil the flesh at the entrance of the Tent of Meeting and eat it there with the bread that is in the basket of ordination – as I commanded: Aaron and his sons shall eat of it; and what is left over of the flesh and the bread you shall consume in fire (Lev 8:31–32).*

So often, in the Bible and beyond, bread is taken for granted as a component of a meal. You order a bowl of soup and bread shows up on the table, along with olives and a variety of dips if you're in the Middle East. Bread can be viewed as more of a utensil than a food. Or, as with challah on Shabbat, bread can be the star of the show. In this case, certainly, the description highlights bread's importance; it has independent ritual value as the "bread of ordination," and must be eaten or burned exactly like the meat.

Diana Lipton

Shemini

Leviticus 9:1–11:47

The Vegetarian Ideal in the Bible*

Gary A. Rendsburg

Parashat Shemini, especially chapter 11, includes the most prominent treatment of permitted and forbidden animals in the Torah (the parallel text in Deuteronomy 14 is less detailed). Even after millennia of discussion, however, there is still no consensus as to why certain animals are permitted and why others are forbidden. The view I am presenting here builds on the work of other scholars before me.

We begin by recalling that the world was created with both humans and animals commanded to eat only vegetation (Gen 1:29–30, 2:9, 2:16 emphasized more in the first creation account, but present in the second one as well). Accordingly, we posit a vegetarian ideal, in line with a harmonious world established at creation. The humans could not live up to these standards established by God, and the Genesis narrative quickly moves on to disobedience (Gen 3:6), violence (Gen 4:8; 23), and improper sexual relations (Gen 6:1–4).

The result is the great flood, after which God lowers the bar for humanity, allowing for the eating of meat (Gen 9:3), though with

* This essay is based on the author's earlier and more detailed article, "The Vegetarian Ideal in the Bible," in L. J. Greenspoon, R. A. Simkins, and G. Shapiro, eds., *Food and Judaism* (Studies in Jewish Civilization, vol. 15; Omaha: Creighton University Press, 2005), pp. 319–334, available at the author's website, http://jewishstudies.rutgers.edu/faculty/core-faculty-information/gary-a-rendsburg – click on "Complete List of Publications," see Article no. 112.

the one important proviso: no consumption of blood (9:4). It is this latter point, I believe, which allows us to understand the Torah's rationale in permitting certain species, while prohibiting others. In general, the permitted animals are all herbivores, as we may see from analyzing the various sub-divisions.

The permitted land animals are the three domesticated cloven-hoofed ruminants (sheep, goats, cattle), to which may be added one wild animal, the deer, including the many individual species subsumed in that category, such as the gazelle and the antelope (listed in Deut 14:5) – all of them herbivores.

Fish must have fins and scales in order to be eaten, and this description therefore excludes the various scavengers on the river bed or the ocean bed, such as crabs, lobsters, shrimp, and crayfish.

The Torah does not provide traits for the permitted birds, but from the list of the 20 forbidden species, including eagles, vultures, owls, and so on, we may conclude, as does the Mishnah (Hullin 3:6), that birds of prey are forbidden, while other birds, such as doves, pigeons, and quail are permitted.

Finally, we may note that four species of locusts are kosher, even though most Jewish communities no longer eat these creatures – and that these locusts are the plant-eaters par excellence!

Now, to be sure, there are some problems with this approach. For example, other mammalian herbivores are not allowed, such as horse, donkey, rabbit, hyrax, etc. Moreover, certain water fowl, such as ducks, eat fish in addition to their grazing on plants at the water's edge. We also know that some larger fish eat smaller fish, in addition to plankton and so on. So the explanation proffered here is not perfect, yet I believe that it underscores a major theological point.

The permission granted to humanity to eat meat is a compromise of the vegetarian ideal, for it requires the taking of life. But in so doing, man is not allowed to eat blood, which is the symbol of life (again, see Gen 9:4, and especially Lev 17:11; Deut 12:23). Hence, the omnivores (pigs, etc.) and carnivores (cats, eagles, etc.) of the world are not to be eaten – lest we ingest blood through the backdoor, as it were, by eating an animal which itself has eaten an animal.

To put this in other terms: humankind is unable to live up to the vegetarian ideal set forth at creation, but Israel wishes to adhere to that ideal, even in compromised fashion. Hence, Israel consumes only those animals which themselves have not killed other animals or consumed the flesh thereof.

The vegetarian ideal which inspired ancient Israel is not limited to texts of Torah (creation, dietary laws, etc.), however. It appears again, in all its splendor, in the description of the end of days, as envisioned by the prophet Isaiah (ch. 11). In Isaiah 2, the prophet describes the anticipated world peace as the harmony among nations: "nation shall not take up sword against nation" (2:4) (amongst other well-known passages). In chapter 11 the visionary thinker paints more or less the same picture, but he does so by projecting the faunal world onto his canvas. The natural enemies, the animals that prey and the animals that are preyed upon, are paired off, as an exemplar of what the world will be like in this period of perfect harmony. "The wolf shall dwell with the lamb, the leopard lie down with the kid; the calf, the beast of prey, and the fatling together, with a little boy to herd them. The cow and the bear shall graze, their young shall lie down together; and the lion, like the ox, shall eat straw" (Isa 11:6–7).

Thus, in Isaiah's portrayal of the future world, the animals will return to their vegetarian state. Wolves, leopards, and lions no longer will prey upon their traditional foes, sheep, goats, and cattle. The lion will have to learn to eat straw like the ox. We will return to the paradise of creation. Isaiah understood the matter well, and when he sought to highlight what the end of days would be like, he settled upon vegetarianism, just as the text of Genesis 1–2 focused on this point in the two versions of creation.

Even more remarkable perhaps is my final point. Isaiah's words were reused about 160 years later by the prophet Second Isaiah, living in exile in Babylon around 540 BCE, as the culminating verse in one of most glorious passages in the entire Bible. In chapter 65 the prophet presents his view of a new heaven and a new earth (v. 17), a world in which all troubles would be forgotten (v. 16). In this new world order, Jerusalem will be a joy, there will be no more weeping and wailing, a man who fails to reach one hundred years of age will be reckoned as one accursed, people will plant vineyards and enjoy the fruit, and they shall be blessed by the LORD (vv. 18–24). And then the final lines: '"the wolf and the lamb shall graze together, and the lion shall eat straw like the ox . . . In all my sacred mount nothing evil or vile shall be done – said the LORD" (v. 25). This crucial passage, as cited both in Isaiah 11 and in Isaiah 65, speaks volumes. It epitomizes the vegetarian ideal which permeates the spirit of the Bible and the life of ancient Israel.

GARY A. RENDSBURG serves as the Blanche and Irving Laurie Chair in Jewish History at Rutgers University. Previously he taught at Cornell University, and he has served as Visiting Scholar at the Hebrew University, the University of Pennsylvania, the University of Sydney, the University of Oxford, and the University of Cambridge. Professor Rendsburg teaches and publishes on all aspects of ancient Israel: primarily language and literature, but also history and archaeology. His forthcoming book is entitled *How the Bible Is Written* (CDL Press, 2016).

> *And the LORD spoke to Aaron, saying: Drink no wine or other intoxicant, you or your sons, when you enter the Tent of Meeting, that you may not die. (Lev 10:8–9)*

With the exception of the nazirite vow (Num 6:1–8), which puts wine and intoxicants off-limits for that special category of men and women dedicated, even sometimes from the womb (e.g., the birth of Samson in Judges 13), to the service of God, the Bible does not generally problematize alcohol – though it is sometimes associated with drunken foreigners, as in Esther 1. Why, then, are Aaron and his sons prohibited from drinking alcohol when they enter the Tent of Meeting? One answer concerns context; alcohol belongs at a feast, but not in a space dedicated to the service of God. Another concerns correct procedure; alcohol makes it difficult to execute instructions precisely. Yet another concerns personal safety. It has just been established quite graphically through the deaths of Nadab and Abihu (Lev 10:1–7) that God will exact the death penalty for a priest who does not follow the correct procedure. Allowing a drunken priest in the Tent of Meeting, then, would be, to say the least, to put a stumbling block before the blind.

> *Moses spoke to Aaron and to his remaining sons, Eleazar and Ithamar: Take the meal offering that is left over from the LORD's offering by fire*

> *and eat it unleavened beside the altar, for it is most holy. You shall eat it in the sacred precinct, inasmuch as it is your due, and that of your children . . . But the breast of elevation offering and the thigh of gift offering you, and your sons and daughters with you, may eat in any clean place, for they have been assigned as a due to you and your children from the Israelites' sacrifices of well-being. (Lev 10:12–14)*

A sharp distinction is made between two different kinds of offerings, where they may be eaten and by whom. The meal offering is of an order of holiness that allowed for eating, but only in a sacred space. That constraint effectively ruled out some eaters: the daughters of the priests, who were not permitted to enter the designated space. Perhaps that's why, with reference to the breast of elevation offering (10:14), the daughters are explicitly mentioned. Since the "sacred space" rule does not apply here, and since priests and their families depended on the sacrificial cult for sustenance, it was crucial to make it clear that females were included.

> *Then Moses inquired about the goat of sin offering, and it had already been burned! He was angry with Eleazar and Ithamar, Aaron's remaining sons, and said, "Why did you not eat the sin offering in the sacred area? For it is most holy, and He has given it to you to remove the guilt of the community and to make expiation for them before the Lord. Since its blood was not brought inside the sanctuary, you should certainly have eaten it in the sanctuary, as I commanded." (Lev 10:16–18)*

This narrative stands out. Instead of eating something they shouldn't have eaten, Aaron's surviving sons *don't* eat something they *should* have eaten. This reversal of the norm underscores the complexity of attitudes towards food in the context of the sacrificial cult. Sometimes the priests and their families eat specified parts of a sacrificial animal as a source of food, as in verse 14 above. On other occasions, sustenance has nothing to do with it. Moses is not angry with Eleazar and Ithamar because they missed their dinner, but because they failed to observe the proper protocol with regard to sin offerings.

Diana Lipton

Tazria'

Leviticus 12:1–13:50

You are what you give someone else to eat

Amit Gvaryahu

Parashat Tazria' does not deal with food. The laws of birth and the various bodily afflictions it relates deal with other aspects of the human body: with what the body expels or what grows on it, not what enters it. The connection between food and Tazria' can, however, be found in two other places – in the haftarah, the weekly reading from the Prophetic books (2 Kgs 4:43–5:19), and in the Mishnah.

Let us begin with the Mishnah. Leviticus 13:12 discusses the status of a person whose entire body is covered in disease, "wherever the priest can see." From this verse the rabbis learned that there are parts of the human body which are not viewed by the priest, and that disease in these places does not render the person impure. The Mishnah describes the way in which a man or a woman must stand in front of the priest in order to properly show him their skin:

> *How is the disease to be seen? The man shows himself as one who hoes and as one who harvests olives. And the woman as one who kneads and as one who nurses her son. (Mishnah, Nega'im 2:4)*

Men and women need to be seen in two different working positions, in which different body parts are exhibited, as detailed in the Sifra (*Nega'im,* p.63b ed. Weiss).

These working positions are ones in which both the man and woman are preparing food. There is an interesting statement here on how people are perceived. The diagnosis of this disease is arguably is the situation in which people were the most exposed to their communities, through the eyes of the rabbis, who identify the disease, and the priest, whose job it is to determine whether the diseased skin is pure or impure, according to the rabbis' instructions. But what is it that the rabbi or the priest sees? A man or a woman engaged in the production of food – whether in the production of food from the soil, in kneading, or in breast feeding.

There is, then, an interesting statement in this Mishnah regarding the relationship between someone's body, their personality, and their food. When a person's body is inspected in order to determine whether or not anything is out of order, it is inspected like the body of a worker engaged in food production. This is not a trivial statement. In our world we find many descriptions of people – verbal, material or graphic – but they barely ever describe working people, and certainly not people who are working to produce food. In this context, the sharp gender division of the Mishnah is also unfamiliar to us today: while we are used to seeing sharply gendered bodies, this gendering is rarely in the context of productive work, but rather in the context of the objectification of the human body.

In the world of the Mishnah, the above-mentioned activities were often undertaken naked. This is certainly true regarding the nursing woman, but also of kneading women, while men who were tilling the earth or harvesting olives often wore very little. The body was of course exhibited naked to the priest, so that clothes did not conceal the disease. A body the skin of which is being inspected is an object which must be viewed and diagnosed, but the owner of this naked body is a man or a woman. While they are viewed "nude" – without clothes, status, wealth, or even identity to hide their disease – the Mishnah takes the trouble to identify, in this nakedness, the person working to feed others. The human body, in its abstract form, is the body engaged in feeding.

In our haftarah, in 2 Kings 5, Naaman, the commander of the Aramean army, falls ill with leprosy. However, he refuses to recognize that the disease strips him of all of his former possessions and honor. First, he offers Elisha money in exchange for healing him, but then he refuses to immerse himself in the Jordan River, as Elisha commands him to. "I thought," he [Naaman] said, "that he would surely come out to me, and would stand and invoke the LORD his God by name, and would wave his hand toward the spot, and cure the affected part,"(2 Kgs 5:11). After all, Naaman claims, what is so special about the Jordan?! However, when he finally follows Elisha's instructions and immerses in the Jordan, "his flesh became like a little boy's, and he was clean" (v. 14). The leprosy forces Naaman to realize that he is nothing but "a little boy" in its face and that his money and the various rivers over which he holds sway cannot help him.

Immediately before the healing of Naaman is another story, in which Elisha, the "man of God," engages himself in feeding:

> *"A man came from Baal-shalishah and he brought the man of God some bread of the first reaping – twenty loaves of barley bread, and some fresh grain in his sack. And [Elisha] said, "Give it to the people and let them eat." His attendant replied, "How can I set this before a hundred men?" But he said, "Give it to the people and let them eat. For thus said the LORD: They shall eat and have some left over." So he set it before them; and when they had eaten, they had some left over, as the LORD had said." (2 Kgs, 4:42–43)*

Following our interpretation of the Mishnah, we now find another interesting connection between leprosy, its healing, and the production of food. Elisha, the "man of God," knows how to feed many people with a small amount of food. This contrasts with the working man, who requires additional toil in order to produce more food. If the working man is the one who falls ill with leprosy, and his work defines the limits of the body for the purposes of viewing his disease, the "man of God" is capable of breaking these boundaries: he does not require the work, and is capable of healing leprosy as well. This "man of God," therefore, is one who is able to transcend physical boundaries through the power of his spirit, and by using this power to feed others.

According to this interpretation, we can understand the story of Elisha's servant, Gehazi, in 2 Kings 5. Gehazi doesn't understand why Elisha refuses payment from Naaman, and chases after the Aramenian commander to tell him that Elisha has requested money after all. Naaman gladly gives Gehazi money, as well as clothing, but Elisha reacts in anger and curses Gehazi that "the leprosy of Naaman shall cling to you and to your descendants forever." And as [Gehazi] left his presence, he was snow-white with leprosy" (2 Kgs 5:27). Gehazi's inability to understand the importance of giving up possessions and social standing in order to be healed from leprosy leads him to take the mantle of the "man of God" and use it as a status symbol. However, unlike Elisha, the real "man of God," capable of transcending physical boundaries, this misuse of the title by Gehazi renders him identical to Naaman, who likewise refused to be stripped down in order to be healed. Thus, Gehazi is punished, not with ordinary leprosy, but rather with "the leprosy of Naaman."

The Mishnah instructs us that, even when afflicted with leprosy, the naked man is none other than the man who feeds; the haftarah demonstrates that the inability to feed freely is, perhaps, the root cause of the illness.

AMIT GVARYAHU is a Ph.D. candidate at the Hebrew University. He has taught at Yeshivat Hadar, Drisha, Yeshivat Talpiot, and the Pontifical Gregorian University in Rome. He lives in Jerusalem with his wife Yedidah and his son Benjy.

> *When a woman at childbirth bears a male, she shall be unclean seven days; she shall be unclean as at the time of her menstrual infirmity. (Lev 12:2)*

The analogy in this verse with menstruation indicates that at least one component of a woman's uncleanness after giving birth is discharge. This is the first of many references to various types of female and male discharge that render a person unclean (see Lev 15:2–4, 16, 18, 19, 25). It's interesting to note that while excrement is considered unclean and defiles the camp – it must be buried outside (Deut 23:13–14) – there seem to be no circumstances in which excrement defiles a person. Without being too graphic, it's easy to think of cases – dysentery, for example – where that could have been different. What does this have to do with food? Short of the kind of miracle attributed to the wilderness wanderers by rabbis, what goes in – food – must come out.

Diana Lipton

Metsora'

Leviticus 14:1–15:33

Food Subsidies

Uri Gabbay

In this week's portion, we learn that the leper was required to go through a long process of healing and purification. The process began with purification rituals undertaken by the priest on the leper's behalf, after which the leper shaved his hair and spent seven days outside his tent. On the eighth day the leper returned to the priest in order to undergo the final rite of purification, which was accompanied by sacrifices and bread offerings. The leper himself had to supply these sacrifices, as specified in the parasha: "On the eighth day he shall take two male lambs without blemish, one ewe lamb in its first year without blemish, three-tenths of a measure of choice flour with oil mixed in for a meal offering, and one log of oil" (Lev 14:10).

This is no small number of sacrifices and bread offerings! What if the leper was poor and couldn't afford all these offerings? This is one of the few places in which the Bible provides a cheaper and more considerate alternative to the sacrifice: "If, however, he is poor and his means are insufficient, he shall take one male lamb for a guilt offering, to be elevated in expiation for him, one tenth of a measure of choice flour with oil mixed in for a meal offering, and a log of oil; and two turtledoves or two pigeons, depending on his means, the one to be the sin offering and the other the burnt offering" (Lev 14:21–22).

Similar cases of alternatives for sacrifices can be found in only two other places in the Bible, in Leviticus 5 (in the matter of oaths and impurity) and Leviticus 12 (in the sacrifice of the woman who has recently given birth). In both these cases the sacrifices which must be brought are connected to the social standing of the person bringing them.

A similar correlation between the social standing of the sacrificing person and the offering they must bring existed in ancient Mesopotamia. An Akkadian prayer to the god of the sun and justice, Shamash, known to us from several tablets in cuneiform script from the seventh century BCE, opens with the following words:

You arose, Shamash, in the cedar mountain.
The gods rejoice in you, mankind is happy with you.
The diviner brings you cedar,
The widow – cheap flour for roasting,
The poor woman – oil,
The rich man in his wealth brings a lamb.

In the world of ancient Mesopotamia, sacrifice was not perceived as a unilateral action, but rather functioned as a conduit of communication between man and god. On one side stood man, who gave of his own to god, and on the other, god, who returned the favor to man (through various signs which the priest or diviner interpreted), informing him whether or not his sacrifice had been accepted. Just as each man brought a different sacrifice, depending on his social status, thus god received the sacrifice in a manner relative to each man and corresponding to the substance of his sacrifice, whether through the signs visible in the liver of the lamb brought by the rich man, in the oil floating on the water brought by the poor woman, or in the shape of the heap of flour brought by the widow.

In the Bible, this personal social conception was preserved in the case of the leper. At times it is actually the lack of material equality – as in the case of the leper's sacrifice – which creates real equality of opportunity. Biblical law does not specify one law for all regarding the leper's sacrifice. Just as anyone can become a leper, so all people must have equal opportunities to purify themselves from leprosy.

This equal opportunity is expressed through the social distinction guiding the sacrifice which each person must bring.

URI GABBAY teaches Assyriology at the Hebrew University, Jerusalem. His main subjects of research are Sumerian and Akkadian religious and scholarly texts.

> *The LORD spoke to Moses, saying: This shall be the ritual for a leper at the time that he is to be cleansed. When it has been reported to the priest, the priest shall go outside the camp. (Lev 14:1–2)*

Parashat Tazria' mentioned several times what the priest should do with a person or object diagnosed with leprosy: "*hisgir* [him or it] for seven days" (Lev 13:4). Some translations render *hisgir* as "isolate" This fits well with modern ideas of how to deal with contagious diseases, but "shut out," the more familiar translation of this Hebrew verb, would be better. As is confirmed in verse 2 above, "the priest shall go outside the camp," the lepers were not placed in an isolation unit of some kind, but *shut out* of the camp altogether. Neither Tazria' nor Metsora' give any indication of how they survived out there, but the haftarah for Metsora', 2 Kgs 7:3–20, gives a glimpse of the challenges they faced with regard to food. King Ben-Hadad of Aram has besieged the cities of Samaria (2 Kgs 6:1). Within the city gates, the food shortages are so severe that mothers are eating their children (2 Kgs 6:26–30). Meanwhile,

> *There were four men, lepers, outside the city gate. They said to one another, "Why should we sit here waiting for death? If we decide to go into the town, what with the famine in the town, we shall die there; and if we just sit here, still we die. Come let us desert to the Aramean camp. If they let us live, we shall live, and if they put us to death, we shall but die." (2 Kgs 7:3–4)*

It transpires that the Arameans, terrified by the *sound* sent by God of an approaching army, have abandoned their camp. They enter the camp, eat and drink, and loot the Aramean tents. An interesting paradox emerges from this story with regard to what is now known as "food security." In normal circumstances, the situation of the lepers outside the gates is extremely precarious. They depend on people inside to bring them food from inside, and could so easily be abandoned. At a time of crisis, such as war, however, their situation outside the gates is less precarious than that of those inside. The healthy residents are trapped inside and could starve to death, while the lepers, rendered in some sense "liminal" by their illness, are free to move between the warring factions and find food.

DIANA LIPTON

'Aharei Mot

Leviticus 16:1–18:30

Know What You Eat

Shani Tzoref

When I was taught the biblical basis of kashrut at high school, the passages we studied were the lists of kosher and non-kosher animals and the prohibition against "cooking a kid in its mother's milk." Parshat 'Aharei Mot includes some kashrut laws which are less frequently part of the modern Halakha curriculum, but merit reading through a contemporary lens.

Leviticus 17:3–4 states:

> *"If anyone of the house of Israel slaughters an ox or a lamb or a goat in the camp, or slaughters it outside the camp: and does not bring it to the entrance of the Tent of Meeting to present it as an offering to the Lord before the Lord's tabernacle, bloodguilt shall be imputed to that man: he has shed blood; that man shall be cut off from among his people."*

The Talmud describes a debate between Rabbi Ishmael and Rabbi Akiva about the subject of this law, which continues through medieval times to contemporary commentators. Rabbi Ishmael follows what seems to be the plain sense of the verses, prohibiting the consumption of meat unless it is part of a sacrificial offering. This interpretation is supported in the Septuagint, in the Samaritan tradition, and in some of the Dead Sea Scrolls, including the Temple

Scroll and *Miqsat Ma'ase HaTorah*. In Rabbi Ishmael's understanding, the Israelites in the wilderness – the narrative framework for Leviticus – were not permitted to eat *ḥullin* ("profane slaughter" in rabbinic terminology; also called *basar ta'ava* – "meat of craving" or "of lust"). Any Israelite wanting to eat meat in the wilderness period would have needed to bring a *shelamim* sacrifice, and eat from the permitted portions of this sacrifice.

An injunction against eating non-sacrificial meat sounds like something we would expect more from Michael Pollan than the Torah: "Eat food. Not too much. Mostly Plants" (*The Omnivore's Dilemma*). In fact, one challenge that has been posed to Rabbi Ishmael's reading is that the continuation of the passage declares that this law "shall be to them a law for all time, throughout the ages" (v. 7). This is problematic since Deuteronomy 12, which legislates for a time when the Temple is standing and the nation is settled in the Land, allows for the consumption of "the meat of craving." Putting academic considerations aside, I would like to suggest a homiletic reading: a biblical restriction on eating "Meat of Craving" can offer a lesson that is applicable in every generation, perhaps especially our own.

The Rambam suggests limiting meat consumption according to one's financial means and desire, and the *Shulchan Aruch* advises avoiding meat for ascetic reasons. These and similar models are especially relevant in the modern era, since the twentieth-century saw meat become an accepted component of the ordinary daily Western diet. In the twenty-first-century, there is growing awareness of the hazards of that development, from nutritional, ecological, and humanitarian perspectives. It is precisely such awareness which may be the most important lesson we can take from the *kashrut* laws in our parsha and their parallels. The passage in Leviticus 17 continues with a prohibition against consuming blood:

> *". . . For the life of the flesh is in the blood, and I have assigned it to you for making expiation for your lives upon the altar; it is the blood, as life, that effects expiation. Therefore I say to the Israelite people: No person among you shall partake of blood, nor shall the stranger who resides among you partake of blood. . . . Any Israelite*

or any stranger who resides among them hunts down an animal or a bird that may be eaten, he shall pour out its blood and cover it with earth. For the life of all flesh — its blood is its life. Therefore I say to the Israelite people: "You shall not partake of the blood of any flesh, because the life of all flesh is its blood. Anyone who partakes of it shall be cut off." (vv. 11–14)

A connection between the consumption of meat as a concession to human weakness and a prohibition of the consumption of blood has also been identified in Genesis 9:3–4, where the permission to eat meat is presented as a novelty granted to Noah in the wake of the flood. In Genesis, the restriction is tied to negative observations about human nature and susceptibility to violence, and is associated with the prohibition against murder. In Leviticus, the law is explained in terms of atonement and sanctity.

This prohibition against consuming blood is essential to the process of koshering meat, so familiar to many of our grandmothers, but not generally a part of the culinary repertoire of today's kosher consumer. Among contemporary criticisms of the industrialization of meat "production", alongside concerns of *tza'ar ba'alei ḥaim* (cruelty to animals), is the disconnection of the consumer from the powerful act of animal slaughter. A similar observation may be made concerning the convenience of avoiding the labor-intensive process of salting meat to remove the blood. This increasing depersonalization is very far from the graphic descriptions in Torah, which attach great importance to acknowledging blood as the life-force, associated with holiness and divine worship. Perhaps this parasha can serve as an incentive to reduce our consumption of meat and to heighten our awareness of the sources of all of our food. Most of us are likely to continue to be market consumers of food, rather than to hunt, gather, or grow the bulk of what we eat. As Pollan notes, "The more knowledge people have about the way their food is produced, the more likely it is that their values . . . will inform their purchasing decisions."

SHANI TZOREF is currently a Fellow at the Qumran Institute of the University of Göttingen. A specialist in the Dead Sea Scrolls, she has taught Biblical Studies and Ancient Judaism at universities in Israel, Europe, the U.S. and Australia, including Yeshiva University, the Hebrew University, and the University of Sydney. Dr. Tzoref's academic awards include a Fulbright Fellowship (1994), and a Rothschild Fellowship (2006) at Hebrew University.

> *And if anyone from the house of Israel or of the strangers who reside among them partakes of any blood, I will set My face against the person who partakes of the blood, and I will cut him off from among his kin. For the life of the flesh is in the blood, and I have assigned it to you for making expiation for your lives upon the altar; it is blood, as life, that effects expiation. (Lev 17:10–11)*

Among the explanations given for the prohibition against drinking blood, this one stands out. Unlike the others, it is utilitarian: Don't consume blood because it was intended for a higher purpose. Don't eat that chicken soup now; I made it for Shabbat dinner. In contrast to those explanations that emphasize blood as the life essence of what was once a living creature (see e.g., vv. 13–14 below), this one emphasizes blood as the essence of what that creature has the potential to become: a sacrifice to remove human guilt.

> *And if any Israelite or any stranger who resides among them hunts down an animal or a bird that may be eaten, he shall pour out its blood and cover it with earth. For the life of all flesh – its blood is its life . . . Anyone who partakes of it shall be cut off. (Lev 17:13–14)*

The reference to hunting indicates that the subject here is what occurs outside the camp, away from visual and tangible reminders of the demands of the sacrificial cult. Just as people can be tempted to be more lenient with their dietary restrictions – whether motivated by religion or health – when on vacation or away from their communities, so too a hunter, alone in the desert, with no-one to see, could have been tempted to break the prohibition against consuming blood. These verses make it clear that context is immaterial; it makes no difference where, when, or who is watching.

> *Any person, whether citizen or stranger, who eats what has died or has been torn by beasts shall wash his clothes, bathe in water, and remain unclean until evening; then he shall be clean. (Lev 17:15)*

Experience suggests that the food we eat affects our bodies *inside* – a feeling of fullness, a stomach ache, and so forth. So why does this response to eating meat from an animal that died of unknown causes, or was the prey of another animal, specify that even clothes must be washed? In contrast to discharge (see Lev 15), nothing is envisaged exuding from the body. Perhaps there's a sense that, as with hunting in the wild in verses 13–14 above, eating is not a private matter. We can't just swallow the evidence; it's written on our bodies and even our clothes.

> *Do not defile yourselves in any of those ways [incest], for it is by such that the nations that I am casting out before you defiled themselves. Thus the land became defiled; and I called it to account for its iniquity, and the land spewed out its inhabitants. (Lev 18:24–25)*

This is one of several occurrences in which the land is described as if it were a human being. Just as people become defiled, so the land becomes defiled (by their defilement!), and just as people vomit when they swallow something inedible, so the land will vomit, spewing out the people.

DIANA LIPTON

Kedoshim

Leviticus 19:1–20:27

Food and Justice

Paula Fredriksen

Leviticus 19, at first glance, looks like it's in need of a good editor. Torts, property law, ritual protocols, animal husbandry, agricultural prescriptions, issues surrounding income inequality, advice on anger management – all these issues, by our current categories of meaning quite unrelated, come jumbled together in this chapter, framed by a pronouncement rather than an explanation: "I am the Lord." And the whole comes wrapped in the idea of "holiness": the people are to live by these injunctions so that they can be "holy," since their God is holy too.

Commentators have long noted that much of this section of Leviticus recapitulates the Ten Commandments given in the Sinai covenant. Those teachings traditionally divide into the "two tablets" of the Law, the first five relating duties toward God, the second five, proper relations between people. Backlit by the Ten Commandments, the categories of Kedoshim begin to fall into coherent clusters, the spiritual/religious cluster relating to piety, and the social cluster, relating to justice. Indeed, "piety" (toward God) and "justice" (toward neighbor), in the late Second Temple period, was a common two-word code for the Ten Commandments and, by extension, for the whole Law.

Yet Kedoshim not only gives more detail to the commandments of the second tablet: it radicalizes social justice in two ways. Leviticus

19:18 binds the individual to society with the instruction specifically to *love*: "Love your neighbor as yourself; I am the LORD." Leviticus 19:34 extends this injunction to the "*ger ha-gar*": "The stranger who resides with you . . . you shall love him as yourself, for you were strangers in the land of Egypt: I the LORD am your God." Love the neighbor *and* the stranger, the two without distinction, in-group and out-group, "us" and "them."

"Love"?

Standing on this side of the 19th and 20th centuries, which spanned the rise of Romanticism to the invention of psychoanalysis, it can be difficult for us to make sense of this word "love" in the context of Kedoshim. We too easily, even unselfconsciously, register "love" as an index of sentiment, of authenticity or depth of feeling, of some sort of deep emotional and psychological attachment. Those connotations can cloud concepts of "love of self" and of neighbor/stranger: the first teeters toward narcissism, the second toward a generalized, indeed an unfocused good will.

However, context gives content. Kedoshim tells us how to understand this word "love," and it has to do not with psychological states, but with concrete actions. No stealing (Lev 19:11). No lying (Lev 19:12). Just law courts, weights, and measures (Lev 19:15, 35). No grudges, no vengeance (Lev 19:17–18). Respect elders (Lev 19:32). No taking advantage of the disadvantaged (Lev 19:14).

In the middle of this stand two injunctions, ostensibly about farming, but more profoundly about social justice:

> *When you reap the harvest of your land, you shall not reap all the way to the edges of your field, or gather the gleanings of your harvest. And you shall not pick your vineyard bare, or gather the fallen fruit of your vineyard; you shall leave them for the poor and for the stranger: I the LORD am your God. (Lev 19: 9–10)*

Not all of what we have actually belongs to us. By having all that we have, we are obligated to share with the poor and the most fundamental care of the poor is feeding the poor. No matter what individual effort we put into our own work, the fruits thereof, our "harvest," are finally God-given. In grateful recognition, we assume this responsibility to feed the hungry: part of our harvest is actually theirs. Here, at this place in Kedoshim, food is "love," and "love" is food.

What good luck for English literature that Shakespeare did not really understand Leviticus 19:9–10! His lack of understanding is brilliantly, beautifully on display in Portia's speech in *The Merchant of Venice.* "And earthly power doth then show likest God's/When mercy seasons justice." *Pace* Portia, the opposite of justice is not mercy; the opposite of justice is arbitrariness. Mercy, Kedoshim teaches us, however, *is* Justice, the second tablet of the Law, the pursuit of holiness in and through social relations: feeding the hungry, thus loving the neighbor.

PAULA FREDRIKSEN is the Aurelio Professor of Scripture Emerita at Boston University and Distinguished Visiting Professor of Comparative Religion at the Hebrew University, Jerusalem. A graduate of Wellesley College, Oxford University and Princeton University, she has published widely on the social and intellectual history of ancient Christianity, and on pagan-Jewish-Christian relations in the Graeco-Roman world. Her most recent work investigates the ways that ideas about God, humanity, and the world shift and grow during the charged period between Jesus and Augustine in *Sin: The Early History of an Idea* (2012).

> *When you sacrifice an offering of well-being to the* LORD, *sacrifice it so that it may be accepted on your behalf. It shall be eaten on the day you sacrifice it, or on the day following; but what is left by the third day must be consumed in fire. If it should be eaten on the third day, it is an offensive thing, it will not be acceptable. (Lev 19:5–7, see also Lev 7:16–18)*

Almost all the food we buy today has a use-by date, treated by some consumers as if given on Sinai and to be obeyed to the letter, by others as a rough guide, and by yet others as something to be ignored. Parashat Kedoshim has something similar; it leaves no doubt that the expiration date is to be taken seriously. Sacrifices of well-being may be eaten on the day they are sacrificed or the next day, but leftovers that still remain on the third day must be burned (Lev 19:5). Clearly this goes beyond the demands of health and hygiene, so what motivates the three day rule? Time often functions in rituals as a property that intensifies the "magic." It's fairly routine for an initiate to prepare a special formula and say, "drink it and your problems will be solved." It's much less common for the initiate to say, "to solve your problems drink this potion within three days, after which it will have precisely the opposite effect." Once time is added to the equation, the potion ceases to be a simple cure, and even after it has been dispensed, the threat of reversal means that the potion's power remains in some sense in the hands of the dispenser. The three day stipulation in Kedoshim ensures that the remains of the sacrifice are not simply absorbed into the storeroom as ordinary food, but retain their special holy quality until the moment they are eaten or burnt.

> *. . . You shall not let your cattle mate with a different kind; you shall not sow your fields with two kinds of seeds; you shall not put on cloth from a mixture of two kinds of material. (Lev 19:19)*

Two of the three prohibitions against mixing mentioned here are connected to food: different breeds of cattle must not interbreed, and fields must not be sown with mixed seeds. No single explanation captures the significance of these laws. In the context of the book Leviticus, concerned with a special kind of separation, Israel is less a bordered area on a map (as it is in Deuteronomy) than an essential cog in a universal wheel – the law against mixing makes sense as a reinforcement of the need to be different. It also serves to underline the requirement to maintain the natural order as God created it, each creature and plant with the capacity for self- regeneration (Gen 1:11–12): no new species created. Intentionally or otherwise, the prohibition against mixing suggests that there is no unimportant stage of food production. Alongside selecting an appropriate species of animal or plant in the first place, slaughtering or harvesting it correctly, and preparing it properly for consumption, farmers must be ever vigilant that the species of cattle or crops in their care remain exactly as they began and do not lose their key identifying features.

> *You shall not eat anything with its blood. You shall not practice divination or soothsaying. (Lev 19:26)*

Elsewhere the prohibition against consuming blood along with meat seems to be linked to an awareness that blood represents the life-force of a living being (Deut 12:23). In Kedoshim, however, the context suggests a different rationale. Consuming blood is the first in a list of forbidden activities that includes divination, shaving side-growth, and gashing or incising the flesh. It seems to be prohibited here not solely because blood was regarded as the essence of life, but because consuming blood was a distinctive ritual practiced by the surrounding nations from whom Israel must keep themselves apart and whom they should not emulate.

> *You shall not falsify measures of length, weight, or capacity. You shall have an honest balance, honest weights, an honest ephah, and an honest hin. (Lev 19:35)*

While the warning against using false weights and measures as a form of cheating could theoretically apply to many areas of life, in practice it is mainly an issue in relation to food. Weights and measures were used in the sale and purchase of seeds, grain, fruits and vegetables, oil, and meat, as well as baked goods such as bread. Falsifying them was not the ancient equivalent of fiddling tax returns (unacceptable as that is!), but as brutal as stealing food – directly or indirectly – from someone else's plate.

> *. . . You shall possess their land, for I will give it to you to possess, a land flowing with milk and honey (Lev 20:24)*

This is one of 15 occasions in the Torah (24 in the entire Tanakh) upon which the land of Israel is described as a land of milk and honey. This time the description is embedded in a warning against adopting the practices of the nations that God drove from the land before he gave it to Israel (Lev 20:23). The reference to milk and honey is especially evocative in this context. All the forbidden practices of the nations specified here concern the failure to separate clean from unclean animals (Lev 20:25). The reward for rejecting the foods that God finds bad, and eating those He finds good, is a land that flows endlessly with two kinds of good, pure food.

> *When you enter the land and plant any tree for food, you shall regard its fruit as forbidden. Three years it shall be forbidden to you, not to*

be eaten. In the fourth year all its fruit shall be set aside for jubilation before the L*ORD; and only in the fifth year may you use its fruit – that its yield to you may be increased,* (Lev 19:23–25)

This is the second of three sets of instructions in the Torah concerning fruit trees. The first is, of course, the first negative commandment of all: don't eat the fruit of the tree of knowledge (Gen 2:16–17). This time, the fruit in question is forbidden only for a limited time, and contains several comparisons with the other dietary laws. These instructions are interesting in several respects. First, unlike the dietary laws but like other agricultural laws, they apply only in the land of Israel ("when you enter the land"). Second, they include a rare reference to the idea that following the Torah's agricultural laws will lead to an increased yield. The third respect in which they are interesting is not evident from the above translation. Where the New Jewish Publication Society translation follows many others in suggesting that fruit should be regarded as "forbidden" for three years, the Hebrew reads literally that it should be rendered "uncircumcised." This unexpected adjective creates a resonance between the rules in parashat Kedoshim and the third set of instructions concerning fruit trees in parashat Shofetim (Deut 20:19–20). Here in Leviticus, fruit is described as "circumcised," a verb elsewhere applied to male humans.

The laws about waging war in Deut 20:1–20 conclude with the instruction that, unlike non-fruit bearing trees, fruit trees must not be cut down during the process of besieging a city because the trees of the field are not "men," who can withdraw from their attackers (Deut 20:19). Anthropomorphizing and gendering trees in the context of war, a predominantly male enterprise in this context, helps us reflect on the fertility that is lost and potentially preserved in this military pursuit. These two sets of laws about fruit trees are gender-specific, inviting comparisons with men – and not women – providing a two-directional image of a male body that provides fruit and so must be circumcised.

Diana Lipton

'Emor

Leviticus 21:1–24:23

Gleaning, Rosh HaShanah and the World to Come

Chaim Milikowsky

In the world of midrash, special attention is paid to unexpected juxtapositions – verses which are adjacent to each other without obvious justification. As readers of midrash would expect, various explanations for the placement of specific verses can be offered by students and scholars of the Bible, but the voice of the midrash still retains its biblical ground. One such juxtaposition occurs in parashat 'Emor, in the midst of the section detailing Israel's festival days. In Lev 23:22 Israel is commanded: "When you reap the harvest of your land, you shall not reap all the way to the edges of your field, or gather the gleanings of your harvest; you shall leave them for the poor and the stranger: I the Lord am your God." Verses 23–25 proceed to present the festival that occurs on the first day of the seventh month, the festival we call Rosh Hashanah. What conceivably connects the commandment of gleaning, "gifts to the poor," to the celebration of Rosh Hashanah?

According to *Va-yikra' Rabbah* 29:2, a very important communication from God should be deduced from this juxtaposition. The midrash elucidates it by means of a verse from Jeremiah: "For I am with you to deliver you – declares the Lord. I will make an end of all the nations among which I have dispersed you; but I will not make an end of you! I will not leave you unpunished, but will chastise you in measure (Jer 30:11). This verse is connected midrashically to Lev 23:22 in that both contain words from the Hebrew root *kalah* (*kaf, lamed, heh*) meaning "complete, waste away, perish." And so according to the midrash, God says: "I will make an end (*kalah*)" of the wicked nations of the world "who wholly reap (*mekallim*) their fields"; but Israel even when they also "wholly reap (*mekallim*) their fields" (see the Margulies edition of *Va-yikra' Rabbah*) "I will not make an end (*kalah*) of them; [rather] I will chasten them with suffering in this world in order to cleanse them for the World to Come; and when will this be? – in the seventh month, on the first day of the month, on the Day of Judgment, on Rosh Hashanah."

The gleaning (*leket*) of the field and the edges of the field, as well as everything else which must be left to the poor, have become in the world of this midrashic exposition the very basis for determining righteousness and wickedness. It is only by stretching out our hands and giving what was originally ours to others, to those who need it, that we become worthy of being God's people.

CHAIM MILIKOWSKY is Professor of Talmud at Bar Ilan University and Chair of the Talmud Department. His two volume critical edition of, commentary on, and introduction to, the rabbinic chronography *Seder Olam* was published in 2013 (Hebrew).

> *Speak to Aaron and say: No man of your offspring throughout the ages who has a defect shall be qualified to offer the food of his God . . . He may eat of the food of his God, of the most holy as well as of the holy; but he shall not enter behind the curtain or come near the altar, for he has a defect. (Lev 21:17, 22–23)*

This is a rare occurrence in which sacrificial offerings are describes as God's "food." In general, the nature of God's engagement with sacrifices is limited to His responsiveness to their pleasing odor; there is no suggestion that they might fulfill a nutritional need or satisfy an appetite. It's interesting, then, that this rare exception occurs in the context of a priest disqualified by a defect from making offerings. Is it possible that the rare description of the sacrificial offering as "food" reflects a desire to portray the disqualified priest – who must nevertheless eat to live – as a guest at God's table instead of the chef or *maitre d'*?

> *No man of Aaron's offspring who has an eruption or a discharge shall eat of the sacred donations until he is clean. If one touches anything made unclean by a corpse, or if a man has an issue of semen, or if a man touches any swarming thing by which he is made unclean . . . the person who touches shall be unclean until evening and shall not eat of the sacred donations unless he has washed his body in water. As soon as the sun sets, he shall be clean; and afterward he may eat of the sacred donations, for they are his food. (Lev 22:4–7)*

These verses suggest two different ways of thinking about the relationship between "sacred donations" and the person offering them. Regarding food, there can be no contact with an unclean vessel – the body of a priest defiled by discharge, or some other source of uncleanness. Would we prepare a delicious, fresh meal and store the leftovers in a dirty container? From the perspective of the priest, what's at stake here is his sustenance. It is therefore essential that the rules concerning defilement by discharge and so forth include a mechanism for becoming clean again by the evening. For these donations "are his food"; he can't be expected to fast indefinitely!

> *He shall not eat anything that died or was torn by beasts, thereby becoming unclean. I am the Lord. (Lev 22:8)*

It seems odd that this prohibition is repeated here specifically in relation to Aaron and his sons. No-one, whether citizen or stranger, is permitted to eat meat from animals that died of a natural cause or were the prey of other animals (see Lev 17:15). A possible explanation for the repetition is that the prohibited meat has two different functions in the above verse. Most obviously, it is a source of uncleanness, like discharge (Lev 22:5). More pertinently, perhaps, it rules out an alternative source of food for the priest. If he can't eat sacred offerings, he might have been tempted to eat meat from animals deemed unfit for sacrifice, such as those that died of natural causes. But that's not an option; he must wait patiently until sunset, when he will be clean again and can eat the sacred donations (v. 7).

> *No lay person shall eat of the sacred donations. No bound or hired laborer of a priest shall eat of the sacred donations; but a person who is a priest's property by purchase may eat of them; and those that are born into his household may eat of his food. If a priest's daughter marries a layman, she may not eat of the sacred gifts; but if the priest's daughter is widowed or divorced and without offspring, and is back in her father's house as in her youth, she may eat of her father's food. No lay person may eat of it: but if a man eats of a sacred donation unwittingly, he shall pay the priest for the sacred donation, adding one-fifth of its value. (Lev 22:10–14)*

Even nuclear families in the West today can be complex organisms: parents, step-parents, biological parents, adoptive parents, siblings, half-siblings, adopted siblings, "siblings" from previous marriages . . . In non-Western societies, where families are not typically nuclear, they can be even more complex, and the same goes for ancient societies. Food is one way of determining who belongs to a particular family unit. Viewed from one angle, these verses explain whom the priest, as the head of his household, is obliged to feed. Viewed from another angle, they show who can lay claim to being a member of the priest's household, namely those he is required to feed.

> *When you sacrifice a thanksgiving sacrifice to the Lord . . . it shall be eaten on the same day; you shall not leave any of it until morning . . . (Lev 22:29–30, see also Lev 7:15)*

One explanation for the time-bound nature of eating the meat of a thanksgiving sacrifice is that it makes it difficult to turn sacrificial meat into a commodity. The priest can't save the leftovers and distribute them the next day, with or without payment. Another is that eating the meat of the sacrifice is not a bonus for the priest, but part of the sacrificial process. Since the sacrifice won't be complete until he has finished eating, he must eat it all in a timely fashion.

> *And on the fifteenth day of that month [the first] the Lord's Feast of Unleavened Bread. You shall eat unleavened bread for seven days. (Lev 23:6)*

Like working for six days (do we have to work on the six days, or is it just an option?) and resting on the seventh, the command to eat unleavened bread for seven days is ambiguous. The focus could be the unleavened bread itself, in which case eating it every day would be essential. Or the focus could be the leavened bread that's prohibited during these seven days, in which case eating unleavened bread was a means of highlighting a negative prohibition rather than a positive obligation.

> *Until that very day, until you have brought the offering of your God, you shall eat no bread, or parched grain, or fresh ears; it is a law for all time throughout the ages in all your settlements. (Lev 23:14)*

What would this be like? Eating the produce of the new harvest without first making an offering to God would be like planning a lavish banquet to honor a great leader, and forgetting to serve it to her.

> *And when you reap the harvest of your land, you shall not reap all the way to the edges of your field, or gather the gleanings of your harvest; you shall leave them for the poor and the stranger. (Lev 23:22)*

For those of us who live in cities, the closest we come to experiencing a successful harvest may be that feeling before Passover when our fridge and cupboards are full of Kasher l'Pesah food and we know we won't go hungry – far from it! – over the festival after all. You can't let your anticipation of eating and being satisfied make you greedy and complacent, this law is saying. Find a way to give food to people who won't otherwise be able to eat.

DIANA LIPTON

Be-Har

Leviticus 25:1–26:2

Brotherly love

George Savran

Near the end of Leviticus, a book devoted largely to ritual concerns and often directed at a priestly audience, we come to a chapter that is breathtaking in its scope. In Leviticus 25 all Israel is addressed, not simply the *kohanim*, the priests. The subject, moreover, extends beyond immediate personal and calendric concerns to a broader expanse of time and space, namely the agricultural cycle for the entire land of Israel. In describing the fallow year cycle of seven years (*shemitah*) and fifty year cycle of the Jubilee year (*yovel*), the chapter lays out a theology of time and space intimately tied the land and its productivity. A celebration of divine control of the land, it offers as well a unique solution to the problem of debt that was (and is) an all too frequent factor in the growing of food.

At the center of this spatial and temporal complex are two central issues: how can the community continue to feed itself during the years when there will be no harvest? Moreover, what is a person's responsibility to his "brother" – be it a sibling, a clan member, or a fellow Israelite – when that brother falls into debt and is unable to sustain himself and his family? Both issues concern the well-being of the community. Regarding the first, a (hypothetical) question is posed in Lev 25:20: "What are we to eat in the seventh year?" The question is answered by a divine promise that God will grant an exceptional blessing in the sixth year which will allow for ample stores of food during the fallow period. This could be seen as a miraculous occurrence in the sixth year, or as an indication that the natural fertility of the earth will be sufficient to feed the community, provided proper steps are taken to ensure that all will be fed. The reply to the second question lays out appropriate responses to the different stages of destitution, which include selling one's land to cover debt, being forced into being a tenant farmer on one's own land, and, most severe, being sold into temporary slavery outside the community. In each case we are instructed how to preserve the dignity of the person in straits and are given the steps necessary to remedy the situation and redeem the person's land. Most striking is the command in Lev 25:36 – "let him live by your side as your kinsman" (*veḥai aḥikha immakh*) – indicating that the person *in extremis* must be nourished and supported. Even if the person is indentured to you as "a resident alien" (Lev 25:35) (*veheḥezaqta bo ger vetoshav*) it is your responsibility to see to his welfare in no uncertain terms. Another person's disadvantage should not be seen as an excuse to exploit the situation to one's own advantage.

As we read this text today, our frame of reference must go beyond the land of Israel and extend past a seven-year cycle. The question "What will we eat?" is no longer hypothetical, but is an existential cry of anxiety about world hunger, and the urgency of large-scale malnutrition and starvation must be addressed on a global level. The idea of the blessing ordained in Lev 25:21 is that there is sufficient food to sustain an ever-growing world population only if we accept responsibility for the "kinsman" beyond our tribal and national definitions. The command *veheḥezaqta bo* in Lev 25:35 should be read as Rashi suggests: "Don't abandon him, for if he falls it will be difficult to raise him up." And the command that "you let him live by your side as your kinsman" can become a real possibility when we organize ourselves effectively to work towards the eradication of world hunger, making use of the broadest range of humanitarian and technological means at our disposal.

With proper distribution of surplus crops from affluent countries, the application of technological advances in agriculture, and the conservation of natural resources for food production, eradicating world hunger is not an impossible task. By taking responsibility for one's brother and properly organizing our efforts, the question "What are we to eat in the seventh year?" need not be a cry of desperation.

GEORGE SAVRAN received his Ph.D. from Brandeis University in 1982. He has taught at Wellesley College, Indiana University and the Hebrew University of Jerusalem. He is presently director of Biblical Studies at the Schechter Institute for Jewish Studies in Jerusalem, where he has taught since 1996. His books include *Telling and Retelling: Quotation in Biblical Narrative* (1989) and *Encountering the Divine: Theophany in Biblical Narrative* (2005).

> *But you may eat whatever the land during its sabbath will produce – you, your male and female slaves, the hired and bound laborers who live with you, and your cattle and the beasts in your land may eat all its yield. (Lev 25:6)*

As strong as the imperative is against exploitation of the land, so is the imperative against wasting food. The Israelites cannot cultivate their land during its sabbatical year, but nor can they leave to rot what it produces naturally. This imperative points to a vicious circle that exists in many western societies. The more we exploit – using damaging, dangerous and, when it comes to workers and animals raised for food, often cruel methods to increase productivity – the more we waste. The more we waste, the more we exploit.

> *It [the Jubilee year] shall be holy to you: you may only eat the growth direct from the field. (Lev 25:12)*

This assumes an intimate connection to the land that most of us cannot easily replicate. You can eat its produce in the Jubilee year, the fiftieth year, the sabbatical of sabbaticals, but you have to go to the field itself to get it. In some circles, there's no value to reinterpreting a law that cannot be kept, but for those who think differently, it's worth considering how we can reproduce the intimacy required here. One way is to foster a sense of the source of the food we eat, beyond supermarket shelves.

You shall observe My laws and faithfully keep My rules, that you may live upon the land in security; the land shall yield its fruit and you shall eat your fill, and you shall live upon it in security. (Lev 25:18–19)

In many circles today, "Food Security" is a very important idea. It's an academic discipline all of its own; people write books about it and do degrees in it. At its core is the awareness that, from tiny villages through large cities to entire continents, we cannot rely on an adequate food supply. The term "security" is traditionally associated with the threat posed by enemy military or terrorist forces. These verses show that the connection between security and food is as least as well established.

DIANA LIPTON

Be-Hukkotai

Leviticus 26:3–27:34

Starvation, now and then

Sandra Jacobs

The reality of food poverty, even in relatively stable Western countries, is shocking in its enormity, yet shockingly low on the agenda of world leaders. The accounts of starvation in our own times nevertheless pale alongside the extreme images depicted in parashat *Be-Ḥukkotai.*

The parasha opens with a conditional demand for obedience which characterizes mood of the entire portion: "If you follow My laws and faithfully observe My commandments, I will grant your rains in their season, so that the earth shall yield its produce and the trees of the field their fruit" (Lev 26:3–4).The promised reward of wealth and success contrasts dramatically with the harsh punishment threatened for disobedience that follow. Among the medieval commentators, neither Rashi nor Rashbam comment on the explicit threat issued in Lev 26:29, "You shall eat the flesh of your sons and the flesh of your daughters." Ibn Ezra observes simply, "there is no famine as fierce as this." Retreating into social convention, Hizkuni offers a pragmatic escape from the text's difficulties by explaining that some interpret this verse as referring to well-born families who marry off their children to unsuitable partners in exchange for money.

Within the Bible, however, there is considerable support for a literal interpretation of Lev 26:29. Near-identical threats appear in Deut 28:53–57; Jer 19:9; Lam 2:20 and 4:10, not to mention the depiction of the cannibal mother(s) in 2 Kgs 6:26–30. Likewise in post-biblical antiquity, Josephus goes to inordinate lengths to provide vivid corroboration of this promise, notably in his account of the destruction of Jerusalem in the summer of 70 CE (*Bellum Judaicum, VI 199–219).* Mary, daughter of Eleazar, is portrayed killing, roasting, and eating her own son, to the revulsion of the local rebels. This scene is arguably no more than dramatic rhetoric, lacking historical basis and engineered by Josephus to corroborate the fulfilment of God's punishment of his people. Inevitably the actions of this Mary were viewed by the early Church fathers as a fulfilment of apostolic beliefs, if not an undisputed "gospel truth."

Yet was Lev 26:29 intended as a deterrent evoked, rather than a punishment experienced? Our ancestors' desire to demonstrate its historical veracity sits uneasily alongside Rashi's resounding silence. Perhaps he thought that his silence offered the best chance of excising starvation from our collective memories, thus easing our communal pain? Yet for ancient Israelites, the divine threat that mothers would eat their children must have generated profound fear and a desire to avert this promised outcome. We, by contrast, remain shamefully indifferent and unresponsive to the images of hunger and starvation that flood our media every day – and equally blind to the reality of refugee infant corpses, recently washed ashore on our local beaches.

SANDRA JACOBS is a Visiting Researcher in the Theology and Religious Studies Department at King's College, London. Her revised doctoral dissertation, *The Body as Property: Physical Disfigurement in Biblical Law* (Bloomsbury Press, 2014), sold out in its first year and was reprinted in paper-back in 2015.

> *If you follow My laws and faithfully observe My commandments, I will grant your rains in their season, so that the earth shall yield its produce and the trees of the field their fruit. Your threshing shall overtake the vintage, and your vintage shall overtake the sowing; you shall eat your fill of bread and dwell securely in your land. (Lev 26:3–5)*

This is one of the Bible's most evocative visions of plenty. Security is once again associated with having sufficient food, not with safety from enemies.

> *You shall eat old grain long stored, and you shall have to clear out the old to make room for the new. (Lev 26:10)*

This is another kind of vision of plenty, not in the fields, but in the store house. Far from having to worry about whether the grain supply will hold out until the new crops have been harvested – a pressing fear in a society like ancient Israel, the obedient Israelites will not even get a chance to finish eating the old grain before the new grain arrives.

> *But if you do not obey Me and do not observe all these commandments . . . you shall sow your seed to no purpose, for your enemies shall eat it. (Lev 26:14, 16)*

Not only will the disobedient Israelites be prevented from eating the produce of the seeds they sowed, they will have to endure the sight of their enemies eating it.

> *When I break your staff of bread, ten women shall bake your bread in a single oven; they shall dole out your bread by weight, and though you eat, you shall not be satisfied. (Lev 26:26)*

"Staff of bread" seems to be a metaphorical term suggesting support. Bread is the staple food that allows a person to walk upright. In this context, though, it may have sexual undertones, suggesting impotence as well as hunger. Even though ten women are baking his bread, the disobedient Israelite will never feel full.

DIANA LIPTON

Be-midbar

Numbers 1:1–4:20

The Set Table

Simon Goldhill

As the wilderness seems to be no place to set out on a hunt for food, let alone for recipes to excite the palate, so parashat Be-midbar ["in the wilderness"] seems at first sight to offer a poor return for the foodie. Bar the cattle of the Levites, which are taken in redemption (Num 3:45) – and not eaten – and the mention of the meal offering (Num 4:16) – also not eaten – there is nothing mentioned in this week's parasha that is even edible (for someone who keeps kosher at any rate). Yet there are at least two ways in which Be-midbar goes to the heart of a Jewish relationship to food.

Sefer Be-midbar explicitly continues the story of Sefer Shemot: we are in the second month of the second year after leaving Egypt, and the Israelites are "in the wilderness." The command from God is to take a census. The census lists the tribes and numbers the men of the community, and sets out the order in which they are to camp and make their march. It also lays out the duties of the individual groups with regard to the Mishkan, the Tabernacle. It offers an intensely detailed structure of a community, leading up to the avodah, service, of the community with regard to the central site of religious ritual, where the sacrificial cult is practiced.

The threat posed by the wilderness is that it is without order, without markers of direction, with no organized relation between food and its production and consumption, food and religious practice. "In the wilderness" thus provides a significant framing description for the detailed expression of the social order of a community, leading up to the rituals of avodah which stand at the center as a ritualized – ordered, sanctified – expression of why the production and consumption of food plays an integral role in this sense of sanctified social order. The narrative of parashat Be-midbar is the antithesis of its opening frame: "in the wilderness." Food and order are integral for Judaism – the opposite of wilderness. One of the most influential codes of Jewish law is known as the *Shulchan Aruch*, "the Set Table." The very title links the order of food and the order of religious living, integrally. It is not by chance that the disorder that is about nearly to destroy the Israelites on their march is precisely an uncontrolled lust for the food of their past life as slaves: "The riffraff [*asafsuf*] in their midst felt a gluttonous craving; and then the Israelites wept and said "If only we had meat to eat!" (Num 11:4).

A midrash on this week's parasha takes this point importantly further. Be-midbar Rabbah (5:2) glosses the verse "Do not let the group of Kohathite clans be cut off from the Levites" (Num 4:18), with Prov 22:22: "Do not rob the wretched because he is wretched. . . ." "How can you rob someone who has nothing?" ask the rabbis. By failing to give them what you are obliged to give: gleanings, the forgotten sheaves, the poor man's tithes. That is, a rich man who does not support those who are needy is actively robbing the poor. The social order, which a religious attitude to food demands, is impossible to maintain without a heightened sense of social justice. Observance of rituals of kashrut without a powerful commitment to justice, concludes the midrash, leads to the wrath of heaven.

SIMON GOLDHILL is the director of CRASSH, Cambridge University's Centre for Research in the Arts, Social Sciences and Humanities; Professor in Greek Literature and Culture at Cambridge; and Fellow of King's College, Cambridge. Simon's research interests include: Greek Tragedy, Greek Culture, Literary Theory, Later Greek Literature, and Reception. His latest book is *Victorian Culture and Classical Antiquity: Art, Opera, Fiction, and the Proclamation of Modernity*. He directs the European Research Council-funded project: The Bible and Antiquity in Nineteenth-Century Culture. [Editor's note: I can attest that Simon is also a gourmet cook!]

Upon it they shall place all the vessels that are used in its service: the fire pans, the flesh hooks, the scrapers, and the basins – all the vessels of the altar . . . (Num 4:14)

So many components of the Mishkan seem alien to the modern reader, but the altar vessels mentioned here are familiar to anyone who has been in an old-fashioned butcher's shop. Many items connected to food preparation have remained constant through the centuries.

DIANA LIPTON

Naso'

Numbers 4:21–7:89

Bitter water

Ishay Rosen-Zvi

Numbers 5 includes one of the strangest episodes in the Torah. It also describes what is, without a doubt, the most surprising incidence of eating (or rather drinking) in scripture. The passage treats the case of a woman whose husband, without any actual proof, suspects her of adultery. The Torah rules that the suspicious husband must bring his wife to the priest in the Tabernacle, where she undergoes a divine "ordeal." This includes imbibing an unusual potion – "holy" water into which the priest has mixed dust from the Tabernacle's floor (which was, unlike the Temple floor, unpaved).

But the water has a third ingredient: the priest writes the text of an oath on a piece of parchment, which, after being read to the woman, is rubbed off into the water. The oath written on the parchment says that if the woman has indeed betrayed her husband, the holy water will enter her bowels and cause "her belly to distend and the thigh to sag" (Num 5:22; this probably refers obliquely to a miscarriage). If, however, the woman has not committed adultery, she will be absolved by the ordeal of the water and shall be "able to retain seed" (Num 5:28) – i.e. she is promised future fertility. This potion, with the dust from the Tabernacle and the ink from the parchment, is called "the water of bitterness that induces the spell" (Num 5:24), and its drinking is supposed to cause the woman to react as described in the parchment which was rubbed off into it.

What is the meaning of this strange act of drinking? Since we are dealing with a divine ordeal it would appear that the oath itself, written with God's name, is supposed to act upon the woman's body. But how? Ezekiel the prophet is commanded to eat a scroll containing prophecies, and thus to internalize them, as described in the following passage:

> *"So I opened my mouth, and He gave me this scroll to eat, as He said to me, "Mortal, feed your stomach and fill your belly with this scroll that I give you." I ate it, and it tasted as sweet as honey to me." (Ezek 3:2–3)*

It is difficult to know whether what is being described here is a prophecy, a dream, or a real event, but in any case, it seems wrong to demand of an ordinary woman, who comes to the Tabernacle only because her husband suspects her of cheating on him, what is required of a prophet, whose whole being is committed to his prophecy. Therefore, the Torah comes up with a creative solution: the parchment is rubbed off into the water, which the woman then drinks – in a similar fashion to the dissolving of a medicine in water in order to aid its digestion by children or the sick.

On first reading, the story is an extremely troubling one. An ordinary woman, whose husband suspects her without any real basis, must undergo a humiliating ceremony, one that even endangers her life, with the sole purpose of laying *his* fears to rest. It goes without saying that the Torah offers no parallel ceremony intended to put women's minds at rest regarding their husbands! However, the biblical commentator Moshe Greenberg has suggested an original explanation for the ceremony [M. Greenberg. *Ezekiel*, New York, 1983]. Greenberg points out two interesting phenomena in this passage: first, in divine ordeals we know from the ancient Near East and the Middle Ages, the accused imbibes a poisonous drink or engages in a dangerous activity, such as being thrown into deep water or fire, and his very survival from this danger testifies to his innocence. Not so in this case, where there is no poisonous ingredient in the water the suspected woman drinks, but only water, dust, and ink. Second, the passage ends with the surprising expression: "The man shall be clear of guilt; but that woman shall suffer for her guilt" (Num 5:31). Why does the man, the husband, need to be cleared of guilt? Of which crime is he guilty?

Based on this verse, Greenberg claims that the entire passage is intended to protect the woman at its center. A woman whose husband suspects her of adultery might suffer violence or even murder at his hands or the hand of the community. In order to protect her, the Torah states that the husband is not permitted to act on his own. If he suspects her, he must bring her to the priest, who is the only one empowered to deal with the suspicion. Only if the husband acts thus will he be cleared of his guilt. The priest gives the woman a harmless potion to drink, and furthermore, the Torah says that if she afterward bears a child, this is proof of her innocence. In other words, the ceremony protects not only the woman, but also the fetus she may be carrying.

We have thus learned that the strange act of drinking found in Naso' could be a wise method adopted by the Torah to protect a defenseless woman (and her unborn child!) from lynching. And we have learned, further, that texts are always open to new interpretations, and that what appears, from one angle, as a misogynist and "primitive" text, can be revealed from another as a cunning procedure intended to aid society's most vulnerable members.

ISHAY ROSEN-ZVI is an Associate Professor and the Head of the Talmud and Late Antiquity section of the Department of Hebrew Culture Studies at Tel-Aviv University, where he teaches Talmudic literature and culture. His main interests are midrashic hermeneutics; the formation of the Mishnah; Temple rituals in rabbinic literature; and gender and sexuality in late antiquity. Among his recent publications are: *Demonic Desires: YETZER HARA and the Problem of Evil in Late Antiquity* (2011); *Body and Soul in Ancient Judaism* (2012); and *The Mishnaic Sotah Ritual: Temple, Gender and Midrash* (2012).

The LORD spoke to Moses, saying: Speak to the Israelites and say to them: If anyone, man or woman, explicitly utters a nazirite's vow, to set himself apart for the LORD, he shall abstain from wine and any other intoxicant; he shall not drink vinegar of wine or of any other intoxicant, neither shall he drink anything in which grapes have been steeped, nor eat grapes fresh or dried. Throughout his term as nazirite, he may not eat anything that is obtained from the grapevine, even seeds or skin. (Num 6:1–4)

Just as the Israelites were required to take on dietary restrictions that underlined and reinforced their separation from the nations, so too nazirites were required to take on an additional dietary restriction that underlined and reinforced their separation from other Israelites. Special dietary laws make explicit the differences between those who keep them and those who don't, and the inability to accept hospitality and share other people's food limits the potential for social interaction.

The prohibition of alcohol for nazirites seems to have an additional component that it does not share with the laws of kashrut. Not drinking alcohol, with its strong association with joy and celebration, is a form of deprivation; the nazirite vow thus entails giving up a source of pleasure. Even if Jews who keep kosher feel from time to time that they are missing out on something, it seems obvious that deprivation – where that occurs – is an unintended side-effect of the dietary laws, not a central motivation.

This is the ritual for the nazirite: On the day that his term as nazirite is completed, he shall be brought to the entrance of the Tent of Meeting. As his offering to the Lord he shall present: one male lamb in its first year, without blemish . . . After that the nazirite may drink wine. (Num 6:13–14a, 20b)

There are (at least) two different ways of understanding "After that the nazirite may drink wine." On the one hand, it can be read as no more than a statement that what had been prohibited while the vow was operative is now permitted. On the other hand, it can function as part of the ceremony that ends the vow – indeed its symbolic crowning moment. On this second reading, "After that the nazirite may drink wine" functions similarly to "The groom may kiss the bride" at the end of some marriage ceremonies. Now that they are married, the bride is permitted to the groom, but that moment at a wedding is far more than the signal that a ban has been lifted.

Diana Lipton

Be-ha'alotekha

Numbers 8:1–12:16

Food appreciation

Joel Hecker

Numbers is filled with narrative episodes recounting the travels and travails of the people of Israel once the fireworks of exodus and revelation have passed. Much of the law has been communicated to them and now they learn about their responsibilities to perform the commandments; the flexibility and limits of the law; the difficulties of a nomadic existence; and about God's wrath. Complaint is the most frequent tone of Israel's rhetoric, as they lament the lack of luxuries they imagine was their lot while slaves in Egypt. Thus we read in parashat Be-ha'alotekha: "If only we had meat to eat! We remember the fish that we used to eat free in Egypt, the cucumbers, the melons, the leeks, the onions, and the garlic. Now our gullets are shriveled . . ." (Num 11:4–6).

The Israelites' fanciful and selective memory seduces them into griping about the miraculous food – manna – that descends for them daily. In the biblical description,

> *Now the manna was like coriander seed, and in color it was like bdellium. The people would go about and gather it, grind it between millstones or pound it in a mortar, boil it in a pot, and make it into cakes. It tasted like rich cream. When the dew fell on the camp at night, the manna would fall upon it (Num 11:7–9).*

The dependability and strangeness of this food has intrigued scholars from ancient times through to the modern day. In recent years, scholars have suggested that the Bible's manna might refer to a natural substance formed by the activity of a type of plant lice upon the yellowish-white flaky sap of the tamarisk tree, commonly found in the wilderness of northern Arabia (Brevard S. Childs, *The Book of Exodus: A Critical, Theological Commentary*, Philadelphia, Westminster Press [1974], 282).

In rabbinic legend, the manna becomes a magical phenomenon: precious stones and jewelry fell along with it; adopting multiple tastes like mother's milk; manifesting multiple colors like a demon; age-appropriate taste and texture; the ability to be absorbed throughout the body's limbs without need for elimination; encased in a box-like structure of dew; bearing enormous proportions; and so on (Babylonian Talmud, Yoma 75–76a). For medieval mystics, the consumption of manna becomes a symbol for the internalization of divine wisdom, a transformation of holiness into corporeality (*Sefer ha-Bahir* 127–128; Nahmanides on Exodus 16:6; *Zohar* 1:157a–b; Joseph of Hamadan, *Sefer Tashaq*, 309).

While it is commonly thought that our experience of taste begins at the tongue's taste buds, what the pre-modern approaches demonstrate is that our most powerful organ of taste resides in the mind. How we think about food, imagine it, and experience it depends largely on the mindset. When eaten appreciatively, the plainest food can be transportive; when eaten by desert riffraff, even the most miraculous food can seem paltry. Ultimately, the Torah's aim with this story is to instruct us about humility and gratitude, the starting points for transforming our attitudes toward food, food production, and dining.

JOEL HECKER is translator of *The Zohar: Pritzker Edition*, Vols. 11–12 (Stanford University Press, 2016, 2017) and serves as Associate Professor of Jewish Mysticism at the Reconstructionist Rabbinical College. He is also the author of *Mystical Bodies, Mystical Meals: Eating and Embodiment in Medieval Kabbalah* (2005).

Did I conceive all this people, did I bear them, that You should say to me, 'Carry them in your bosom as a nurse carries an infant,' to the land that you have promised on oath to their fathers? Where am I to get meat to give to all this people, when they whine before me and say, 'Give us meat to eat!' (Num 11:12–13)

It's easy to read Moses' words here as no more than a rebuke to God for attempting to offload His responsibilities: You created this problem, now You deal with it. In fact, however, Moses is presenting God with a brilliant analogy demonstrating that he is physically unable to feed the people. Just as it is pointless to ask a woman to breastfeed a hungry child unless she has recently conceived and given birth – she will have no milk, so it is futile to ask Moses to provide sustenance for the whining Israelites – he has no meat.

And say to the people: Purify yourselves for tomorrow and you shall eat meat, for you have kept whining before the LORD and saying, 'If only we had meat to eat! Indeed, we were better off in Egypt!' The LORD will give you meat and you shall eat. You shall eat not one day, not two, not even five days or ten or twenty, but a whole month, until it comes out of your nostrils and becomes loathsome to you . . . (Num 11:18–20a)

Getting what you wanted works particularly effectively as a punishment when it comes to food, especially the kind of food that typically provokes strong desire. (It's easy to imagine, You want chocolate? Here's chocolate! It's less easy to imagine, You want lettuce. . . .) In this context, however, there's more at stake. The people have uttered the lowest form of ingratitude: we were better off in Egypt. They seem to be implying that God is unable to provide them with even a little of what they had in abundance under Pharaoh. At the same time as punishing them for failing to be grateful, God shows beyond doubt that the lack of meat in the wilderness is not a reflection of what He can or cannot do.

But Moses said, "The people who are with me number six hundred thousand men; yet You say, 'I will give them enough meat to eat for a whole month.' Could enough flocks and herds be slaughtered to suffice them? Or could all the fish of the sea be gathered for them to suffice them?" (Num 11:21–22)

In a different context, Moses' words could be quite poetic: I love you more than all the tea in China. In this context, however, his expansive talk of flocks, herds, and fish underlines his skepticism. Where in the desert, which has neither pasture nor water, will he be able to find meat and fish to feed six hundred thousand? What's interesting is that God does not perform miracles in the wilderness with ordinary food, as might have been expected. There's no little lamb or small bucket of fish that turned out to be sufficient to feed multitudes. It's rather the food itself – manna – that's miraculous.

> *A wind from the LORD started up, swept quail from the sea and strewed them over the camp, about a day's journey on this side and about a day's journey on that side, all around the camp, and some two cubits deep on the ground . . . The meat was still between their teeth, nor yet chewed, when the anger of the LORD blazed forth against the people and the LORD struck the people with a very severe plague. That place was named Kibroth-hattaavah, because the people who had the craving were buried there. (Num 11:31, 33–34)*

The scene presented here is grotesque by any measure – mounds of rotting flesh as far as the eye could see. God strikes the people with a plague before they can even chew, let alone digest, the meat they had been craving. And, to add insult to injury, the place where they died and were buried was named in memory of their unsatisfied appetites.

> *And Aaron said to Moses, "O my lord, account not to us the sin which we committed in our folly. Let her not be as one dead, who emerges from his mother's womb with half his flesh eaten away." (Num 12:11–12)*

Does Aaron's image of a stillborn baby emerging half eaten from its mother's womb belong with the Bible's devastating depictions of cannibal mothers? They were driven to eat their children by the threat of starvation during a siege or famine. This mother ate her baby before it was even born.

DIANA LIPTON

Shelah-lekha

Numbers 13:1–15:41

Risk and Reward, Reward and Risk

Athalya Brenner

When the Israelites camp in the wilderness of Paran, probably in the Sinai Peninsula, God orders Moses to send twelve men, leaders of their tribes, to "tour," or "scout," the southern part of the land of Canaan which, according to the divine plan, they are about to enter.

Moses is a cautious leader. The land is not empty. Its inhabitants must be conquered, and it must be fertile in order to support the newcomers from the moment of entry. He chooses twelve men and gives them a detailed mandate, from which it transpires that they are to be spies, not just "tourists." Their task is twofold: on the one hand, to find out the military strength of the land, its inhabitants and its cities; and on the other hand, to examine its food production and bring back samples.

The "spies" are gone for forty days. Since it is the end of the summer, they come back bearing samples of summer fruit. The verdict shared by ten of them, as they spoke to Moses and the congregation members upon their return, is clearly pessimistic: the land is naturally fertile. It "flows" with milk and honey and has abundant fruit, but will be impossible to conquer by military means. The people want to return to Egypt. Only two of the touring spies, Joshua and Caleb, favor the quest because of the land's natural food production and God's support.

God's verdict concerning this lack of trust is: all Israel will roam the desert for forty years, a year for every day of the spies' journey, until all die. Of the wilderness generation, only Joshua and Caleb will enter the Promised Land.

Interestingly, the land is typified by foodstuff (as much as its inhabitants are typified by their military prowess). It is abundantly fertile. As elsewhere in the Five Books, it "flows with milk and honey" (see for example, Exod 3:8 and 17; 13:5; 33:3; Num 14:8; 16:13–14; and seven occurrences in Deut) before Israel's entry. Outside the five books, this formula is rare (see Josh 5:6; Jer 11:5; 32:22; Ezek 20:6 and 15; and see also "curds and honey" in Isa 7:22). The milk is probably that of sheep or goats, naturally flowing in the birthing season; the honey is probably date honey, again available without special effort or cultivation. (Bee honey is known, for example in the stories of Samson [Judg 14] and Jonathan [1 Sam 14], but it is rarer). In other words, the impression is transmitted that the land, much like the female lover in the Song of Songs ("Honey and milk are under your tongue," Song 4:11), is effortlessly, potentially fecund. Just eat: the food awaits you in immediately edible form.

This picture of plenty is further enhanced by the choice of other plant food brought back by the spies. They carry a gigantic bunch of grapes, requiring two people to carry it between them, which was plucked near the Eshkol River. "Eshkol" means bunch or cluster in Hebrew. The exact location is uncertain, but it is probably in the south Judean hills. They also bring some pomegranates and figs. A quick glance at the list of the "seven species," the products characteristic of the land, will probably explain why these three are chosen. The full list, as in Deut 8:8, has a land of "wheat and barley, of vines, figs, and pomegranates, a land of olive trees and honey." While all these species are depicted as native to the land, the three kinds of fruit – grapes, pomegranates and figs – are there to be eaten, with no processing or hard work needed in order to turn them from plant to food. A return to paradise, but for the power of the local inhabitants? Incidentally, or perhaps not, the food that characterizes the southern region of Canaan is totally different from the typical Egyptian food, which is fish, meat, and vegetables (mentioned in last week's parasha, Num 11:5).

But grapes have added value, of course. They can be processed into wine. Perhaps this is why the bunch brought back to the desert achieves such mythological proportions: wine making and non-excessive wine drinking are viewed positively in the Bible. The spies have made a good choice. Indeed, the southern Judah Hills region is even now a center of viticulture, still developing. (At last count, the area had about 25 boutique wineries; names to watch and buy include Tzorah, Tepperberg, Barkan, Castel, Psagot and Flam [www.wine-searcher.com/regions-judean+hills]. You can even book tours of vineyards and wine-tastings in the Judean Hills and neighboring areas [www.israelwinexp.com].) In addition, the neighboring Lachish area is a major grower of grapes for the local market as well as for export.

The two interested "tourists" who carried back the great bunch of grapes as proof of the land's fertility (were those Joshua and Caleb, the optimists?) are still very much with us today, since an abstracted image of them serves as the logo of Israel's ministry of tourism (see below, on the left). They also appear in Israeli philately. A postage stamp from 1954 depicts them in a similar manner (below, right).

As for the object of search and scouting, a full stamp series of the "seven species" was designed by Zvi Narkiss and published for the High holidays in 1959. The images on the two stamps on the first row, on the right, and on the second row the first and third, are mentioned in our parasha. Another series of stamps on the same subject was published in 1983.

Yet another relevant area is numismatics. From the beginning of the Israeli state, its coins carried images of its age-old food produce, including vine, date, pomegranate, and the other "species." Below is an image prepared by Yehuda Malachi (under the Creative Common license), presenting such Jewish/Hebrew coins from antiquity until modernity.

Grapes, pomegranates, figs, dates, goat or sheep milk, and honey. A ready feast, waiting for the believer. If only, if only, the risks were not so great.

ATHALYA BRENNER is Professor Emerita of Hebrew Bible/Old Testament at the University of Amsterdam and now at Tel Aviv University. She has published extensively on feminist criticism of the Hebrew Bible, transdisciplinary approaches, Semitic philology and computer applications in the Humanities. She is the compiler and editor of three ground-breaking series: the 20-volume *Feminist Companion to the Bible*, *The Bible in the 21st Century* (8 volumes), and *Texts@Contexts* (5 volumes so far).

> *". . . And take pains to bring back some of the fruit of the land." – Now it happened to be the season of the first ripe grapes. (Num 13:20)*

The scouts are instructed to bring back a report about several different aspects of the land they are about to conquer: general appearance, population, urban settlement, agricultural potential, and topography. When it comes to the fruit of the land, however, Moses asks for samples. Perhaps this has to do with fruit's relative portability (though, given the size of the grapes, less portable than Moses probably anticipated). But it happens to reflect an almost universal interest among travelers in bringing home food from foreign countries. For reasons that are hard to explain, exotic foods often embody or encapsulate the spirit of the place they came from, and create a semi-mystical connection between the place and the eater. Perhaps it's partly that, unlike other souvenirs, food does not remain external – an object only to look at or touch. We eat it, and it becomes part of us.

> *". . . The county that we traversed and scouted is one that devours its settlers . . ." (Num 13:32)*

The scouts were commissioned to find out how easy it would be to conquer the land, and how well it would support them once they had (Num 13:17–21). Their report implied that even if they could defeat the large – in number and in size – population, they would never be able to conquer the land itself. To be sure, they could grow food, but would they have time to eat it before the land ate them?

> *The LORD spoke to Moses, saying: Speak to the Israelite people and say to them: When you enter the land to which I am taking you and you eat of*

> *the bread of the land, you shall set some aside as a gift to the* Lord*: as the first yield of your baking, you shall set aside a loaf as a gift; you shall set it aside like the gift from the threshing floor.* (Num 15:17–20)

A home video that went viral on YouTube a few years ago showed an exchange between a toddler sitting in a highchair and his mother, who was attempting to feed him. He had just worked out that the chicken on his plate was . . . chicken. Their interchange is moving. It's also indicative of entire generations who grow up knowing nothing of the origins of the food that ends up on their plates. They could not point on a map to the countries that produce it; they could not identify it in its raw state; they have no idea of the processes by which it became edible, nor of the people involved in that processes. They eat unthinkingly. The separation between their food and its source is almost total. Clearly, this would not have been possible in the ancient world, but nevertheless, the command to set aside as gifts both a loaf and a portion of the grain from the threshing floor functions effectively to prevent our damaging and delusional state of disconnect.

Diana Lipton

Korah

Numbers 16:1–18:32

Food and Revolution

Noam Mizrahi

Parashat Korah combines several literary components. One striking story, which gives its name to the whole parasha, tells of Korah, who leads a group of two hundred and fifty priests in challenging Aaron's ritual authority. At the end of the story, this group is killed by a divine fire which consumes them at the entrance to the Tent of Meeting. The story of Korah's rebellion begins in Numbers 16, and is picked up again at the beginning of Numbers 17, in an account of what became of the copper rods that the rebels were holding at the time of their deaths. It is interwoven with a second, similar but distinct narrative, the tale of Dathan and Abiram, two men from the tribe of Reuben who rebel against Moses' political authority. Numbers 16 closes with the story of how the earth opens and swallows Dathan and Abiram and their families. Numbers 17 continues with a miraculous sign in the shape of Aaron's flowering rod that is tied to the Korah narrative. The parasha closes at the start of Numbers 18 with a series of laws that define the roles of the priests as compared to those of the Levites (see the end of Numbers 17) and organize the income of both groups.

Food plays a central role in parashat Korah, and is particularly prominent in the legal section that ends the reading. As usual in the ancient world in general and the ancient Near East in particular, the sources of income specified for the Temple workers are framed in terms of food allocation, namely the sacrifices or parts of sacrifices given to the priests to eat, and the tithes from the agricultural produce that are the lot of the Levites. Food related images also appear in the other sections of the parasha, and their appearances are characterized by specific details worth noting. The most dramatic examples appear in the story of Dathan and Abiram (Num 16), and are concentrated at the two ends of the tale told about them: at the beginning are the harsh complaints they level against Moses, and at the end is the description of their dreadful punishment.

Dathan and Abiram's challenge to Moses' leadership is grounded in their disappointment that the promises he gave have not been fulfilled. Their words open and close with the defiant statement "We will not come," in reaction to Moses' summons that they should come before him (Num 16:12, 14). But the crux of their claim against Moses is found in the images of food at the center of their speech: "Is it not enough that you brought us *from* a land flowing with milk and honey to have us die in the wilderness, that you would also lord it over us? Even if you had brought us *to* a land flowing with milk and honey to, and given us possession of fields and vineyards . . . we will not come!" (Num 16:13–14). This claim is couched in deeply ironic language – the phrase "land of milk and honey" is frequently used to describe the Promised Land (see, for example, Exod 3:8, 17), but here it is used to describe Egypt, with the Land of Canaan explicitly excluded.

From the precise wording of their complaint we understand that Dathan and Abiram are not concerned with physical hunger. It is instructive to compare what they say with the wording of the Israelites' complaint in parashat Beshallah: "In the wilderness, the whole Israelite community grumbled against Moses and Aaron. The Israelites said to them, "If only we had died by the hand of the Lord in the land of Egypt, when we sat by the fleshpots, when we ate our fill of bread! For you have brought us out into this wilderness to starve this whole congregation to death" (Exod 16:2–3). While this complaint also opens with a glorification of life in Egypt, beyond what we can assume was actually the case, we learn from its closing that it stems from a real hunger and need – and indeed God responds immediately, raining down bread "from the sky" for the people (Exod 16:4). In contrast, the verses in our parasha make no mention of hunger. Indeed, the reverse is true. Dathan and Abiram's words sound like the complaint of spoiled people who have been cut off from the continuous free-flow of luxury items – this in light of verses that teach us that milk and honey were considered luxuries in biblical times (see, for instance, Isa 7:22; Ps 81:17; Song 4:11).

Dathan and Abiram, it appears, are willing to undermine the entire political order of the Israelite camp, and even to deny the authority of their divinely-chosen leader, because they can no longer fulfill their desire for caviar and champagne. This is not the desperate cry of a multitude bowing under the burden of limited sustenance in the desert, but rather a whining complaint from those who have the benefit of wealth and are demanding to retain their privilege at all costs, while turning a blind eye to the very real distress of their brothers.

This may explain the unusual phrasing of the severe punishment meted out, not only to Dathan and Abiram, but to their entire families and even their possessions. The exterior aspect of the story is that of a political drama: the challenge to Moses' leadership is nothing but a rejection of the leadership of the God who appointed him. Thus Moses defines their words as "provocation" (Num 16:30), that is, an act of rebellion, and the breaking of a covenant (see for example Deut 31:20 and Jer 14:21), and his framing of their future punishment is a proof that all his actions are indeed undertaken at God's commandment (Num 16:28–29). In the description of the enactment of this punishment we can find an additional, deeper level, since it is couched not in political terms, but rather in mythic imagery in which the bowls of the earth are depicted as a predatory animal that swallows the rebels. This is already evident in Moses' warning: "But if the Lord brings about something unheard-of, so that the ground opens its mouth and swallows them up with all that belongs to them, and they go down alive into Sheol" (Num 16:30), and appears in greater detail when this miraculous punishment takes place: "and the earth opened its mouth and swallowed them up with their households, all Korah's people and all their possessions. They went down alive into Sheol, with all that belonged to them; the earth closed over them and they vanished from the midst of the congregation" (Num 16:32–33).

If political conflict was the main point of this story, the Bible could have contented itself with a simpler description, such as the one found in a poetic version of the story in Psalms: "The earth opened up and swallowed Dathan, closed over the party of Abiram" (Ps 106:17). In the prose version in Numbers, however, the earth opens up its mouth, and swallows not only the rebellious individuals but also their families and their belongings, all of whom are described as going "down live into Sheol." In other words, the narrative version, unlike the poem in the Psalms, presents Dathan and Abiram's punishment in a powerful image of being swallowed alive and devoured by the earth.

A close parallel to this language can be found in a prophecy in Isaiah in which the prophet decries the upper classes who are engaged in revelries and warns them of the punishment of the destruction of the Temple, which is described in terms strikingly similar to those used in Korah:

> *"Ah, those who chase liquor from early in the morning, and till late in the evening are inflamed by wine. Who, at their banquets, have lyre and lute, timbrel, flute, and wine; but who never give a thought to the plan of the Lord, and take no note of what He is designing. Assuredly, my people will suffer exile for not giving heed, its multitude victims of hunger and its masses parched with thirst. Assuredly, Sheol has opened wide its gullet and parted its jaws in a measureless gape; and down into it shall go, that splendor and tumult, that din and revelry. Yea, man is bowed, and mortal brought low; brought low is the pride of the haughty. And the Lord of Hosts is exalted by judgment, the Holy God proved holy by retribution" (Isa 5:11–16).*

In both cases, the relationship between the sin and its punishment is one of measure for measure, according to the principle of "Out of the eater came something to eat" (Jud 14:14). Dathan and Abiram's actions, on the one hand, and those of the revelers mentioned in Isaiah's prophecy, on the other, are dictated primarily by their refined tastes. The first are interested in honey and milk and the second in wine and liquor, but all are members of a "high society" that spends most of its time partying. It is for this reason that the rebels are sentenced to become food themselves – prey for an insatiable earth that, in the hands of God, serves as a tool for social justice.

Modern-day readers can find in the story of Dathan and Abiram not only an allegory of political struggle but also a warning of the disastrous results of social polarization and economic inequality. The Bible, in its way, formulates its lesson in the form of a story and uses tangible images in place of the abstract terms we use nowadays. But this cultural difference should not cloud the text's fierce warning: those who blindly and stubbornly hold on to economic privilege while averting their eyes from the needs of their communities are destined to be consumed in a revolution that will shake the earth to its very core.

NOAM MIZRAHI teaches in the Department of Hebrew Culture Studies in Tel Aviv University. His research focuses on Hebrew linguistics, textual criticism and literary and theoretical aspects of the literature of the Bible and the Dead Sea Scrolls.

> *Moses sent for Dathan and Abiram, sons of Eliab; but they said, "We will not come! Is it not enough that you brought us from a land flowing with milk and honey to have us die in the wilderness, that you would also lord it over us? Even if you had brought us to a land flowing with milk and honey, and given us possession of fields and vineyards, should you gouge out those men's eyes? (Num 16:12–14)*

The Bible often uses agricultural differences to underscore contrasts between Israel and Egypt. Defining – though not necessarily positive – episodes in Israel's history hinge on a decision to travel to Egypt in search of grain when there was famine in the land (Abraham and Sarah in Gen 12:10, and Joseph's brothers in Gen 42:1–3), or on a warning *not* to seek food in Egypt (Isaac in Gen 26:1–3, and the people of Judah in Jer 42:13–22). Israel's agriculture relied on rain and was therefore precarious, whereas Egypt's depended on the Nile and was reliable, and farming in Israel entailed hard labor, whereas Egypt's was more like market gardening (Deut 11:10–11).

Nevertheless, the Bible presents the land of Israel positively in terms of its capacity to sustain its population. The evocative phrase that encapsulates all that is good about Israel with respect to food occurs several times: a land flowing with milk and honey. It is shocking then to read that very phrase applied to Egypt (Num 16:12). Not surprisingly, these subversive words come from the mouths of Dathan and Abiram, the Israelites who, along with Korah, rebelled against Moses and Aaron. One aspect of their rebellion involved challenging Moses' unique relationship with God, from which stemmed his right to rule over them (Num 16:3). They do precisely the same with the land of Israel. As they present it, there is nothing unique about being a land flowing with milk and honey; even Egypt is such a land.

Noam Mizrahi's reading of parashat Korah generates an important distinction concerning the role of food in popular uprising. Challenges to authority which emerge from the kind of food deprivation that amounts to cutting back on the caviar are likely to be ineffective and short-lived. Mass starvation, by contrast, can be a catalyst for genuine revolution, especially when extreme hunger is trivialized by pampered, bloated leaders. A significant early event of the French Revolution (1787–1799), the co-called Women's March on Versailles (1789), started among women rioting against bread shortages in the Paris marketplaces, and the four words that came to encapsulate the cruel indifference of the French ruling elite were Marie Antoinette's "Let them eat cake." Revolution was ignited in 2010 in Tunisia and neighboring Arab countries when a poor street vendor set himself alight after the authorities confiscated the scales he used to weigh vegetables. A case that seems at first glance to fall in between is Israel's 2011 "cottage cheese uprising," which began when a Bene Brak shopper noticed that the price of a tub of cottage cheese had risen 75% since price controls were lifted the previous year. Knesset Members who had no clue about the cost of cottage cheese quickly learned the price, and that it was twice as expensive in Israel as in most European countries. For Israel's poor, what was once a staple had become a luxury. Clearly, cottage cheese was more than cottage cheese in this debate. It stood as a symbolic representative of many other overpriced food items, and as an evocative term in a language for speaking about injustice in general. Was it coincidental that the food item on every Israeli's tongue during the socio-economic protests of summer 2011 was cottage cheese, the simple, healthy, accessible-to-all foodstuff that best reflects the still resonant image of a land flowing with milk and honey?

> *The Lord spoke further to Aaron: I hereby give you charge of all My gifts, all the sacred donations of the Israelites; I grant them to you and to your sons as a perquisite, a due for all time. (Num 18:8)*

Thus begins a set of detailed instructions about how Aaron and his sons, along with the Levites with whom they will work in the Temple, will be compensated for their services (Num 18:8–32). Aaron and his sons (but not their female family members) are entitled to eat meal, sin, and guilt offerings (Num 18:8–10); every member of the family who is clean is entitled to eat gift and elevation offerings (Num 18:11); and the same applies to the first fruits – oil, wine, grain –and the first-born of clean animals (Num 18:12–18). Finally Aaron and his sons are entitled to a portion of the tithes that Israelites make to the Lord. Like the yield of the threshing floor or vat, they and their households may eat their portion anywhere (Num 18:30–32). It seems to be because they will never be permitted to own property (Num 18:20, 24), and are therefore deprived of the means of supporting and sustaining themselves, that they are essentially paid in food.

> *And the earth opened its mouth and swallowed them up with their households, all Korah's people and all their possessions. (Num 16:32)*

Here is a reversal even more shocking than the description of Egypt as a land flowing with milk and honey (Num 16:12). As a rule, people who behave well are rewarded by being able to eat the earth's good food (see Deut 11:13–15, the second portion of the Shema). Here in Korah, the people behave appallingly and precisely the opposite occurs: the earth eats them.

Diana Lipton

Hukkat

Numbers 19:1–22:1

A Thirsty Land

Amira Meir

Parashat Hukkat opens with the commandment of the Red Heifer and the laws of death impurity, and goes on to report in brief on about thirty-eight of the forty years the Israelites wandered in the Sinai desert. The motif of water appears in different contexts throughout the parasha: the Red Heifer pericope; the passage that details the laws of impurity of death and the purification rite with its "water of separation;" the story of Meribah; in Moses' request that the king of the Edomites allow the Israelites to pass through his land; the story of the Canaanite king of Arad; the song of the well; and the tale of the war with Sihon, the Amorite king. In fact, water is mentioned twenty-two times in the eighty-six verses of the parasha.

Water was part of the void that predated the creation of the world, with the commandment "let there be an expanse in the midst of the water, that it may separate water from water" (Gen 1:6), appearing only on the second day of creation. From then to this day water carries a negative connotation: the "water [which] is bad" (2 Kgs 2:19), the "waters that cannot be relied on" (Jer 15:18), and the "seething waters" (Ps 124:5), whose destructive power can be witnessed in the biblical flood and elsewhere, as well as a positive aspect: the "well of spring water" (Gen 26:19; Song 4:15) that is the basis for all life.

The figure of Miriam is also linked to water. At the beginning of the book of Exodus we meet Miriam when she has "stationed herself at a distance to learn" (Exod 2:4) what happens to her brother Moses, who has been placed in a basket in the reeds at the riverbank. After the parting of the Red Sea, Miriam sings with the Israelite women of God who hurled "horse and driver" into the sea (Exod 15:21). And upon her death we are told, "Miriam died there and was buried there. The community was without water" (Num 20:1–2). This juxtaposition led the rabbis to say that it was because of Miriam's merit that the Israelites were provided with water in the desert:

> *"Three good leaders had arisen for Israel, namely: Moses, Aaron, and Miriam. And for their sakes three good things were conferred [upon Israel], namely, the Well, the Pillar of Cloud and the Manna; the Well, for the merit of Miriam . . . When Miriam died the well disappeared." (Babylonian Talmud, Ta'anit 9a)*

Siftei Ḥaḥamim, a compilation of interpretations of Rashi's biblical commentary collected in Prague in the 17th century by R. Shabtai Meshorer Bas, claims that "because Miriam waited for Moses at the riverbank to see what would become of him when he was laid there in the basket, she merited the well, that is, God gave the Israelites water for her merit" (*Siftei Haḥamim* on Num 20:2). This apparently refers to the same well that was given to the Israelites because of Miriam's merit: "while she was alive, [it] provided water for the encampment. When Miriam died . . . there was no water for the community, for the well had disappeared" (Tosefta *Sotah* 11:1). In other words, Miriam's life story is intertwined with the story of the provision of water for the Israelites in the desert. Because Miriam stood at the bank of the river to watch over her brother Moses, the Israelites had water during their years of desert wandering. Parashat Hukkat, in which her death is reported, is thus linked particularly closely to the motif of water in the wilderness, regarding which Miriam had special significance.

AMIRA MEIR earned her Ph.D. in medieval Jewish commentary on pentateuchal poetry at McGill University. She served as head of Biblical

Studies at Israel's Beit Berl College, taught at Hebrew Union College in Jerusalem and New York, University College London, the Gregorian University in Rome, and has lectured in many Italian universities. Her publications deal mainly with Biblical Commentary.

> *Why did you make us leave Egypt to bring us to this wretched place, a place with no grain or figs or vines or pomegranates? There is not even water to drink! (Num 20:5)*

Wandering in the wilderness, the people think of Egypt. In this context, the grain, figs, vines and pomegranates are less like food to eat than aesthetic adornments for the land (see Hosea 2:10–15). By no means bare – it's not the Sahara – the wilderness is definitely underdressed. Egypt, by contrast, was decked up to the nines. Some find distasteful the notion of food used decoratively – a bowl of lemons instead of a vase of flowers, for example. But food has always decorated the land.

> *Thus you shall produce water for them from the rock and provide drink for the congregation and their beasts . . . Out came copious water, and the community and their beasts drank. (Num 20:8, 11)*

Food often differentiates people from other people: who eats what, where, when, how, and with whom. Still more, it divides humans from animals. Only very rarely – probably under duress – would people and non-domestic animals eat the same food, from the same source, prepared in the same way, at the same time, in the same place. Water, by contrast, unites all living creatures. There's nothing unnatural about the scene evoked by this verse – Israelites and their animals pressing forward as one in their desperation to drink the cool, clear liquid that came gushing out of the rock.

> *Allow us, then, to cross your country. We will not pass through fields or vineyards, and we will not drink water from wells. (Num 20:17)*

> *"We will keep to the beaten track," the Israelites said to them, "and if we or our cattle drink your water, we will pay for it." (Num 20:19a)*

> *Israel now sent messengers to Sihon king of the Amorites, saying, "Let me pass through your country. We will not turn off into fields or vineyards, and we will not drink water from wells." (Num 21:21–22)*

Why did Moses promise the kings of Edom and the Amorites that the Israelites would not pass through fields and vineyards as they crossed their lands? A clue to a possible answer lies in his additional undertaking not to drink from the wells. A law in Deut 23:25–26 specifies that someone who enters a neighbor's vineyard can eat grapes but not collect them in a vessel. Similarly, someone who enters a field can pluck ears of grain by hand, but cannot use a sickle. Allowing travelers to eat a few grapes or a handful of grains was a form of hospitality. Moses understood that the Edomites and Amorites were not inclined to be hospitable, and thus sought to reassure them that the Israelites had no expectations on that score.

> *"Why did you make us leave Egypt to die here in the wilderness? There is no bread and no water, and we have come to loathe this miserable food." (Num 21:5)*

What is the matter with Mary Jane?
She's crying with all her might and main,
And she won't eat her dinner – rice pudding again
What *is* the matter with Mary Jane?

What is the matter with Mary Jane?
I've promised her dolls and a daisy-chain,
And a book about animals – all in vain –
What *is* the matter with Mary Jane?

What is the matter with Mary Jane?
She's perfectly well, and she hasn't a pain;
But, look at her, now she's beginning again! –
What *is* the matter with Mary Jane?

What is the matter with Mary Jane?
I've promised her sweets and a ride in the train,
And I've begged her to stop for a bit and explain –
What *is* the matter with Mary Jane?

What is the matter with Mary Jane?
She's perfectly well and she hasn't a pain,
And it's lovely rice pudding for dinner again!
What *is* the matter with Mary Jane?

(Alan Alexander Milne 1882–1956)

DIANA LIPTON

Balak

Numbers 22:2–25:9

Non-kosher sex

Laliv Clenman

Moabite women, eating sacrifices made out to foreign deities, prostrating and even binding themselves to the god Baal-peor; the beginning of Numbers 25 is a busy time for the Israelites. These verses describe not only the intimate connection between the Israelites and Baal-peor, but also the intimacy of food and sexuality, linking both to a consumption and adoption of idolatrous worship. The attachment of the people, though perhaps only of the males in this case, to a different deity is brought about through the act of eating sacrificial foods. The sacrificial food appears to be rendered accessible through the invitation of the Moabite women, after whom the people, again perhaps the men, follow. The "*zenut*" of the Israelite men after the Moabite women may have been promiscuous, idolatrous, or both. The acts of consumption, be they sexual, edible, or idolatrous, are all bound up with the betrayal of the divine.

It is against this backdrop that Zimri and Cozbi enter our parasha, seemingly uninvited from some other time or place, some other theatre. The union of Zimri, a Simeonite chief, and Cozbi, a Midianite daughter of a Midianite chief, may have simply been a diplomatic marriage between a prominent Israelite and a similarly high-ranking woman, hailing from a nation nowhere specifically prohibited. Then again, there is nothing simple about marriage or food. The Jerusalem Talmud, Sanhedrin 10:2 (28d–29a) understands the challenge which their match presents through the lenses of food and purity. The rabbis' daring question is posed by Zimri:

> *He [Zimri] said to him [Moses], "Is your Zipporah not Midianite? And are her hooves not cloven? Is this one pure and this one impure?" (Jerusalem Talmud, Sanhedrin 10:2 [28d])*

If woman is food, to be eaten by man, she must be either fit or unfit for eating – kosher or non-kosher, a calf or a camel. Of course no human is kosher, being neither ruminant nor hooved beast of any variety, but the construction of woman as a category of either fit or unfit animal transfers discussions of human existence and unions between male and female into a hierarchical binary (human as eater /animal as food), as well as into a clear legal structure (laws of kashrut). Likewise, Midianite women have no particular form of *tumah*, ritual impurity, though associating the female Other with a *tumah* to be avoided is a complex manoeuver. We might also understand this in the vein of the fitness of woman as sacrificial food (perhaps as in Lev 7:19), such that she becomes both sacrifice and sexual comestible. The answer to whether or not Moses and Zimri are permitted to eat of their Midianite women might be as simple as determining the kashrut of a pig over a goat, as plain as avoiding unnecessary exposure to sources of *tumah* or as straightforward as avoiding eating sacrificial food that has become contaminated with impurity.

What, then, is the correct mix for kashrut and purity in the male consumption of female as food, sacrifice, "Other?" Pinḥas brings his own answer in the form of the elimination of the source of the question, piercing through the coupled bodies of Zimri and Cozbi. In a beautiful talmudic irony, the Babylonian Talmud, Sanhedrin 82b tells us that the tribes were shocked by Pinḥas' act, ridiculing him en masse. Why? Because Pinḥas himself was born of a Midianite mother and an Israelite father. The Jerusalem Talmud never really resolves Zimri's pointed challenge as to why Zipporah is kosher for Moses but Cozbi is not kosher for Zimri, and even asserts that Pinḥas' act was not according to the will of the Sages (Jerusalem Talmud, Sanhedrin 11:7 [27b]). This is a world where gender, sexuality, identity, worship and food, the relationships between those who eat and those who are eaten, are far more complex than any ingredient list and set of instructions would allow.

LALIV CLENMAN is Lecturer in Rabbinic Literature at Leo Baeck College, London and teaches Jewish Studies in Department of Theology & Religious Studies at King's College London. She conducted her doctoral research in Rabbinics and Hebrew and Aramaic language and literature at the University of Toronto, and her current work focuses on the nature of talmudic and midrashic discourse, as well as problems of identity and status, including intermarriage, gender, sexuality, the construction of Jewishness and the impact of halakhah on the individual.

> *"Now this horde will lick clean all that is about us as an ox licks up the grass of the field." (Num 22:4)*

As presented here by King Balak, eating is a weapon. The Israelites are a gorging ox that eats not simply to satisfy its hunger, but also to prevent anyone or anything else from eating. Paradoxically, the image of "licking clean" is a complete reversal of Israel's laws of *peah* and gleaning (e.g., Lev 19:9), which demand that a field should never be razed bare. We must leave leftovers in the pot, as it were, to feed the poor.

> *They shall devour enemy nations, crush their bones . . . (Num 24:8)*

As above, eating is construed here as an act of violence. The reference to bones brings the metaphor to life: first eat the flesh, and then come the bones.

> *While Israel was staying at Shittim, the people profaned themselves by whoring with the Moabite women, who invited the people to the sacrifices for their god. The people partook of them and worshiped that god. (Num 25:1–2)*

The method of worship specified here is sacrifice. The Moabite women invited the Israelite men to sacrifices for their gods, but, although the Israelites are said to have worshipped that god, there is no indication that they made sacrifices. Rather, the order in which events are reported suggests that they worshipped the Moabite god by eating the sacrifice. It's interesting to ponder whether the Moabites saw themselves as worshipping when they ate sacrificial meat, or whether this was an Israelite understanding of Moabite religion, based on the significance of eating (by the priest) in Israel's own sacrificial cult.

Diana Lipton

Pinhas

Numbers 25:1–30:1

"To Change Your Consciousness, Change your Menu"*

Susan Handelman

Here follows one of the most famous and eloquent quotes in the history of food writing, by a pioneer in the field, the eminent American writer Mary Francis Kennedy Fisher (1908–1992). It's also a personal favorite; I read it aloud at the beginning and conclusion of a university course I teach called "Food for Thought: Food and Literature:"

> *People ask me: Why do you write about food, and eating and drinking? Why don't you write about the struggles for power and security, and about love, the way others do?*
>
> *They ask it accusingly, as if I were somehow gross, and unfaithful to the honor of my craft.*
>
> *The easiest answer is to say that, like most other humans, I am hungry. But there is more than that. It seems to me that our three basic needs, for food and security and love, are so mixed and mingled and entwined that we cannot straightly think of one without the others. So it happens that when I write of hunger, I'm really writing about love and the hunger for it, and warmth and the love*

* A fuller version of this essay entitled *'Don't Forget the Potatoes': Imagining God Through Food* is forthcoming in the volume *Imagining the Jewish God*, edited by Kenneth Koltun-Fromm and Leonard Kaplan (Lexington Press, 2016).

> *of it and the hunger for it . . . and then the warmth and richness and fine reality of hunger satisfied . . . and it is all one.*
>
> *I tell about myself, and how I ate bread on a lasting hillside, or drank red wine in a room now blown to bits, and it happens without my willing it that I am telling to you about the people with me then, and their other deeper needs for love and happiness.*
>
> *There is food in the bowl, and more often than not, because of what honesty I have, there is nourishment in the heart, to feed the wild or more insistent hungers. We must eat. If, in the face of that dread fact, we can find other nourishment, and tolerance and compassion for it, we'll be no less full of human dignity.*
>
> *There is a communion of more than our bodies when bread is broken and wine drunk. And that is my answer, when people ask me: why do you write about hunger, and not wars or love. (M.F.K. Fisher, "Foreword," The Gastronomical Me)*

"M.F.K. Fisher" as she was known, was far ahead of her time when she began writing about food in the 1920s. It's taken a long while for academia to catch up and make "Food Studies" a respected part of the curriculum. But our Rabbis understood long ago that food is always about something else, that every meal has a story. They saw in the "dread fact that we must eat" a deep spiritual meaning. Or, as the talmudic scholar I study with puts it, our ancient Sages understood that "in order to change your consciousness, you have to change your menu." Granted, he's French and wants to turn upside down his countryman Descartes' famous pronouncement "I think, therefore I am." But even a philosopher has to eat. Without that nourishment, there is neither "I think" nor "I am." In Jewish sensibility this need becomes the gateway to faith and moral consciousness. I'd like to reflect on the connection between food, faith, and philosophy in parashat Pinhas using the insights of another French rabbi, R. Léon Ashkénazi (1922–1996), a leader of post-war French Jewry.

Where is the food in our parasha, Pinhas? Pinhas comes after the high drama of the previous week's episodes: Balak and Balaam's talking donkey; curses turned to blessings; the people's sexually idolatrous sins with the Midianite and Moabite women; the subsequent punishing plague. One of the sinning couples is caught *in flagrante delicto* in front of the Tent of Meeting. Phinehas takes his spear and kills them both in one fell swoop. That leads to the end of the plague that has killed 24,000. Our parasha opens in the aftermath. The narrative pace suddenly slows; we catch our breath. Phinehas receives the covenant of peace and priesthood. We are now in the last eleven chapters of the book of Numbers; the Israelites are preparing for war with the Midianites and entrance of a new generation into the Promised Land.

Finally, come two long chapters on food, prefaced by Numbers 28:1: "The LORD spoke to Moses, saying: Command the Israelite people and say to them: Be punctilious in presenting to Me at stated times the offerings of food due Me, as offerings by fire of pleasing odor to Me." Chapters 28 and 29 establish the public calendar for the sacrificial system to be instituted in the Land. We are given long lists and exhaustive details of sacrifices made up of animal, meal, and drink. We are told specific offerings for each weekday, the Sabbath, New Moon, and all the major festivals: Passover, Shavuot, Yom Kippur, Rosh Hashanah, Yom Kippur, and Sukkot. This material was later added to the Jewish liturgy; each list is read on its appropriate festival. Jewish tradition holds that God counts our reading of these passages as equal to our bringing the offerings to the Temple. But where are elevated thoughts like those of M.F.K. Fisher about food here?

Let's first consider why food is such a key vehicle for religious consciousness, and then explore the deeper meaning of the sacrificial meals in the Temple. Rabbi Ashkénazi, in analyzing the religious significance of food, stresses that Jewish tradition knows and speaks of God first of all as the *Creator*. That's where the Bible begins; it establishes our essential mode of being in the world as "creature." The foundation of moral consciousness also begins here: that is, to recognize oneself as created, as given existence gratuitously by the Creator. The project of our lives, then, becomes to morally earn that existence. "Food, this need constantly to nourish and sustain ourselves, reminds us of our finitude in a way that no abstract philosophy can," Rabbi Ashkénazi stresses.

Philosophical or rational proofs for the existence of God via the idea of creation are secondary important clarifications. They follow varying intellectual trends; they can be more or less persuasive to various intellectual elites. But they can't serve as a means of primary religious consciousness accessible to everyone. As he puts it: "that fundamental experience of being created comes from the fact that a person has to eat in order to live"; "the presence of the highest values depends, at the end of the day, on the fact of physical and food . . . that's a philosophical scandal and true mystery." ("Foi et Morale", *Ki Mitsion II: les mo'adim,* 37–41, my translation).That's why, R. Ashkénazi continues, the midrash in *Genesis Rabbah* 30:8 describes Abraham teaching his new faith in the Creator and One God by inviting guests to his tent, feeding them, and redirecting them to thank – not him – but God, who is the source of creation and existence. Food, which enables them to perpetuate their existence, helps them to recognize God as the Being who gave them that existence.*

Now how does the formal sacrificial system of food offerings laid out in our parsha relate to all the above? The early chapters of Leviticus set forth aspects of the sacrificial system dealing with expiation of sins. Commenting on these passages, Rabbi Ashkénazi writes that every offence or error, of whatever sort, comes from the fact that our essential nature involves an appetite for pleasure (sometimes called in Hebrew, "*yetzer hara*"). But that appetite is *necessary* to ensure the functioning of our physical life; and that physical life enables our consciousness. So we are inevitably thrust into an economic and moral dilemma as we try to satisfy our hungers. We're exposed to the constant risk of fault by the simple fact of living life in the world. No wonder, then, that in the biblical narrative, the first sin of the first human (Adam) is tied to a problem involving food. Let it be clear, though: this is no doctrine of "original sin" but an existential

* There are two seemingly opposite dimensions to human existence, he notes: the "what" (Heb. *"mah"*), one's physical body given over to deterministic natural law; and the "who" (Heb. "*mi"),* one's consciousness, and intellect. The physical connection between the world and the person is food, "By the sweat of your brow, shall you get bread to eat" (Gen 3:19). Food is the world that is transformed into the human. When a person ceases eating, he or she first loses the "who," and then the "what" through death. (*Sod ha-Ivri*, 62–64).

condition of our being as created by God and placed in a world with others who also need to sustain their existence.

M.F.K. Fisher, describing the "dread fact that we must eat," also reminds us that the world includes many "wild, more insistent hungers." If, "in the face of that dread fact," she continues, "we find other nourishment, and tolerance and compassion for it, we'll be no less full of human dignity." How does one achieve that? Rabbi Ashkénazi gives a surprising answer. Jewish law, he argues, compensates for the existential, moral, and economic problem through the Temple ritual, which is that of a "meal, in the obtaining of which, no fault has been committed." The *kodashim,* the consecrated food offerings, have been removed from the market economy of exchange and surplus value. In this sense, he continues, one could describe the cult of the High Priest of the Temple of Jerusalem as the "perfect man, dressed in perfect garments, in the perfect house, nourished by the perfect meal." In other words, "if we could live or emulate the holiness of the priest exempted from the risks of the economic life, our meal would also be without fault." The ordinary Jew participates by bringing these sacrifices to the Temple priests from his own flocks or grains or fruits. These offerings are then slaughtered or burned on the Temple altar, and in certain cases partially eaten by the priests. In Rabbi Ashkénazi's view, the entire act generates a certain form of consciousness; it creates the possibility for an existence untainted by the existential, moral, and economic problem, and allows for renewed good conscience (*Ki MiTsion: Notes sur la Paracha*, vol 1; 215–217; 223–225).

After the destruction of the Temple, the Pharisees saved Judaism by extending the holiness of the ritual Temple meal to every Jewish home; the table becomes the substitute for the altar; prayers take the place of sacrifices, and so forth. Leviticus 19:2 proclaims, "You shall be holy, for I, the Lord your God, am holy." That is simultaneously a promise and a commandment; holiness becomes the model for all Israel. What do we do today, when the animals, plants, and drink that come to our tables/ altars have become dangerously degraded through modern industrial food production and factory farming? When the soil has become contaminated through chemical alteration; when what are euphemistically called "confinement animal feeding operations" raise animals for slaughter in cruel and environmentally damaging conditions? According to Jonathan Safran Foer, "Animal agriculture makes a 40% greater contribution to global warming than all transportation in the world combined; it is the number one cause of climate change" (*Eating Animals*, 42). What do we do when, despite all our advances in producing more food more cheaply, almost a billion people go hungry, and affluent Westerners fall ill due to diseases connecting to overeating? Food writer Ruth Reichel puts it well: "While half the world goes hungry, the other half is killing itself with calories, (*Why Food Matters*, The Tanner Lectures on Human Values, 14).

We need our religious traditions to help us restore the balance; to make sure, as Abraham did, that others are sought out, welcomed in and fed; that those who sit at our tables and worship with us recognize and bless the ultimate Source of all nourishment. We need to remember the precariousness of our condition as creatures, and our responsibility to protect the delicate web of life on earth that sustains us. And yes, we need also to satisfy our hungers; there will always be economic and moral dilemmas in doing so. But studying the offerings of our parasha, and symbolically enacting those ancient holy meals in the Temple in our homes can help guide us on our path.

Susan Handelman teaches in the English Department at Bar Ilan University, Israel. Her many publications on Jewish themes include *The Slayers of Moses: The Emergence of Rabbinic Interpretation in Modern Literary Theory* (1982), *Fragments of Redemption: Jewish Thought and Literary Theory in Benjamin, Scholem and Levinas* (1991), and *Make Yourself a Teacher: Rabbinic Tales of Mentors and Disciples* (2011).

> *In the first month, on the fourteenth day of the month, there shall be a passover sacrifice to the* Lord*, and on the fifteenth day of that month, a festival. Unleavened bread shall be eaten for seven days. (Num 28:16–17)*

It's logical to assume that the explicit command to eat unleavened bread has a silent partner: an unstated command not to eat leavened bread. However, avoiding leaven is not the inevitable corollary of eating unleavened bread. Perhaps unleavened bread, rather than the prohibition against leaven, is emphasized here because the broader context is sacrificial offerings, not dietary rules that emerged from Passover's historical origins. Alternatively, it's possible that the emphasis on unleavened bread here preserves the memory of an ancient spring festival that became absorbed into Passover – perhaps the very festival that Moses and Aaron begged Pharaoh to let the people celebrate in the wilderness (Exod 5:1–3). We can only speculate. Nonetheless, it's worth bearing in mind the significant difference – practical and psychological – between being required to eat and being forbidden from eating.

DIANA LIPTON

Mattot

Numbers 30:2–32:42

"To Bind his Soul with a Bond": When a Woman Stops Eating

Nili Wazana

Parashat Mattot opens with the laws of vows (Num 30:3–17). A vow (*neder*) is a future commitment made of one's own free will. In most cases the vow is accompanied by a condition, as in the case of the vow Jacob makes in Beth El: "Jacob then vowed a vow, saying, 'If God remains with me, if He protects me on this journey that I am making, and gives me bread to eat and clothes to wear, and if I return safe to my father's house'" (Gen 28:20–21). When the condition is met, the person making the vow must fulfill it immediately, as we hear in the following warning brought in biblical wisdom literature: "When you make a vow to God, do not delay to fulfill it . . . It is better not to vow at all than to vow and not fulfill" (Eccl 5:3–4; see also Deut 23:22–24).

The majority of biblical stories surrounding vows relate to "gift vows," in which the person vowing makes a commitment to give of his possessions – like Jacob in Beth El (Gen 28:22); to bring a sacrifice – like Jephthah (Judg 11:30–31); or even to dedicate a child to divine service, like Hannah (1 Sam 1:11). Our parasha, however, relates to a different type of vow, a vow of prohibition. This type of vow does not involve the relinquishing of belongings, but rather of physical enjoyment, through a commitment to an ascetic practice. A special kind of prohibition vow is that of the *nazir*, in which a person is sanctified by abstaining from cutting his/her hair, drinking wine and coming into contact with impurity (Num 6:5–21).

In Mattot, after we read the general rule "If a man makes a vow to the LORD or takes an oath imposing an obligation on himself, he shall not break his pledge. He must carry out all that has crossed his lips" (Num 30:3), the Bible lays out a set of test cases which relate exclusively to women: what happens when a woman takes a vow of prohibition in her father's home or in her husband's presence, and what is the status of the vow when the woman is a widow or a divorcee; in which cases can a father or a husband annul the woman's vow of prohibition and under what circumstances does it stand. The basic rule of thumb we learn in these cases is that the person taking the vow must be legally independent – when they are not, the head of their family must give their assent for the vow, at the very least through silent agreement. However, if the law here examines the status of vows of dependents, why are sons not mentioned?

The biblical passage describing the vows does not detail the contents of a vow of prohibition, but we can glean some information from the expressions used to describe it. Alongside the expression "binding the soul with a bond," which is repeated eleven times in the passage, there also appears the description of a vow which is said to require "self-denial," "to afflict the soul" (Num 30:14). This affliction of the soul is a familiar term from the laws of Yom Kippur and from the words of Isaiah, "Why, when we fasted, did You did not see? When we starved our bodies, did You pay no heed?" (Isa 58:3; see also Ps 35:13). Afflicting one's soul is, first and foremost, an act of fasting. The Talmudic discussion of what vows of affliction the woman has undertaken mentions an abstention from eating fruit (Babylonian Talmud, Nedarim 79a); on the Sabbath, the husband is not required to explicitly annul his wife's vow, but rather "he says to her 'Take and eat it,' 'Take and drink it,' and the vow becomes automatically void" (Babylonian Talmud, Nedarim 77b).

Anorexia nervosa is common primarily among young girls. Despite the fact that the phenomenon has been expanding recently, there were also people in antiquity – primarily women, and primarily young ones – who starved themselves. This may help explain why the laws of vows in Mattot devote fourteen verses to exploring the validity of a vow of prohibition undertaken by a woman in particular, and sums the discussion up by saying "those are the laws that the LORD enjoined upon Moses between a man and his wife, and as between a father and his daughter while in her father's household by reason of her youth" (Num 30:17). The laws of vows transfer the responsibility for a dependent woman's statements onto others, her father or husband. Perhaps this special law is intended to place a "responsible adult" between the woman's commitment to afflict herself and the possibility that she might deteriorate into a state of dangerous self-starvation.

NILI WAZANA is Senior Lecturer at the Hebrew University of Jerusalem in the Department of Bible and the Department of Jewish History and Modern Judaism. Her research relates to the study of the Bible in the context of the Ancient Near East. In addition, Nili works on the cultural history of the biblical period and the ideological development of biblical literature. Recent publications include *All the Boundaries of the Land: The Promised Land in Biblical Thought in Light of the Ancient Near East* (Eisenbrauns, 2013).

> *The Reubenites and the Gadites owned cattle in very great numbers. Noting that the lands of Jazer and Gilead were a region suitable for cattle, the Gadites and the Reubenites came to Moses, Eleazar the priest, and the chieftains of the community, and said . . . "the land that the LORD has conquered for the community of Israel is cattle country, and your servants have cattle. It would be a favor to us," they continued, "if this land were given to your servants as a holding; do not move us across the Jordan." (Num 32:1–5)*

Moses' first response to the request of the tribes of Gad and Reuben to remain on the wrong side of the Jordan is to compare them with the spies whose negative report discouraged the people from conquering the land (Num 32:6–15). The Gadites and Reubenites assure Moses that, far from being afraid to join the conquest, they are willing to go ahead as "shock-troops" (Num 32:17). Matters are resolved, and these two tribes, along with half the tribe of Manasseh, are assigned land that formerly controlled by Sihon, king of the Amorites, and Og, king of Bashan (v. 33). Yet still, something seems amiss. First, it's a bad sign that this episode is reminiscent of the encounter between Abram and Lot, also featuring livestock, which ends with Lot choosing the "well-watered" plain of Jordan, "like the garden of the LORD, like the land of Egypt," while Abram remains in Canaan (Gen 13:7–13). Since the plain of Jordan included the cities of Sodom and Gomorrah – which the LORD had not yet destroyed (v. 10) – this cannot be good news for Lot. The association of the plain of Jordan with Eden and Egypt (v. 10), two places associated with both plentiful food and expulsion, is also ominous. Second, the tribes of Reuben and Gad base their choice on human logic instead of divine. In the bigger scheme of things, that constitutes a failure of conviction that, regardless of how bad things might look, God will put food on the table.

DIANA LIPTON

Mase'ei

Numbers 33:1–36:13

Food, Land, and Politics

Adi Marili

Parashat Mase'ei opens with an itinerary of the Israelites' travels through the Sinai desert. The extremely long list catalogues all the places in which they encamped. The reference to all these temporary homes creates the sense of a never-ending journey, a feeling which intensifies the importance of acquiring a homeland – a single, permanent place that offers a sense of belonging and responsibility, along with personal, economic, and emotional security.

In striking contrast to the list of transitional encampments through which the Israelites passed in the desert, is the description of the Promised Land. In place of locations at which the tribes paused briefly are the names of cities, mountains and rivers that form the borders of the land to which they have been travelling. The Israelites were unfamiliar with the names of all these places; they must have sounded exotic. It's unlikely that they could begin to envisage the paths and passes that Moses listed in detail. We can only guess at their emotions when confronted by this long list of names that defines not a route, but the place that will eventually be their home.

Alongside the preparation for the division of the land into tribal and family estates (a division which would take place only after the Israelites entered the land), God also takes care of those who have no landed domain – collectively and individually. First, God commands the Israelites to set aside land from their future estates for cities for the Levites. Although the tribe of Levi receives no independent territory in Israel, the Levites are given space to create cities and build homes. Second, God commands the allocation of the cities of refuge. Even people who have committed accidental manslaughter or who are charged with murder are given a roof over their heads and ground on which to stand. For individuals in constant flight from a blood avenger, the city of refuge is not just a place to sleep. At the most basic level, the city protects them, ensuring that their blood will not be spilled; at a deeper level, the city enables them to create a community that sustains itself from its own land.

Land provides people with a place to build shelter, to make a living, and, in an agrarian economy, to sustain themselves. By virtue of these material advantages, the inhabitants attach symbolic and social significance to their land. Following the divine commandments mentioned above, the heads of the Giladites begin to worry about their estate. In the parashah, Pinhas, the daughters of Zelophehad – a man who died without male progeny – demanded to receive their father's inheritance. They understood that the landed estate would preserve its owner's name for posterity, and thus in order to keep their father's name alive wished to maintain their possession of their familial property. God accepted this request and decreed that the daughters would inherit their father without condition: "you should give them a hereditary holding among their father's kinsman" (Num 27:7). The usual practice was that a man's sons inherited his land, along with which was passed the family name. This practice preserved the center of economic and political power in exclusively male hands, providing men alone with the right and ability to guarantee their livelihood. The divine decision regarding the daughters of Zelophehad, however, transferred these patriarchal rights into female hands.

The heads of the Menashite families come before Moses in order to appeal this precedential decision. They claim that giving inheritance rights to women will diminish their estate, since when the women marry, all of their belongings – both portable and property – will become their husbands' possessions. Unlike the sisters, who are worried that their father's name will be erased from the tribal lineage, which is imprinted on his land, the leaders of the tribe are concerned about their future loss of land – an economic and political loss which would also lead to their diminished authority among the other tribes. In this case, Moses does not ask God for a decision (as he did when confronted with the sisters' request). He adjudicates on his own, ruling that the sisters must limit their choice in spouses to men from their own tribe. This decision limits the basic rights conferred by God onto the daughters of Zelophehad – the right which allowed them to hold on to their father's land and keep his name; and, on a symbolic level, the right which revolutionized the existing situation and gave them economic and political equality with their male counterparts.

The implementation of the divine commandment, with no reservations, would have destabilized the patriarchal social order according to which the Israelites lived, and Moses – as the person responsible for the social order – could not allow this. He therefore limited the revolutionary extent of God's commandment, specifying that women must choose spouses from amongst their own tribe.

Struggles over the basic right to have a roof over one's head and the ability to sustain oneself with dignity are unfortunately not unfamiliar to our generation. The entity which was once defined as an estate or landed inheritance is now an apartment or a home. But the symbolism embedded in the ancient and modern terminologies is the same. Both agricultural land and apartments in high-rise buildings enable us to provide for ourselves and our families with dignity. The ability to sustain ourselves and produce our food directly from the earth, and the security provided by four walls belonging to us, to which we can return after the day's work in the office that generates money to buy our food, are one and the same.

ADI MARILI is a doctoral candidate in the Bible Department of Bar Ilan University and a lecturer at The David Yellin Academic College of Education. Her research focuses on notions of gender in biblical society, using the analytical tools of anthropological linguistics. By examining the differences in the treatment of certain body organs when relating to males and to females, she gains unique insight into the social thought of ancient Israel.

> *They set out from Alush and encamped at Rephidim; it was there that the people had no water to drink. (Num 33:14)*

Only two of the long list of wilderness locations in which the Israelites encamped on their way from Egypt to the Promised Land are mentioned in connection with events that occurred there: Rephidim and Mount Hor (Num 33:38). Given how often the people complained about the lack of water and food, it's curious that one location is singled out. Still more curious, is that the place mentioned is Rephidim and not Kadesh (Num 33:36), where the people complained about water, and Moses struck the rock twice instead of speaking to it, forfeiting his place in the Promised Land (Num 20:1–13). A possible explanation emerges from the list's reference to what happened at Mount Hor: Aaron died there. It's reported near the end of Deuteronomy that Moses died in the land of Moab and was buried at an unspecified location near Beth-peor (Deut 34:5–6), but neither Moses' death, nor its approximate location, is mentioned in this list in Numbers. By memorializing Rephidim (Exod 17:1–7), instead of Kadesh, as the place where the people complained and Moses struck the rock, the list loosens the link between Moses' demise and the Israelites' need for water. This list of locations lends no support to the reasonable speculation that Moses died of other people's thirst.

DIANA LIPTON

Devarim

Deuteronomy 1:1–3:22

Peace and Plenty

IAN GAMSE AND TAMRA WRIGHT

The book of Deuteronomy opens with what appears to be a review of the Israelites' history since leaving Egypt. But it is soon apparent that the purpose is not merely to recount the events: Moses jumps backwards and forwards in time, and is clearly selective in not only which stories he tells but how he tells them.

The theme of food appears twice in the parasha. First, we are reminded how the spies "took some of the fruit of the land" and brought it back to the camp (Deut 1:25). Second, Moses recounts how he sent emissaries to Sihon, King of the Amorites, asking for peaceful passage through his territory and offering to buy food and water from him on the way – an offer that Sihon rejects "because the LORD had stiffened his will and hardened his heart in order to deliver him into your power" (Deut 2:30).

It would be easy to draw a simple contrast between the two stories: the wicked spies take fruit from the land of Israel without regard for its owners, while the virtuous Moses is prepared to pay for whatever the Israelites eat or drink as they pass through Sihon's country – rather than, for example, relying on their own provisions, or assuming that roadside wells are ownerless. But this would be to ignore a crucial detail in the Sihon story: Moses assures us that Sihon rejects the offer of peace not freely but under divine coercion. So isn't the offer itself empty?

Rabbi Simha Bunim of Peshisha raises this question in his comments on Parashat Hukkat in *Kol Simḥa* (p. 94). He cites a midrash, *Be-midbar Rabbah* 19:27, which quotes two verses in Psalms: "Trust in the LORD and do good" (Ps 37:3) and "Shun evil and do good, seek amity and pursue it" (Ps 34:15). The midrash sees an example of pursuing peace in the Sihon story: "even though the Holy One, blessed be He, had said to them (Deut 2:24) 'Begin the conquest, go to war with him,' they pursued peace." The point, according to Rabbi Simha Bunim, is that the moral action must be performed; the offer of peace must be genuinely made – even if the possibility of its acceptance would appear to contradict God's promise. Moses knows that his offer will be rejected, but making that offer, speaking the language of peace, makes the world a better place.

And perhaps this is his criticism of the spies: they may indeed have been entitled to take the fruit of the land which God had declared would soon be theirs. But they missed the opportunity to "seek peace and pursue it" – and there, according to Jewish tradition, is the starting point for the chain of calamities that we remember on Tisha b'Av.

TAMRA WRIGHT and IAN GAMSE wrote this commentary as a wife-husband team. Dr. Tamra Wright is the Director of Academic Studies at the London School of Jewish Studies and a Visiting Lecturer at King's College London. She has published works on Emmanuel Levinas and other contemporary Jewish philosophers. Ian Gamse is a Jewish educator and investment banker. This commentary is dedicated to the memory of Ian Gamse's father, Yekutiel Natan ben Chayim v'Eta Rachel. This was the last piece of Torah that Ian shared with him.

What food you eat you shall obtain from them [the Edomites] for money; even the water you drink you shall procure from them for money. Indeed, the Lord *your God has blessed you in all your undertakings. He has watched over your wanderings through this great wilderness; the* Lord *your God has been with you these past forty years: you have lacked nothing. (Deut 2:6–7)*

It's easy to think that blessings are free, but the conjunction of verses here indicates otherwise. In one breath, Moses warns the Israelites that they must pay for the food they eat, and even the water they drink, as they pass through Edom. In the next breath, he reminds them that God has blessed them throughout their time in the wilderness, and that they've always had what they needed. Food does not have to be like manna, falling gratis from heaven, to be a blessing. It's a blessing even when you have to pay for it.

Then I sent messengers from the wilderness of Kedemoth to King Sihon of Heshbon with an offer of peace, as follows, "Let me pass through your country. I will keep strictly to the highway, turning off neither to the right nor to the left. What food I eat you will supply for money, and what water I drink you will furnish for money; just let me pass through . . . (Deut 2:26–28)

Food is often the focal point of the relationship between travellers and the places in which they are travelling. If the travellers are tourists, their need to eat represents an opportunity in both directions; the tourists experience local cuisine (unless they insist on international restaurant chains), and the residents benefit economically. For many tourists, eating is a highlight of their trip, and may even be its main aim. If the travelers are refugees, their need to eat creates a burden on the local population; food must be supplied, but payment cannot be expected. Moses' message to the Amorite king shows that the Israelites are neither tourists – wandering off the beaten track in search of the best artisanal pita – nor refugees, unable to pay for what they need and depending entirely on local hospitality.

Diana Lipton

Va-'Ethannan

Deuteronomy 3:23–7:11

Food to . . . live for in the Ten Commandments

Chaim Hames

Parashat Va-'ethannan contains the second rendering of the Ten Commandments found in the Pentateuch. The commandments appear without any reference to the events related to the giving of the commandments on Sinai as found in Exodus 20. In addition, when the two renderings are set side by side, they appear to be two quite different versions of the commandments. Biblical commentators over the generations have worked hard to explain how can there be so many differences if these commandments are the divine fiat.

The fifth commandment (Deut 5:16), well known to parents and children alike, focuses on the obligation to honor one's parents. In the rabbinic understanding of the commandments, as well as in the popular imagination, there were two tablets each containing five commandments (if this was indeed the case, the side containing the second five would have looked pretty empty compared to the side containing the first five). This puts the fifth commandment on the side of the tablets containing the commandments that are considered to be between God and humankind (the other five commandments focus on relations between human beings that allow for a just society). This seems to be counter-intuitive as honoring one's parents is so clearly connected to inter-personal relations. Some of the commentators explain that this demonstrates the importance of the commandment, in that by honoring your parents, you are actually honoring God.

This is the actual wording of the fifth commandment in English (more substantial than Exod 20:12; my translation): "Honor your father and your mother, in order that your days shall be lengthened and in order that things should go well for you upon this earth (ground) that the LORD, your God, has given you." Honoring one's parents is a divine fiat which has an immediate reward if performed properly. Yet, because it is not a one-time deed, but an ongoing process continuing even after a parent's death, the practical implementation of the promised reward is not necessarily immediately apparent.

The promise of long life and prosperity are, naturally, dependent on having the wherewithal to allow them. Interestingly, this promise also appears in other contexts where the issue of food is central; one of them at the end of the second paragraph of the Shema, recited twice a day in the evening and morning services (Deut 11:13–21). This paragraph emphasizes that teaching the commandments to one's children, keeping them, and loving God, will be rewarded by rain that falls in the right seasons and bountiful harvests. These are the sine qua non for the prosperity and long life promised in the last verse of the paragraph. The keeping of another commandment, that of sending the mother bird away from her young offspring or eggs before taking them from her nest (Deut 22:6) and presumably using them for food, also assures long life and prosperity. Hence, honoring one's parents is intimately connected with physical sustenance.

This is perhaps not surprising. As young children, we are unable to care for ourselves and we are almost totally dependent on our parents to provide us with food, lodging, an education, and hopefully, love. As we grow up, acquire the skills necessary for making our way in the world and then set up our own families, our parents also age and move into a different phase of life whereby they become more dependent on us. In essence, the cycle of life is embedded in this fifth commandment, hence the reward for those who uphold it.

CHAIM [HARVEY] HAMES is head of the Department of General History at Ben-Gurion University of the Negev and the Director of the

Center for the Study of Conversion and Inter-Faith Encounters. His research interests include Medieval and Renaissance Jewish and Christian mysticism and philosophy, apocalypticism, inter-religious polemics, and conversion. Chaim's books include *Like Angels on Jacob's Ladder: Abraham Abulafia, the Franciscans, and Joachimism* (2008) and *I (do not) Believe: Israel and Judaism – Past, Present, Future* (2011) [in Hebrew]. These words of Torah are dedicated to the memory of his father, Asher Anshel ben Hana ve-Aharon ha-Levi, who died on 5th Sivan 5774 (June 3, 2014).

> *Obey, O Israel, willingly and faithfully, that it may go well with you and that you may increase greatly [in] a land flowing with milk and honey, as the LORD, the God of your fathers, spoke to you. (Deut 6:3)*

H.L.A. Hart, the brilliant and inspiring professor of Jurisprudence in whose sprawling family vacation home I cooked and cleaned when I was an undergraduate, used to say: there's no such concept as earning food. The context in which I heard him say it was playful. A guest – the Harts had constant house parties – would walk into the kitchen at the end of the compulsory afternoon hike through the beautiful Cornish countryside, gaze at the table set with homemade scones, strawberry jam and the local delicacy – clotted cream – and exclaim: "We've earned this." But for Hart, the point was serious; he saw food as a right, not something that can be earned. It's difficult to see how that fits with the Torah's conditionality concerning food. (This wasn't a problem for Hart – he was a Jewish atheist.) Perhaps an answer is that food is a right that, in certain circumstances – such as extreme disobedience or infidelity – can be revoked. This verse is a reminder of that. The milk and honey won't inevitably flow when you get to the land.

> *When the LORD your God brings you into the land that He swore to your fathers, Abraham, Isaac, and Jacob to assign to you – great and flourishing cities that you did not build, houses full of all good things that you did not fill, hewn cisterns that you did not hew, vineyards and olive groves that you did not plant – and you eat your fill, take heed that you do not forget the LORD who freed from the land of Egypt, the house of bondage. (Deut 6:10–12)*

Counter-intuitively in some respects, it's much harder to be appreciative when you have than when you don't have. This is particularly evident in the case of food. How quickly we shift from, "This sandwich tastes fantastic – I was starving," to "Oy, I'm so full; I can't eat another thing." Sometimes, a hint of blame creeps in, as if the sandwich, or the person who provided it, was responsible for our feeling of fullness. It's no surprise, then, that the words immediately preceding the warning against ingratitude in the face of the land's abundance are "and you eat your fill." Could this be why *birkat ha'mazon*, the blessing for meals, comes *after* eating, not, as in some other religious traditions, before? It's easy to feel grateful in anticipation when you don't have food, more challenging when it's already on your plate, and hardest of all when your plate is empty because you've just finished eating.

DIANA LIPTON

'Ekev

Deuteronomy 7:12–11:25

Not By Bread Alone

MARC SAPERSTEIN

Several years ago, I saw an extraordinary play entitled "Not By Bread Alone." The eleven actors, from an Israeli Company called *Nalaga'at* (meaning "please touch"), were all deaf and blind. As the audience entered, the actors were sitting at a long table on the stage, each one kneading dough that would be baked during the course of the performance. At the end, the audience was invited onto the stage to taste the bread. But the main purpose was not for us to eat the delicious warm bread, but to communicate on some level, by touch, with the actors who could not hear our applause or see our smiles.

"Man does not live by bread alone" (Deut 8:3) is the most common translation of six simple Hebrew words. Yet the meaning and message of these words is more complex than it might appear. Here is how Rabbi Joseph Hertz put it in his classic commentary on the Pentateuch and haftorahs:

> *Physical food is not the only thing that ensures man's existence. Apart from the normal sustenance there are Divine forces which sustain man in his progress through life.*

Now this does *not* seem to be the meaning in its original biblical context, which speaks of faith and trust in God when facing unfamiliar food (manna) in difficult circumstances. But let's take the familiar meaning – about the need for the spiritual dimension in life. I remember Professor Krister Stendhal, of Harvard Divinity School, once saying at a faculty colloquium, "This verse means something quite different when you quote it to a group of people who are wealthy, than it does when you quote it to a group of people who are hungry."

That was a powerful insight for me. To the wealthy, who may have inherited fortunes that allow them to enjoy a lifetime of leisure, or who expect annual distributions of more than most of the population will earn in a lifetime of productive labour, the message is: "Don't think that your gastronomic pleasures, your expensive wines, your conspicuous consumption of consumer goods, are what is ultimately important. There is much more to life than this." Most of us would consider that message appropriate.

Quoting the same verse to a group of the countless millions of people on earth who go to bed hungry each night, who do not know where their next meal will come from, the meaning is quite different: "Don't complain that you haven't enough food; it's not the body but the spirit that is most important; you will eventually get your reward in the spiritual realm for your suffering here on earth." I hope that we would never say to a family of Syrian refugees who had lost homes and possessions, and have no money to buy clothing or food, "man does not live by bread alone." Quoting the verse in that context conveys a very different message that is insensitive and repugnant.

For those of us fortunate to have our basic needs fulfilled, it is important to recall that the food on which our lives depend comes from many sources, that we should appreciate having this food at a reasonable cost, and that we should express gratitude to the Power that brings forth from the earth the substance from which other human beings – including even human beings unable to see or to hear – may make bread. This is the message expressed in the verse that comes just shortly after "not by bread alone," the verse that is the basis for our birkat ha'mazon: "When you have eaten your fill, give thanks to the Lord your God for the good land" – or the good earth, or we might add: the good health – "which He has given you" (Deut 8:10).

MARC SAPERSTEIN has taught Jewish History at George Washington University in Washington DC, Washington University in St. Louis, Harvard Divinity School and, most recently, Harvard and Yale Universities. From 2006 to 2011, he served as the Principal of Leo Baeck College, London, and continues to teach there as Professor of Jewish History and Homiletics. He is the author of many books and articles on Jewish history, literature and thought, and is an eminent authority on the history of Jewish preaching. A distinguished preacher himself, this commentary is based on a sermon he delivered at Beth Shalom Reform Synagogue in Cambridge, England.

> *For the LORD is bringing you into a good land, a land with streams and springs and fountains issuing from plain and hill; a land of wheat and barley, of vines, figs, and pomegranates, a land of olive trees and honey; a land where you may eat food without stint, where you will lack nothing; a land whose rocks are iron and from whose hills you can mine copper. When you have eaten your fill, give thanks to the LORD your God for the good land which He has given you. (Deut 8:7–10)*

This is the biblical source of what became known in Jewish tradition as the "seven species," the seven basic food types that the Israelites will find growing when they enter the land. This feast of colors, textures, and tastes, whose constituent foods are to this day ingredients for many local staple dishes, appears immediately after a positive instruction ("Therefore keep . . .") to observe God's commandments and walk in His ways (Deut 8:6), and is followed by a warning ("Take care lest you . . .") about forgetting to keep them (Deut 8:11). At first it looks like part of a familiar pattern in Deuteronomy and beyond: blessings promised as a reward for obedience to the law, followed by curses threatened for disobedience. Yet here the almost inevitable negative that tempers the positive is not a set of curses in response to inappropriate Israelite behavior (disobedience), but rather the prediction that Israelites will respond inappropriately, with hubris, to these blessings. Instead of acknowledging God's essential role in their agricultural bounty and thanking him when they have eaten and are satisfied (Deut 8:10), they will forget God and imagine that they themselves are responsible for this good land with its abundant produce (Deut 8:17).

> *When you have eaten your fill, and have built fine houses to live in . . . beware lest your heart grow haughty and you forget the LORD your God – who freed you from the land of Egypt, the house of bondage . . . who brought forth water for you from the flinty rock; who fed you in the wilderness with manna, which your fathers had never known, in order to test you by hardships only to benefit you in the end . . . (Deut 8:12, 14, 15–16)*

The danger of hubris is underlined here by a graphic contrast: the land versus the desert. The land they are about to enter is flowing with life-giving water – streams, springs, and fountains – and bursting with technicolored produce – golden wheat and barley, green vines, purple figs, ruby pomegranates, green and black olives, and deep brown honey. The desert they are leaving, and to which, by implication, they could return, is a parched and therefore colorless land patrolled by serpents and scorpions. Survival there is possible only because God brought forth water from the "flinty rock" and fed the people with manna (Deut 8:15–16).

Paradoxically, both the land and the desert, as they are described here, yield food without requiring effort on the part of the people. In the desert, God's involvement is evident for all to see – how else could water come from a rock and manna from heaven? In the bounteous land, by contrast, God's hand is invisible, and therein lies the problem. The Israelites do not understand that He is the source of their sustenance and therefore neglect to show gratitude.

> *I had ascended the mountain to receive the tablets of stone, the Tablets of the Covenant that the LORD had made with you, and I stayed on the mountain forty days and forty nights, eating no bread and drinking no water. (Deut 9:9)*

> *I threw myself down before the LORD – eating no bread and drinking no water forty days and forty nights, as before – because of the great wrong you had committed, doing what displeased the LORD and vexing Him. (Deut 9:18)*

Why did Moses fast? A popular answer to this question is that he sought to intensify the spiritual dimension of his encounter with God by ignoring his physical appetites. Foregoing food was a way of withdrawing from the world and immersing himself in the realm of the divine. This answer makes sense with respect to Moses' first ascent (Deut 9:9), a time of hope and expectation, we can assume. It makes less sense with regard to his second ascent, when the priority was less forging a spiritual connection with God and more saving the people from God's threat of total destruction. Fasts, formal and informal, are often associated with lack and the aversion of danger. The childless Hannah refuses to eat every year when she visits the House of the LORD with her husband, his other wife Peninnah, and the children they have together (1 Sam 1:7–8), and Esther institutes a three day fast for all women in response to Haman's plan to kill the Jews of Shushan (Esth 4:16). The second time Moses knows precisely what he lacks – the two tablets of law that he smashed in anger at the end of his first descent – and he has just saved the people from utter destruction in the wake of the golden calf (Exod 32–33). He fasts for forty days and forty nights in the hope that God will overcome *His* anger and replace the broken tablets. Both accounts of Moses' ascents, Exodus 34:28 and Deuteronomy 9:9, open with a reference to fasting and close with the writing of the Ten Commandments. Whether for a leader on behalf of his or her people or for a layperson in distress, food has always been a way to make a demand or express a request.

> *For the LORD your God . . . upholds the cause of the fatherless and the widow, and befriends the stranger, providing him with food and clothing. You too must befriend the stranger, for you were strangers in the land of Egypt. (Deut 10:17a, 18–19)*

Here we learn what it means to love the stranger – feed and clothe him. We may not love everyone we invite to dinner, but nevertheless giving food is an act of love.

> *And what he did to Dathan and Abiram, sons of Eliab son of Reuben, when the earth opened her mouth and swallowed them, along with their households, their tents, and every living thing in their train, from amidst all Israel. (Deut 11:6)*

Another repetition in parashat 'Ekev concerns what happened to Dathan and Abiram, "when the earth opened her mouth and swallowed them, along with their households, their tents, and every living thing in their train, from amidst all Israel" (Deut 11:6). In its original context in parashat Koraḥ (Num 16:31–34), the emphasis is twofold: the terrible punishment inflicted upon the rebels and all those associated with them, including their wives and innocent children (Num 16:27), and God's readiness to affirm Moses' authority (Moses comes up with the idea as a proof that he is acting on divine instruction, v. 30). Both serve as a deterrent for anyone else who had it in mind to challenge Moses' authority. Here, in 'Ekev, the event is mentioned at the end of a list of four types of "marvelous acts" that were witnessed by the wilderness generation but not their children: the signs and deeds (plagues) that God performed in Egypt; God's drowning of the Egyptian army in the Reed Sea; and "what God did" for Israel on their journey to the land (Deut 11:3–5). The reference point of the third category is unclear, but the first two refer explicitly to occasions when God broke laws of nature in order to punish Israel's enemies. This is also the case for the fourth "marvelous act," but what is striking in the case of Dathan and Abiram is that this time the enemies are within. While the earth that opened its mouth and swallowed them was the wilderness, the context here seems to point towards the land of Israel which, as was earlier reported by the spies (Num 13), also has the potential to devour those who forget God's power and disobey his commandments (Deut 11:16–17).

> *Keep, therefore, all the instruction that I enjoin upon you today, so that you may have the strength to enter and take possession of the land that you are about to cross into and possess, and that you may long endure on the soil that the Lord swore to your fathers to assign to them and to their heirs, a land flowing with milk and honey. . . . If, then, you obey the commandments that I enjoin upon you this day, loving the Lord your God and serving him with all your heart and soul, I will grant the rain for your land in season. . . . You shall gather in your new grain and wine and oil – I will also provide grass in the fields for your cattle – and thus you shall eat your fill. (Deut 11:8–9, 13,14a, 15)*

Deuteronomy has a strong claim for being the Bible's most conditional book, and what God most often promises to give or threatens to withhold, depending on Israelite compliance or otherwise with the laws, is food. These verses touch on the main agricultural products of the land of Canaan – the produce of the soil, new grain, wine and oil, and cattle – promising that all these will be abundant *if* the people keep the commandments, the terms and conditions of God's covenant over the land. This focus on food as an incentive or bargaining tool is hardly surprising. Nothing else in an agrarian society is at once so absolutely essential and so obviously beyond human control.

> *For the land you are about to enter and possess is not like the land of Egypt from which you have come. There the grain you sowed had to be watered by your own labors, like a vegetable garden; but the land you are about to cross into and possess, a land of hills and valleys, soaks up its waters from the rains of heaven. (Deut 11:10–11)*

Just as the brief summary of God's "marvelous acts" moves from Egyptians and Egypt to Israelites and Israel, (Deut 8:14–16), so does this brief overview of the agricultural differences skip between the two lands. God reminds the Israelites that He had promised their ancestors (usually understood as the patriarchs but possibly here a reference to the generation who left Egypt) "a land flowing with milk and honey." Now, as they are about to enter this land, God gives more detailed information. It is not, He says, like the land of Egypt, where the grain they sowed had to be watered by their own hand (literally "foot") like a vegetable garden. Rather, rain from heaven will be the land's source of water in the land of Israel (Deut 11:11–14). If this sounds at first like a blessing, it turns out to be mixed. To be sure, there will be crops in abundance – new grain, wine and oil, and grass for the cattle (vv. 14–15) – if the people keep God's laws and worship Him exclusively. If, however, they stray, God's anger will flare up against them. He will shut up the skies so that there will be no rain, the crops will soon perish, and the people too will perish (Deut 11:17). Whereas in Egypt, as portrayed here, hard work yielded direct results, in the land of Israel, it is obedience to God that produces fruits. An Israelite in Israel, unlike an Egyptian in Egypt and perhaps even an Israelite in Egypt (that's a big question), cannot make the choice to be self-sufficient.

DIANA LIPTON

Re'eh

Deuteronomy 11:26–16:17

Ethical Consumption

Eliezer Segal

What follows was inspired by the sixteenth-century exegete Rabbi Moses Alsheikh of Safed. His nuanced reading of the passage combines hermeneutical precision, psychological insight, and a moral responsibility.

Several interpreters regard God's permission to eat meat as a reluctant concession to human weakness. That outlook usually correlates with a view that, in the future redemption, we will be restored to the primordial vegetarianism of the original creation. This passage from Deuteronomy can be read as the source of an ethical context for eating meat. Here, the permission to eat non-sacrificial meat is linked to the enlargement of Israel's borders:

> *When the Lord enlarges your territory, as He has promised you, and you say, "I shall eat some meat," for you have the urge to eat meat, you may eat meat whenever you wish. (Deut 12:20)*

Unlike the situation that prevailed during the wanderings in the Sinai wilderness, when the people were encamped around the tabernacle and could conveniently go there to prepare their meat in the form of "peace offerings" [*shelamim*], the settling of the Promised Land placed considerable distances between most of the populace and the sanctuary. Now the Torah explicitly permitted eating meat even if its spiritual purpose was not reinforced by a sacrificial rite.

The craving for meat is described very precisely in Deut 12:20: [literally] "your *soul* longs to eat meat." Though the Hebrew word *nefesh* has a broad range of possible meanings, traditional commentators often emphasize its theological sense as the "soul" as distinct from the body. This understanding allows for an important insight in relation to the longing to eat meat expressed in Deut 12:20. Although the consumption of meat has been extended from the sacred precincts to the individual home, you must nonetheless strive to retain the spiritual quality of the act and not reduce it to the mere satisfying of a physical urge.

What is the spiritual quality that is evoked by the activity of eating meat? Kabbalistic commentators understood this in light of mystical principles, particularly with the doctrine of reincarnation; by ingesting the flesh of an animal species into a noble human body, one is thereby elevating its metaphysical status. I prefer to understand it in a more ethical manner: food, including the nutritional components of meat, should serve as a source of strength to assist people in doing God's will and increasing goodness in the world. It should not become an irresponsible indulgence in sensuality, or a pretext for cruelty.

Accordingly, it should be clearly understood that when enjoying the permission to eat non-sacrificial meat, we must strive not to lose sight of its essential religious purposes. As Alsheikh puts it with his textual ingenuity:

> *Scripture stated "If the place . . . is too far from you." It is the Temple that is geographically remote from you. However, you should not be the ones who distance yourselves spiritually from the sacred ideals that ought to govern your attitudes to food.*

ELIEZER SEGAL lectures in the Department of Classics and Religion, University of Calgary, Canada on Hebrew Bible, Judaism, and the Abrahamic religious traditions. Alongside extensive scholarly publications on Talmudic philology, Midrash, ritual and ethics, and the encounters between Judaism and Greco-Roman culture, he is the author of the popular children's book *Uncle Eli's Haggadah.*

> *But whenever you desire, you may slaughter and eat meat in any of your settlements, according to the blessing that the* LORD *your God has granted you. The unclean and the clean alike may partake of it, as of the gazelle and the deer. But you must not partake of the blood; you shall pour it out on the ground like water. (Deut 12:15–16)*

In the highly ritualized context of the Mishkan and, later, the Temple, meat created or reinforced hierarchies and distinctions: those who were permitted to eat versus those who were prohibited from eating. The words "the unclean and the clean alike may partake of it," make it clear that these hierarchies and distinctions will not apply when it comes to eating meat in the land. Once all worship has been centralized and there are no local shrines, meat-eating will be democratized.

> *You may not partake in your settlements of the tithes of your new grain or wine or oil, or of the firstlings of your herds and flocks. . . . These you must consume before the Lord your God in the place that the Lord your God will choose. (Deut 12:17a, 18a)*

Once it is established that restrictions on where meat may be eaten are being relaxed, it's crucial to underline the restrictions that still apply. Meat can be eaten where it was hunted and killed, but first fruit tithes must be eaten in the central place that God will choose – the Temple.

> *You shall not eat anything abhorrent. These are the animals that you may eat: the ox, the sheep, and the goat . . . and any other animal that has true hoofs which are cleft in two and brings up the cud—such you may eat. (Deut 14:3–6)*

The Torah contains two accounts of animals that may and may not be eaten. Here lies an interesting difference between them. Leviticus 11 specifies certain categories of animals, fish, and so forth that may be eaten – those that chew the cud and have cloven hooves and so on. But it does not explicitly name a single permitted creature. Only prohibited creatures are named in Leviticus. Deuteronomy 14, by contrast, lists both permitted categories (has fins and scales etc.) *and* names specific permitted animals.

> *But the following, which do bring up the cud or have true hoofs which are cleft through, you may not eat: the camel, the hare, and the daman, for although they have no true hoofs – they are unclean for you; also the swine – for although it has true hoofs, it does not bring up the cud – it is unclean for you. (Deut 14:7–8)*

As in Leviticus 11, particular attention is given to animals that have one but not both of the characteristics in a given category of permitted animals. Perhaps is to discourage laxity ("it's half kosher . . ."), or perhaps it signals the broader risks associated with ambiguity.

> *These may you eat of all that live in water: you may eat anything with fins and scales. But you may not eat anything that has no fins and no scales: it is unclean for you. (Deut 14:9 –10)*

This is low-key in comparison to Leviticus 11:9–12, which emphasizes the prohibited creatures that populate the different kinds of water, and calls them an abomination.

> *You may eat any clean bird. The following you may not eat: the eagle, the vulture . . . (Deut 14:11–12)*

Neither Leviticus 11 nor Deuteronomy 14 offers guidance as to which properties make a bird unclean. They merely list the specific birds ruled to be unclean.

> *All winged swarming things are unclean for you; they may not be eaten. You may eat only clean winged creatures. (Deut 14:19–20)*

Leviticus is more helpful than Deuteronomy when it comes to winged swarming things. It specifies that four-legged winged swarming things *with jointed legs* may be eaten, and proceeds to offer locusts, crickets, and grasshoppers as examples. Deuteronomy gives no guidance about identifying clean winged swarming things.

You shall not eat anything that has died a natural death; give it to the stranger in your community to eat, or you may sell it to a foreigner. For you are a people consecrated to the LORD your God. You shall not boil a kid in its mother's milk. (Deut 14:21)

The food laws in Leviticus do not include the law that concludes Deuteronomy's food laws, namely, the prohibition against boiling a kid in its mother's milk. The Leviticus food laws conclude thus:

These are the instructions concerning animals, birds, all living creatures that move in water, and all creatures that swarm on earth, for distinguishing between the unclean and the clean, between the living things that may be eaten and the living things that may not be eaten (Lev 11:46–47).

These concluding verses sum up what's gone before. Using terminology that recalls the creation of living beings in Genesis 1, Leviticus 11 seems concerned with identifying and maintaining categories and distinctions between different types of living animals (dead animals are not mentioned again at the end) as God created them. The concluding verses of the food laws in Deuteronomy 14 highlight a different kind of distinction – life versus death. To be sure, Leviticus 11 prohibits eating clean animals that died of natural causes and touching the carcasses of unclean animals, but its emphasis is on the uncleanness they transmit (Lev 11:32–40) rather than on death as a category in its own right – the opposite of life. Furthermore, as mentioned above, there is no reference to death in the programmatic conclusion of the Leviticus food laws. The placement of the law concerning the kid boiled in its mother's milk immediately after the prohibition against eating an animal that died of natural causes highlights the role of life and death in the former law. There's something unnatural about cooking a dead baby animal in the milk that sustained it, produced by the mother who gave it life in the first place. It represents par excellence a mixing of categories that should be kept separate, and are presented elsewhere in Deuteronomy in stark opposition (see "Choose life!" in Deut 30:19) – life and death.

You shall consume the tithes of your new grain and wine and oil, and the firstlings of your herds and flocks, in the presence of the LORD your God,

> *in the place where He will choose to establish His name, so that you may learn to revere the* Lord *your God forever. (Deut 14:23)*

How will eating the tithe of the first fruits in God's chosen place teach people to revere God forever? Perhaps by helping them to internalizing the link between what they eat and what God gives. The location of where we eat affects our sense of connection to what we are eating. Food you eat at home feels like yours, most of all if you prepared it yourself, but even if you didn't. You feel responsible for what you serve to others in your home, whether home-cooked or ordered in. Your relationship to food you're served elsewhere is more detached, even if you're paying for it, and definitely if you're a guest at someone else's table. The quality and quantity of the food reflects on your hosts, not you. If the Israelites ate the tithes of first fruits at home, they'd be inclined to feel ownership. Eating them in God's home drives home the point that they're only giving back what was already God's.

> *Should the distance be too great for you, should you be unable to transport them . . . you may convert them into money. Wrap up the money and take it with you to the place that the* Lord *your God has chosen, and spend the money on anything you want – cattle, sheep, wine, or other intoxicant, or anything you may desire. And you shall feast there, in the presence of the* Lord *your God, and rejoice with your household. (Deut 14:24a, 25–26)*

These verses take a giant leap from the agricultural produce that was harvested to a major celebration that, potentially, they merely finance. You can sell what you grow, buy what you want (including alcohol), and consume it in abundance in a festive atmosphere at the place God will choose. This ensures that festivities are not limited by the particular crops a farmer happens to grow; a farmer who does not raise cattle or grow vines can nevertheless celebrate with meat and wine.

> *You shall consecrate to the* Lord *your God all male firstlings that are born in your herd and in your flock . . . You and your household shall eat it annually before the* Lord *your God in the place that the* Lord *will choose. But if it has a defect, lameness or blindness, any serious defect,*

you shall not sacrifice it to the LORD your God. Eat it in your settlements, the unclean among you no less than the clean, just like the gazelle and the deer. Only you must not partake of its blood; you shall pour it out on the ground like water. (Deut 15:19–23)

A defect renders a male firstborn eligible to be slaughtered like any other clean animal (Deut 12:15–16) and eaten at home instead of at the place God will choose. Clearly, this law was open to abuse. Animals could be maimed intentionally, rendering them unfit for sacrifice and available to be slaughtered at home and eaten at will.

You shall not eat anything leavened with it [the Passover sacrifice]; for seven days thereafter you shall eat unleavened bread, bread of distress – for you departed from the land of Egypt hurriedly – so that you may remember the day of your departure from the land of Egypt as long as you live. (Deut 16:3)

As Marcel Proust famously expounded in his meditation on the madeleine in the first chapter of *Remembrance of Things Past*, food stimulates memory. Eating cake crumbs soaked in tea takes Proust back to childhood visits with his aunt, when she would soak the same shell-shaped cakes in her real or lime-flower tea and share a crumb or two with her nephew. On many occasions since then, Proust had seen the distinctive little cakes in bakery windows, but only now, when he tastes one, do his childhood memories come flooding back. Food also attracts memories, and they attach themselves to it. Eating unleavened bread, poor bread, matzah, evokes the memory of leaving Egypt, even for those – hundreds of generations later – who were there only in spirit. This verse offers a clear resolution to possible ambiguity about whether the main goal was abstaining from leaven for seven days or, alternatively, eating unleavened bread for seven days. Since matzah is explicitly linked to the rush to leave Egypt, only eating matzah can provoke the (collective) memory of that event. Abstaining from leaven may be crucial for other reasons, but it does not serve this purpose.

You shall cook it and eat it [the Passover sacrifice] at the place that the LORD your God will choose. (Deut 16:7)

The original *Pesaḥ* sacrifice was to be made at home and eaten inside the house. One might even say that the home was defined by who was eligible to eat from it – circumcised slaves counted but temporary laborers did not (Exod 12:43–46). This verse in Deuteronomy envisages the time when *Pesah* has been instituted as one of the three pilgrimage festivals, and the head of each household is responsible for making the offering – probably without other family members if the family lives far from Jerusalem – in the place that God will choose. At that point, the *Pesah* sacrifice will no longer function effectively, as it did at the beginning, as a tangible marker of who counts as a family member.

> *After eating unleavened bread six days, you shall hold a solemn gathering for the* L*ORD your God on the seventh day; you shall do no work. (Deut 16:8)*

Shabbat is sometimes described as a reminder of creation (Exod 20:11) and sometimes as a reminder of the exodus from Egypt (Deut 5:15). In this particular formulation, the command to celebrate the Passover festival evokes all three. Six days eating unleavened bread and a seventh day not working recalls both creation and Shabbat, and the unleavened bread recalls the Exodus and the respite from slave labor in Egypt.

Diana Lipton

Shofetim

Deuteronomy 16:18–21:9

Leaders or Landowners?

Suzanne Last Stone

Parashat Shofetim provides a model for the social, religious, and political organization of the Israelite polity. The parasha has often been called the "first Constitution," because it emphasizes the separation of powers and because it subordinates all human power to the authority of the law. The Torah describes an independent judiciary, a monarch forbidden to amass wealth, prophets who will mediate between God and the people, and a priestly group charged with administering the divine service. The priests, the Torah instructs, subsist off the sacrifices to God. They receive an allotment from the people offering sacrifices, including the first fruit of corn, wine, and oil.

At first glance, these food offerings to the priests and Levites seem to be a simple quid pro quo: the priests and Levites perform an essential religious service for the people and, in turn, receive a portion of the sacrifices. However, the verse introducing this obligation suggests that the commandment to provide food to the priests is not only part of the Torah's larger concern for social welfare policy but also part of its limiting of the accumulation of power by those in authority, a specific theme of this parasha. The Torah prefaces this arrangement with the stipulation that the priests and Levites are to remain landless. The tribe of Levi "shall have no portion among their brother tribes; the Lord is their portion (Deut 18:2)." Why does the

Torah deny the Levites the fundamental right to own land and to live self-sufficiently and independently?

This mandate may become more understandable if we consider a story that appears at the end of Sefer Bereshit. When Egypt is ravaged by seven years of famine, the Egyptians are so impoverished that they must sell themselves and their land to the state in return for food. Joseph, the ruler of Egypt second only to Pharaoh, buys all their land and resettles the people of Egypt, who are now essentially indentured servants of the state, into cities. However, the Torah informs us, there was one group of people in Egypt who weathered the famine without difficulty and without dislocation: "Only the land of the priests he [Joseph] did not buy, for the priests had a portion from Pharaoh, and ate the portion which Pharaoh gave them; therefore they did not sell their land" (Gen 47:22). The contrast is striking: while the Egyptian nation lies destitute and landless, the religious leadership sits comfortably, completely detached from the suffering of the people around them.

Perhaps it is to counter this social divide, between the comfort and luxury enjoyed by authority figures and the poverty and struggle experienced by the rest of the population, that the Torah insists that the Levites and priests remain landless. Only by denying the religious leadership land ownership, the Torah argues, will we ensure that religious leaders are sensitive to the suffering and struggles that their people endure. By remaining landless, the Levites and priests may become attuned to the needs of those who are disadvantaged in Israel, and will not become the rich, bloated, and isolated upper class of Egyptian priests.

This point is further driven home if we consider the first time that this law against levitical land ownership appears, not in our parasha, but at the end of the story of Korah's rebellion. It bears emphasizing that Korah is a Levite; someone who already holds a position of authority. Yet, Korah is unsatisfied with what he has, and seeks greater political stature. After the rebellion is quelled, the Torah rules that Levites will subsist on tithes, but will not have their own land (Num 18:23–24). Here again, it seems that the Torah recognizes the danger of investing religious leaders with political power. When religious leadership is conjoined with the state, as in the case of the Egyptian priests, religious leaders are numbed to the needs of the people. Withholding land ownership from the Levites is an extreme measure taken to ensure that religious authority is responsive to the landless, dependent, and needy members of Israel.

SUZANNE LAST STONE is University Professor of Jewish Law and Contemporary Civilization, Professor of Law, and Director of the Center for Jewish Law and Contemporary Civilization at the Benjamin N. Cardozo School of Law, Yeshiva University. She has held visiting positions at Harvard Law, University of Pennsylvania Law, Princeton, Columbia Law, Hebrew University Law, and Tel Aviv Law, with which she is affiliated. Professor Stone is the co-editor-in-chief of *Diné Israel*, a journal of Jewish law, and is on the editorial board of the *Jewish Quarterly Review*.

> *When in your war against a city you have to besiege it a long time in order to capture it, you must not destroy its trees, wielding the ax against them. You may eat of them, but you must not cut them down. (Deut 20:19a)*

Eating an enemy's produce and food supplies can be a means of weakening and ultimately over-powering him. This regulation about fruit trees makes a clear distinction between the locust tactic – eating your enemy out of house and home – and the need to eat during military operations. The general prohibition against destroying fruit trees is followed by a qualification. You may eat their fruit; since they are trees not animals or certain kinds of crops, this will not destroy them. However, you may not cut them down, an act which would certainly cause their end. Even in times of war, long-term sustainability is a concern.

DIANA LIPTON

Ki Tetse'

Deuteronomy 21:10–25:19

All mixed up? A rabbinic difference of opinion on forbidden mixtures

Yehuda Galinsky

In Ki Tetse' we read of the various prohibited admixtures, *kil'ayim*, relating to planting, breeding livestock and sewing clothing:

> *You shall not sow your vineyard with a second kind of seed, else the crop – from the seed you have sown – and the yield of the vineyard may not be used. You shall not plow with an ox and an ass together. You shall not wear cloth combining wool and linen. (Deut 22:9–11)*

These prohibitions are basically parallel to those found already in parshat Kedoshim, where it is stated:

> *You shall observe My laws [ḥukotai]. You shall not let your cattle mate with a different kind; you shall not sow your field with two kinds of seed; you shall not put on cloth from a mixture of two kinds of material. (Lev 19:19)*

Regarding the content of these two passages, the only real difference between the books is that in Leviticus the prohibition concerning animals is formulated in an unequivocal manner, that is, not to crossbreed different animals, whereas in Deuteronomy the prohibition is assumed but not stated explicitly. In its place one finds an additional directive, a biblical *gezeira*, not to plow with an ox and a donkey yoked together. There is in addition one seemingly less significant difference between the two. The Leviticus passage opens with "You shall observe My laws (*et ḥukotai tishmoru*)" which is not found in Deuteronomy. However, what seems at first glance to be somewhat unimportant becomes central in a debate between two medieval commentators in Northern France regarding the significance of the *kil'ayim* prohibitions.

Commenting on the verse in Leviticus, Rashi writes: "You shall observe My laws" – They are the following: "You shall not crossbreed your livestock with different species, etc." These *ḥukim*, "statutes," refer to the Decrees of the [Divine] King, *gezeirot melekh*, which have no rationale. Here Rashi, following the Talmudic sages, reminds us of the distinction between *ḥukim* (ritual laws) and *mishpatim* (social laws). He argues that all of the *kil'ayim* prohibitions fall into the category of *ḥukim* that cannot be understood rationally but must be fulfilled because of the Divine King's command.

In contrast to Rashi, the French exegete Rabbi Joseph Bkhor Shor, a prized pupil of the famous Rabbi Tam, and an important Tosafist in his own right, in his commentary to Leviticus, begs to differ. In his opinion all of these commandments are to be understood rationally, and here we shall focus on his central theme, which relates to the agricultural prohibitions, vegetation and animal alike.

Regarding the prohibition of crossbreeding he writes:

> *Do not breed your animals in a forbidden mixture" [such as] breeding a horse and a donkey or a donkey and a horse, resulting in a mule which I did not create, and you will have thus altered the work of creation. Similarly, any two species, such as a sheep with a goat, for you make yourself into a creator.*

This religious idea of not aggressively tampering with God's world, and of acting as if one were God, is taken up by Rabbi Joseph once again concerning the plant world. So too, he writes:

> *Do not sow your field with forbidden mixtures – such as wheat and fruit seeds, for one is a kind of grass and one is a kind of tree, and*

> *sometimes when they are sown together the two seeds join and issue a plant, something that is a combination of both which was not created. . . . Also, tree grafting alters the law [of creation] (ma'avir ha-ḥok). For it causes an apple tree to produce quince and 'uzradin [i.e. reeds that harden like wood] and create something that is not according to the laws of the world (she-eino ḥok ba-olam) – this is altering the way of the world (meshane minhag ha-olam) and therefore prohibited.*

In Rabbi Joseph's opinion man should not to be too intrusive in his interaction with nature, he is not allowed to alter the law of creation that God had set in the beginning of time. I doubt he was against all innovation, or improving the world with technology, but he most probably would have been against using scientific knowhow to create new animal breeds or new types of plants.

To end I would like to return to the opening verse in Leviticus, "You shall observe My laws." We have seen how Rashi utilized the word *ḥukotai* in order to categorize all the laws of *kil'ayim* as *mitzvot* that lack any rationale, besides fulfilling the will of God. On the other hand, Rabbi Joseph has quite a different interpretation of these words. His reading is in fact ingenious. He writes "You shall observe My laws" – Laws which I already decreed *during the six days of creation* – I do not wish you to alter them, creating new beings in this world which I did not create." The laws, *ḥukim*, that are to be observed are not referring to those given at Sinai but rather to those of nature which were employed by God to create the world!

YEHUDA GALINSKY is a Senior lecturer in the Department of Talmud and Rabbinic Literature at Bar Ilan University, specializing in the field of medieval Jewish rabbinic literature and culture. Among other subjects he has published on varying approaches to "Miracles of the Christian Saints" in medieval Rabbinic literature, and on the different Hebrew Versions of the "Talmud Trial" of 1240 in Paris. He is currently working on a book about late 13th-century rabbinic culture in Northern France.

No Ammonite or Moabite shall be admitted into the congregation of the Lord*; none of their descendants, even in the tenth generation, shall ever be admitted into the congregation of the* Lord*, because they did not meet you with food and water on your journey after you left Egypt . . . (Deut 23:4–5a)*

The problems with Ammonites and Moabites began at their conception; they emerged from the incestuous unions between Lot and his daughters (Gen 19:30–38). But their exclusion from the congregation of Israel is linked to something that seems, at face value, much less serious: their lack of hospitality. Bearing in mind the context, though, the unwillingness of the Ammonites and Moabites to offer food and drink was not so different than Amalek's vicious attack. Lack of hospitality to tired and hungry travelers in a desert can easily produce the same end result as violence with rocks and knives.

When you enter another man's vineyard, you may eat as many grapes as you want, until you are full, but you must not put any in your vessel. When you enter another man's field of standing grain, you may pluck ears with your hand; but you must not put a sickle to your neighbor's grain. (Deut 23:25–26)

Travelers in the ancient world, as in many cultures today, depended on the hospitality of strangers. Sometimes this constituted an invitation to a meal, as when the three "men" stopped to eat with Abraham and Sarah (Gen 18). But often it meant "helping yourself" to food and water along the way. Where was the line between the reasonable – and, in the big scheme of things, reciprocal – use of other people's resources and exploitation? These verses mark it out by with reference to the human hand. You can pick, eat, and carry in your hand as many grapes as you want, but you cannot put them into a vessel. You may pluck ears of grain with your hand, but you can't use a sickle. Is this what it means to live "hand to mouth"?

When you reap the harvest in your field and overlook the sheaf in the field, do not turn back to get it; it shall go to the stranger, the fatherless, and the widow – in order that the Lord *your God may bless you in all your undertakings. (Deut 24:19)*

This verse adds a random, or perhaps providential, element to the strict rules of tithing. In addition to the "tenth" that must be measured and set aside, there is another "non-measurable" component – the sheaf the farmer overlooked. Once he has passed it by, it's no longer his. It belongs to those marginalized members of society who depend on others to provide their food.

> *Remember what Amalek did to you on your journey, after you left Egypt – how, undeterred by fear of God, he surprised you on the march, when you were famished and weary, and cut down all the stragglers in your rear. (Deut 25:17–18)*

Amalek exploited the Israelites in two different kinds of ways, according to this verse. As is usually emphasized, he attacked the weak at the back of the line – the old, the very young, the sick, and so forth. But he also timed his attack so that even the strong were weak – a time when they were tired and extremely hungry. Our capacity to respond to external challenges changes very slowly – mostly over years – during the course of our lives according to our age. State of health can affect us more quickly; from one day to the next, a minor irritation becomes a major obstacle, and vice versa. But hunger – which in itself is a cause of fatigue – can dramatically influence our ability to cope from one moment to the next, and, except in extreme cases, the availability of food and drink can quickly reverse the damage.

DIANA LIPTON

Ki Tavo'

(Deuteronomy 26:1–29:8

The Prayer of Giving

Itay Marienberg-Milikowsky

Parshat Ki Tavo' marks the end of the detailed and complex list of religious laws contained in Deuteronomy 12–26. The legal focus, which was intended to organize Israelite life, in any place and at any time, is now replaced with descriptions of special one-time rituals. These work to strengthen the Israelites' commitment to God and His Torah upon their entry into the Land of Israel. Two of these rituals are the writing of the words of the Torah on stones after crossing the Jordan River (Deut 27:1–9), and the ceremony of blessings and curses on Mounts Gerizim and Ebal (Deut 27:11–26). The latter description includes details of the future in store for the Israelites if they adhere to the word of God, or in the unfortunate case that they do not (v. 28). These ceremonies, while they include familiar elements from the world of holy worship – the construction of an altar on Mount Ebal (Deut 27:5–8) and the prominent role of the Levites in exhorting the nation to refrain from religious misconduct (v. 14) – center on words and narrative; written and oral texts.

From this perspective, it is instructive to reexamine the two *mitzvot* which close the list of laws – the special reading which must be recited over the bringing of the first fruits (*mikra bikurim*) (Deut 26:1–11), and the formula required after the completion of the tithes in the third year of the *shemitah* cycle (*viduy ma'asrot*) (vv. 12–15) – two *mitzvot* which straddle the transition from Deuteronomy's legal corpus and the texts that follow it. On the one hand, both these *mitzvot* are described in meticulous practical detail; on the other, the ceremony and the text are central in both, since both require man, perhaps for the first time, to recite a fixed prayer formula before God. To a certain extent, one can see these two *mitzvot* as a personal ceremony of blessings and curses, in which the individual gives thanks for the beginning of his personal harvest and the blessing that has fallen to him (the *mikra bikurim*) and declares that he has not strayed from all that he was commanded (*viduy ma'asrot*).

The basic placement of these prayers, as described above, might shed light on the world of the commandments in Deuteronomy in its entirety. Anyone who looks at Deuteronomy cannot but sense the new religious ethos it brings to the world. Again and again Deuteronomy mentions the love and care one must have for the stranger, the orphan, and the widow (for example in the laws of the various festivals); it consistently shifts the experience and consciousness of holiness from the priestly domain into the general domain of the Israelites (such as in the laws of tithes); over and over again, daily rituals change their shape (for instance in the laws relating to eating and sex). These three changes share a common characteristic, which some describe, in modern terms, as the social-humanist-liberal turn: the status of the priestly class is diminished, and – at the same time – the individual's responsibilities toward God and towards his fellow man are intensified. A clear example of this development can be found in the description of Shabbat, which in Exodus is explained as a re-enactment of Creation: "It will be a sign between me and the Israelites forever, for in six days the LORD made the heavens and the earth, and on the seventh day he rested and was refreshed" (Exod 31:17), and which in Deuteronomy is depicted as a social duty: "so that your male and female servants may rest, as you do" (Deut 5:14).

However, this new turn, which may garner intuitive identification from members of contemporary Western culture, can act as a double-edged sword; the subject's appearance as a central entity in the world, while it sharpens attention and sensitivity toward the disadvantaged other, also necessarily raises the awareness of those stronger members of society of their own status and position. Indeed, Deuteronomy portrays, again and again, a social order which includes, on the one hand, a wealthy elite, and on the other the needy members of society; and just as it cares for those needy, so also does it protect the rights of the elite. For instance, the *mitzvot* of returning lands to their original owners during the Jubilee year (which, as formulated at the end of Leviticus, strives for almost utopian economic parity and social mobility) are completely missing in Deuteronomy. In their place we find only the requirement to forgive debts during this time (Deut 15:1–11), which creates a clear distinction between the wealthy and the poor, as well as awareness that "there will never cease to be needy ones in your land" (v. 11). A similar process can be identified in the case of another social demand. The *mitzvah* of *pe'ah*, which requires someone a priori to share a bit of his field with others (Lev 19:9), is replaced in Deuteronomy with the more minor *mitzvah* of *shikheḥa* – the prohibition of returning to glean crops which were mistakenly forgotten in the field (Deut 24:19).

This insight enables us to appreciate properly the formative role played by the two prayers which open our parasha. When a person brings the first of his fruits to the Temple, he is required to tie his personal success to a national story which centers on divine rescue:

> *You shall then recite as follows before the Lord your God: "My father was a fugitive Aramean. He went down to Egypt with meager numbers and sojourned there; but he became a great and very populous nation. The Egyptians dealt harshly with us and oppressed us; they imposed heavy labor upon us. We cried to the Lord, the God of our fathers, and the Lord heard our plea and saw our plight, our misery, and our oppression. The Lord freed us from Egypt by a mighty hand, by an outstretched arm and awesome power, and by signs and portents. He brought us to this place and gave us this land, a land flowing with milk and honey. Wherefore I now bring the first fruits of the soil which You, O Lord, have given me." (Deut 26:5–10)*

In our context, the second prayer, recited when one confesses the removal of the various tithes, including gifts given to the poor, is even more significant: one must declare that "I have obeyed the Lord my God; I have done just as You commanded me" (v. 14), and only then may he request of God "Look down from Your holy abode, from heaven, and bless Your people Israel and the soil You have given us, a land flowing with milk and honey, as you swore to our father" (v. 15).

Altruistic generosity does not, on its own, protect one from mistakenly believing that "My own power and the might of my own hand have won this wealth for me" (Deut 8:17). Sometimes, as we know, it can in fact lead to mistaken pride in its most destructive forms. The presence of the poor and needy, in and of itself, encourages the presence of the wealthy. Ki Tavo' therefore teaches us that, in a world in which the value of holiness is constantly diminished, giving alone is insufficient; only the prayer which accompanies it retains the power to remind us of our place and to instruct us in the proper humility before God and our fellow man.

ITAY MARIENBERG-MILIKOWSKY is a graduate of Ein-Zurim and Ma'aleh Gilboa religious kibbutz yeshivot, and has recently completed his Ph.D. in the Department of Hebrew Literature at Ben Gurion University of the Negev. He lectures at several institutions of higher education, and teaches a weekly Talmud class at Beit Midrash Shalom Aleichem in Tel Aviv. Itay lives in Jerusalem with his wife and children, and will spend the 2016-17 academic year as a Research Fellow in the department of Narratology at the University of Hamburg. When this piece first appeared, it was dedicated to Itay's father, Ze'ev, on his birthday. Sadly, it must appear now in loving memory.

> *He brought us to this place and gave us this land, a land flowing with milk and honey. Wherefore I now bring the first fruits of the soil which You, O Lord, have given me. (Deut 26:9–10a)*

As presented here, the land of milk and honey is not the carrot that keeps the Israelites going in the wilderness, or the reward for good behavior, or even the benefit they risk losing if they stray from the path. Its function here is similar to the role of God's reference to Egypt and the house of bondage at the beginning of the Ten Commandments, that is, the source of an obligation. That act – bringing Israel out of Egypt – entitled God to demand loyalty and obedience. Bringing them into a land of milk and honey entitles Him to the first fruits. The gift of sustenance creates the obligation to acknowledge its source and show gratitude.

> *When you have set aside in full the tenth part of your yield – in the third year, the year of the tithe – and have given it to the Levite, the stranger, the fatherless, and the widow, that they may eat their fill in your settlements . . . (Deut 26:12)*

The tithe is not intended to give the Levites and the socially marginalized just enough to survive. Just like everyone else, they must have enough to eat their fill – to eat and be satisfied.

> *. . . You shall declare before the* Lord *your God: ". . . I have not eaten of it while in mourning . . . I have not deposited any of it with the dead." (Deut 26:13a, 14c)*

Like offerings set aside for God, the food set aside for the poor and marginalized must not be used in ways that would defile it. Between these lines lies a glimpse of what must have been popular practices surrounding food and death. Mourners were limited in what they could eat, as suggested also in Ezekiel 24:17, "Do not eat the bread of comforters [literally, men]." And it must have been customary to leave food for the dead, perhaps for their journey, or perhaps in case they revived.

> *Look down from Your holy abode, from heaven, and bless the people Israel and the soil You have given us, a land flowing with milk and honey, as You swore to our fathers. (Deut 26:15)*

Milk and honey are presented here as enduring characteristics of the land, but not sufficient in themselves to sustain its inhabitants. For that, God's continued blessing is required.

> *Your carcasses shall become food for all the birds of the sky and all the beasts of the earth, with none to frighten them off. (Deut 28:26)*

Although a source of uncleanness, a dead body must in normal circumstances be treated with respect. Allowing a human corpse to be eaten by birds of prey and wild animals would have been to equate it with the carcass of an animal, with all that implies about the status of the person who died.

> *Your ox shall be slaughtered before your eyes, but you shall not eat of it . . . A people you do not know shall eat up the produce of your soil and all your gains; you shall be abused and downtrodden continually. (Deut 28:31a, 33)*

This is a severe threat. Not only will the Israelites be starving, and not only will they be forced to watch other people eat the food they had intended to eat themselves, but those other people will be strangers – indeed, their enemies (see Deut 28:49 below).

> *Though you plant vineyards and till them, you shall have no wine to drink or store, for the worm shall devour them. (Deut 28:39)*

Putting food on the table in an agrarian society requires a major investment of time and energy. It's disappointing enough to find that the cheese in the refrigerator has passed its use-by date by the time you take it out to eat it. To discover that the grapes you've planted, tended, and watched over for an entire agricultural cycle have been eaten by worms must be devastating.

> *The LORD will bring a nation against you from afar . . . It shall devour the offspring of your cattle and the produce of your soil, until you have been wiped out, leaving you nothing of new grain, wine or oil, or the calving of your herds and the lambing of your flocks, until it has brought you to ruin. (Deut 28:49a, 51)*

It's hard to say what's most destructive about a war. Sometimes, it's the severe food shortages. Borders are closed, transport is limited, farmers and even farming equipment are commandeered for the war effort, land is ravaged, and the conquerors eat the food that was raised, grown, and stored by the conquered. Indeed, as seems to be the case here, the locust-like devouring of the local food supply can be one of the strategies by which military aggressors seek to weaken and overcome their victims.

> *You shall eat your own issue, the flesh of your sons and daughters that the* Lord *your God has assigned to you, because of the desperate straits to which your enemy shall reduce you. He who is most tender and fastidious among you shall be too mean to his brother and the wife of his bosom and the children he has spared to share with any of them the flesh of the children that he eats . . . And she who is most tender and dainty among you, so tender and dainty that she would never venture to set a foot on the ground, shall begrudge the husband of her bosom, and her son and her daughter, the afterbirth that issues from between her legs and the babies she bears; she shall eat them secretly, because of utter want . . . (Deut 28:53–57a)*

This is not the first time we've heard about straits so dire that mothers and fathers are reduced to performing the most unnatural act imaginable – eating their own children. Yet there's further to fall, lower to sink. So degraded is their humanity, so depraved their instinct to survive, that that these parents have lost all feeling for their remaining family members. Not out of shame, but because of "utter want," they hide the forbidden flesh and eat it alone, in secret.

> *I led you through the wilderness forty years; the clothes on your back did not wear out, nor did the sandals on your feet; you had no bread to eat and no wine or other intoxicant to drink – that you might know that I the* Lord *am your God. (Deut 29:4–5)*

A crucial "side-effect" of food is its capacity to mark out the passage of time. In normal circumstances, our days are punctuated by meals – breakfast, lunch, dinner – and tea and coffee breaks. We become aware that time has passed because we feel hungry or thirsty. In extreme circumstances, our very survival depends on the amount of time we can endure without food or drink. This was one of the miracles of the forty years in the wilderness: there was no correlation between the passage of time and the mechanisms we use to measure it (especially in the age before clocks and diaries). Clothes and shoes did not wear out, *and there were no meals.*

Diana Lipton

Nitsavim

Deuteronomy 29:9–30:20

Social eating

Shira Golani

In parashat Nitsavim, Moses gathers the entire camp: men and women, the elderly and the young, and even those who are not Israelites – the foreigners living amongst them (Deut 29:9–10). All these people are required to stand before Moses and commit themselves (again) to their covenant with God, in preparation for entering the land of Israel (vv. 11–12). It is not only those present who are thus obligated: later generations will also be bound by this pledge (vv. 13–14). Israel's success in settling the land of Israel, as well as the land's fruitfulness, is conditional on their upholding the pledge. Thanks to it God will grant Israel "abounding prosperity in all your undertakings, in the issue of their womb, the offspring of their cattle and the produce of your soil" (Deut 30:9). Without it, the Israelites will be punished: the land will become barren and will cease to produce food for its inhabitants, as was the fate of Sodom and Gomorrah (Deut 29:21–22).

In accordance with the regular practice of naming the parshiyot, the name given to parashat Nitsavim is based on its opening words: "All of you are standing (*nitsavim*) today . . ." (Deut 29:9). However, in this particular case the name also reflects a central idea in the parasha – the personal responsibility – namely, the "standing at the ready" – of each and every person who enters the covenant with God, as a part of the Israelite collective whole. The list of the different groups in the Israelite camp which opens the parasha is unusual in the Bible in general and in the Torah in particular. In most cases, the Torah reports without further qualification that Moses called together the elders, the leaders, the *edah* (congregation), or the whole people. In the long list we find at the opening of our parasha there is a double emphasis: first, the details of the list clarify that the commitment to the covenant includes every single member of the Israelite camp, of all ages, genders and groups, and for all times. Second, the list reflects the idea of individual commitment. Every individual carries a responsibility to the nation, to his tribe, to his family and to himself (v. 17). If an individual decides, even internally, to view him/herself as separated from the nation and to go his/her own way, to insist on benefiting him/herself rather than another, God will personally punish this individual and blot out his/her name from under the heavens (vv. 18–20). This blotting out will also lead to the destruction of the entire land, which will become barren and desolate.

The Torah says of individuals who place their own welfare above that of others that they will cause "utter ruin of the moist and dry alike" (v. 18). This expression, apparently an idiom preserved only here whose exact meaning has been lost, was explained in the Aramaic translations of the Torah, and later on by medieval commentators, as referring to sins. The person who acts according to his own will adds a mistaken transgression to one which was done intentionally. However, before we turn to the metaphorical interpretation, we should note that the metaphor invokes a picture from the world of irrigation, comparing a person or piece of land which have sufficient water to one that thirsts. The message conveyed by this metaphor is that he who strives to obtain peace and a quenching of thirst only for his own home, will eventually find himself in exactly the opposite situation: he will cause collective thirst and hunger, the destruction of the entire land, leaving all its inhabitants without sources of food and water.

Parashat Nitsavim does not close with the destruction and barrenness that will be caused if the Israelites do not keep the covenant. The final word of this Torah portion is not the destruction, but rather the notion of choice. Good and evil, life and death are offered as choices for each and every one. The correct choices made by each and every individual will lead to the fulfillment of all of the blessings promised in the covenant, peaceful inhabitation of the land of Israel, and an enjoyment of all its fruits.

SHIRA GOLANI holds a joint postdoctoral fellowship at the Research Unit Biblical Studies, KU Leuven and the Orion Center for the Study of the Dead Sea Scrolls and Associated Literature, Jerusalem. She completed her Ph.D. in Hebrew University's Bible Department, where she also served as a research assistant in the Hebrew University Bible Project. Her doctoral research focused on Biblical Historiography of the First Temple Period and the Bible in its Ancient Near Eastern environment. Her other academic interests include the Dead Sea Scrolls; scribal techniques in biblical and post-biblical Jewish literature; and textual criticism of the Hebrew Bible.

> *No, the thing [Torah] is very close to you, in your mouth and in your heart, to observe it. (Deut 30:14)*

This verse comes to counter possible objections to keeping the Torah. The Torah is not in an inaccessible place, such as in the heavens, or a remote place, such as across the sea. No intermediary is required to fetch or interpret it. It's as close as imaginable – inside the mouth and heart of each and every Israelite. It's unlikely that, in modern parlance, we would thus equate the mouth and the heart as organs of deep intimacy. Yet their equation has a logic that we recognize in other contexts. Both mouth and heart are associated with romantic intimacy, the heart as the symbol of romantic love and the mouth as a means of expressing it in word and deed. And both are linked to the process of internalizing and making our own. We "take to heart" another person's feelings, and into our mouths we take the food that nourishes and sustains us.

DIANA LIPTON

Va-Yelekh

Deuteronomy 31:1–31:30

Eat your words

Yitzhak Peleg

Parashat Va-yelekh opens with the words "Moses went and spoke these things to all Israel" (Deut 31:1). Where did Moses go? Were these Moses' last words before he "went" from the earth? The Septuagint, the ancient Jewish translation of the Bible into Greek, transposes the Hebrew letters of the first word from "*va-yelekh*" to "*va-yekhal*", and translates this verse as "and Moses finished speaking . . ."

The following discussion will focus on Moses' words in Deut 31:20: "When I bring them into the land [*adama*] flowing with milk and honey that I promised on oath to their fathers, and they eat their fill and grow fat and turn to other gods and serve them, spurning Me and breaking My covenant."

This verse uses the term *adama* to refer to the land of Israel, but *adama* usually refers to *ground* or *soil*, rather than *territory*. The term *aretz* is generally used with reference to territory. In Deut 31:7, for instance, we find: "You shall go with this people into the land (*el ha*-aretz) that the Lord swore to their fathers to give them." In all other twenty biblical occurrences of the phrase "the land of milk and honey," *aretz* is used rather than *adama*, leaving this as the sole occasion on which a different term is chosen.

Should we understand this verse in its literal sense or metaphorically? Does the verse describe the nature of the land, which flows with milk and honey for those who cultivate it, or does it refer to the abundance of milk which will come from the flocks of sheep and herds of cows and of honey produced by bees, rather than directly from the ground? If we follow this latter interpretation, the blessing of "milk and honey" becomes one directed towards the shepherds of the land, not towards its farmers.

Let us return to the verse with which we opened, and note that its continuation carries with it a sense of disappointment. In contrast to what was expected of the Israelites, we are told that they will "turn to other gods and serve them, spurning Me and breaking My covenant." The verse uses the Hebrew conjuction *vav* to introduce this second clause, leading to the popular translation of "*and* [*vav*] they will turn . . ." However, the *vav* can also serve to introduce a contrast – God brings the people into the land of milk and honey, *but* [*vav*] they turn to other gods. It appears that this reading suggests a causal relationship between the two parts – the people turn away from God *as a result of* the abundance that God has given them.

Similarly, in the following chapter: "Jeshurun grew fat and kicked" (Deut 32:15) – the people grew fat and complacent, and therefore revolted against God. If we accept this reading, according to which the connecting *vav* also reads as one of contradiction, we can understand it as an expression of God's disappointment with his people, whose actions are the opposite of his expectations of them. This disappointment calls to mind the divine disappointment expressed at the beginning of the book of Isaiah, in which God says "I have reared children and brought them up – and they have rebelled against Me" (Isa 1:2), as well as the words which appear several chapters later in the name of the owner of the vineyard (i.e. God): "What more could have been done for My vineyard [i.e. the Israelites] that I failed to do in it? Why, when I hoped it would yield grapes, did it yield wild ones?" (Isa 5:4).

Regarding the relationship between God and his people, God later says of the Israelites that they "will forsake Me and break My covenant that I made with them. Then My anger will be flare up against them, and I will abandon them and hide My countenance from them" (Deut 31:16–17) – that is, God will punish the Israelites measure for measure, as is expressed by the use of the words "forsake" and "abandon," the same word in Hebrew. They will leave God, and as a result he will leave them. The notion of "measure for measure" through the use of a single Hebrew term in relation to the crime and the punishment is widespread in the Bible. In the present context I will bring only one example – the verb "to eat" in the story of the Garden of Eden, which is used with reference both to the sin of Adam and Eve – "she took of its fruit and ate. She also gave some to her husband, and he ate" (Gen 3:6) – and to the sin's consequence, in this case the punishment of Adam and Eve: "by the sweat of your brow shall you get bread to eat" (v. 19). Man "ate" from the Tree of Knowledge, and therefore will suffer in providing himself with food.

Finally, in connection with this verb, "to eat," one more note. In my book, *Lekh Lekha* ("Go Forth"), I compare the enjoyment one can derive from a text to the enjoyment of a good meal. The use of eating descriptions in a metaphorical sense is well known in the Bible, as in the case of the scroll that Ezekiel is instructed to eat (Ezek 3:2), or in Jer 15:16. In order to enjoy a meal one should eat slowly, bite by bite. One should focus on each morsel, give it the attention it deserves, chew, wait, digest. It is unhealthy and even unpleasant to eat rapidly, as did Esau upon his return from the field, when he requested of Jacob: "Give me some of that red stuff to gulp down, for I am famished" (Gen 25:30). One should treat each and every word in a text in a similar manner, giving each word the attention it deserves. Even more so is this true in case of the biblical story, which, while it uses few words, carries with it a world of meaning to be savored, taste by taste.

YITZHAK [ITZIK] PELEG is a member of Kibbutz Ein HaShofet. He is a Senior Lecturer in the Bible Department at the Gordon Academic College. Dr. Peleg has published many journal articles. His first book, *Lekh Lekha*, on the travels of the patriarchs of the Bible, was published in 2013; his second book, entitled *Going Up and Going Down: A Key to Interpreting Jacob's Dream (Genesis 28:10–22)*, T&T Clark International Press, was published in 2015.

> *Therefore, write down this poem and teach it to the people of Israel; put it in their mouths, in order that this poem may be My witness against the people of Israel. (Deut 31:19)*

In modern western thinking, the ear is the body part that serves as the access point for the spoken word; someone else speaks and we hear. For the written word, the eye is usually the relevant body part; someone else writes and we see. In biblical thought, however, words – both spoken and written – can be internalized via the mouth. God tells Moses to place the words of His song into the Israelites' mouths. At first glance, this way of thinking seems strange. In modern parlance, the mouth is the exit point for our own spoken words, or words we've memorized, but not a point of entry. There is, however, at least one context in which this notion remains familiar. When we make a statement we later regret or discover to be incorrect, we speak of "eating our words." Words that leave our bodies via our mouths are internalized by other people via their ears. If we ourselves need to re-internalize those words, they enter our bodies the way they left – via the mouth. Perhaps God told Moses to put His words in the Israelites' mouths because He knew from the outset that this process was two-directional. God was already anticipating the moment when the Israelites would return His words – via their mouths – to Him.

> *He will say: Where are their gods, the rock in whom they sought refuge, who ate the fat of their offerings and drank their libation wine? (Deut 32:37)*

This verse articulates the difference between sacrifice as construed in other ancient religions versus the religion of Israel. Other peoples assumed that their gods actually ate and drank what they were offered. For the Israelites, God merely took pleasure in the scent of their sacrificial offerings.

DIANA LIPTON

Ha'azinu

Deuteronomy 32:1–52

Bounty and Warning

Linda Zisquit

In parashat Va-yelekh, according to Rashi's interpretation, God commanded Moses to write down and teach to the Israelites the song contained in parashat Ha'azinu. God gives a prelude to the song's contents and what will happen in the future:

> *Put it in their mouths, in order that this poem may be My witness against the people of Israel. When I bring them into the land flowing with milk and honey that I promised on oath to their fathers, and they eat their fill and grow fat and turn to other gods and serve them, spurning Me and breaking My covenant . . . then this poem shall confront them as a witness. (Deut 31:19–21)*

Then Moses speaks, *Ha'azinu,* "Hear," "Listen," calling to the heavens and earth as witnesses and telling the story of Israel's past, how God bore the people on eagle's wings from a wasteland howling wilderness to a land of oil and wheat and wine. But after that, he predicts, will come a time when the people will become fat, kick, and ungratefully forget God's bounty.

This song of Moses is a poem made up mostly of couplets with a main point stated in the first line and repeated with a slight variation in the second:

Give ear, O heavens, let me speak;
Let the earth hear the words I utter!
May my discourse come down as the rain,
My speech distill as the dew.
Like showers on young growth,
Like droplets on the grass.
For the name of the Lord I proclaim;
Give glory to our God! (Deut 32:1–3)

In the first part of the song, Moses describes God's loving kindness to His people, how he spread His wings, took Jacob from the desert waste, fed him honey from a crag, oil from the rock, cream and milk from the flocks. And then suddenly, a transition:

So Jeshurun grew fat and kicked—
You grew fat and gross and coarse—
He forsook the God who made him
And spurned the Rock of his support." (v. 15)

The movement from a life of plenty to a life in which God is abandoned seems, at first, radical. In fact, the connection between bounty and a warning against serving other gods appears several times in Deuteronomy. As a midrash in *Yalkut Shimoni* says: "Wherever you find eating and being satiated, there you find warning" ('*Ekev*, 851).

For example Deut 6:10-12:

When the Lord your God brings you into the land that He swore to your fathers, Abraham, Isaac and Jacob, to assign to you – great and flourishing cities that you did not build, houses full of all good things that you did not fill, hewn cisterns that you did not hew, vineyards and olive groves that you did not plant – and you eat your fill, take heed that you do not forget the Lord who freed you from the Land of Egypt, the house of bondage.

And Deut 8:7–11:

For the Lord your God is bringing you into a good land, a land with streams and springs and fountains issuing from plain and hill;

a land of wheat and barley, of vines, figs, and pomegranates, a land of olive trees and honey; a land where you may eat food without stint, where you will lack nothing, a land where rocks are iron and from whose hills you can mine copper. When you have eaten your fill, give thanks to the LORD your God for the good land which He has given you. Take care lest you forget the LORD your God and fail to keep His commandments, His rules, and His laws, which I enjoin upon you today.

And again in Deut 11:13–16 (the second paragraph of the Shema):

If, then, you obey the commandments that I enjoin upon you this day, loving the LORD your God and serving Him with all your heart and soul, I will grant the rain for your land in season, the early rain and the late. You shall gather in your new grain, wine and oil – I will also provide grass in the fields for your cattle – and thus you shall eat your fill. Take care not to be lured away to serve other gods and bow to them."

Is this a warning against complacency? Is it human nature to receive what we need and then turn from the provider, become fat, no longer alert to the gifts given, and the needs of others? What is it about us that as soon as we have, we forget, are ungrateful? Are we deaf once the body is full, listening only when we hear our own need? Moses foresees this human phenomenon and prophesies that the children of Israel will not know how to recognize, understand, accept and use the bounty they receive with moderation and generosity.

In the second paragraph of the Shema, the description of bounty is described in singular form (*v'achalta v'savata*, "and you [sing.] shall eat your fill") while the warning is given in the plural form (*hishmaru lachem pen yifteh levavchem, v'sartem v'avadtem elohim aherim*, "Take care not to be lured away [pl.] to serve other gods and bow [pl.] to them.") Is the message then that bountifulness enjoyed only by an individual or a select group without regard to community leads to kicking the provider, serving other gods, an inflated feeling of autonomy and control? The individual who is well-fed and sated may not be open to heeding the words, so the warning is directed to the collective, to be sure the bounty of oil and wheat and wine is shared. And only by keeping our eyes and ears open, "eating" in moderation, can we hear beyond our own needs and turn outward.

On a personal level, a major focus – even obsession – of my life as a writer has been the ongoing conflict between the fullness of my life, on one hand, and an appetite for more – more love, more achievement, more bounty – on the other. I keep learning that if I don't listen to the often inchoate and subconscious warning voices of my poetry to cherish what I have, then blindness, forgetting, loss of self and others can result from a desire for more.

From POROUS by Linda Stern Zisquit*:

"We forgive many things
because we know it passes,
it happens only once."
But repetition—
to pursue a man again knowing the sorrow
to abandon yourself to the four winds
to become filled with their shameful mystery
is a light meal the body digests
metabolizing mineral vegetable so quickly
they leave no trace
only a satisfying lack of fullness:
to crave what cannot fill for the hunger it leaves –
nothing can stop you
like figures lined up in the underworld
each one holding a cracked jar
waiting her turn to pour the water
as it leaks out and flows away
or a girl at the sea's edge
dripping water over her breasts
for the god who one day descends
and wraps himself around her
why don't they stop

* Excerpts from *Porous* reprinted from Linda Zisquit, *Return from Elsewhere* (Outriders Poetry Project, 2014).

doesn't she tire
of desire
they won't stop filling
they can never fill
you can never be filled
. . .
When the body is flooded
nothing can be seen

LINDA STERN ZISQUIT is Associate Professor of English at Bar Ilan University, where she is Poetry Coordinator for the Shaindy Rudoff Graduate Program in Creative Writing. She received degrees from Tufts University, Harvard, and SUNY Buffalo. She has published five full-length collections of poetry, most recently *Havoc: New & Selected Poems* (2013) and *Return from Elsewhere* (co-winner of the Outriders Poetry Project, 2014). Her translations from the Hebrew include *Wild Light: Selected Poems of Yona Wallach* (1997) for which she received an NEA Translation Grant, *Let the Words: Selected Poems of Yona Wallach* (expanded, 2006) and *These Mountains: Selected Poems of Rivka Miriam* (2011) which was a finalist for the National Jewish Book Award in Poetry. Linda runs Artspace Gallery in Jerusalem.

And foaming grape-blood was your drink (Deut 32:14b)

From the perspective of appearance and consistency, it's natural to call grape juice, "grape-blood," especially in a highly poetic context such as this one (see also Gen 49:12). Yet viewed in the light of the Torah's frequent prohibitions against drinking the blood of slaughtered animals, the choice of terminology seems jarring. Wouldn't the negative association of blood rub off and compromise the wine-drinker's enjoyment?

DIANA LIPTON

Ve-Z'ot Ha-berakhah

Deuteronomy 33:1–34:12

Unmixed Blessings

Tova Ganzel

Gastronomical plenty is mentioned twice in Moses' blessings to the Israelite tribes which appear in this week's parasha – once in Asher's blessing: "Of Asher he said: Most blessed of sons be Asher; May he be the favorite of his brothers, *may he dip his foot in oil!*" (Deut 33:24), and again at the conclusion of the blessings: "Israel dwells in safety, untroubled is Jacob's abode, *in a land of grain and wine*, under heavens dripping dew" (v. 28).

This blessing contains an abundance of oil, bread and wine. One will be able to dip one's feet in the abundance of oil that will be found in Asher's land, and while the Israelites live in safety in their land, they will not lack for grain or wine. However, the most significant promise connected to food appears to come at the end of the verse, wherein the Israelites are given the blessing of the dew.

Dew consists of drops of water which form from vapors which cool during the night – hence their poetic description as "the damp of night" (Song 5:2). Dew ensures vitality. In the natural course of things, just as the produce of the land during the winter depends on rain, so its yield during the summer is dependent on the dew. Dew is found in most areas of the Land of Israel in which there are ascending air currents, and appears in the largest quantities following warm days. The raining of the manna in the desert was preceded by the falling of the dew: "When the dew fell on the camp at night, the manna would fall upon it" (Num 11:9), and it seems to have continued to fall after the manna descended as well: "In the morning there was a fall of dew about the camp" (Exod 16:13). In the morning, when the dew evaporated, the manna was revealed to the Israelites: "when the fall of dew lifted, there, over the surface of the wilderness, lay a fine and flaky substance, as fine as frost on the ground" (v. 14). Thus, the dew surrounded the divine food which descended from the heavens.

One might think that there was no need to mention the dew in the blessings given to the Israelites, since it is a natural and dependable daily occurrence in Israel. However, we know from the words of Haggai, a prophet from the beginning of the Second Temple period, that during difficult times for the Jews, the dew, in fact, ceased to fall: "That this why the skies above have *withheld [their] moisture* and the earth has withheld its yield" (Hag 1:10). For this reason, there was no bread, wine or oil for the people: "and I have summoned fierce heat upon the land – upon the hills, *upon the new grain and wine and oil*" (v. 11). In times when those who returned to the land hoped for the success of their venture, they endured a terrible famine which was caused not only by a lack of rain, but also by the cessation of the dew-fall. These difficulties led the people to doubt God's presence in their midst and his relationship with his people, a doubt which was assuaged, in those days, by the promise contained in the prophet's words: "I am with you! – declares the LORD" (v. 13).

In our present reality, since the return of the Jewish people to the Land of Israel, we must hope that we will always merit the blessing of the dew, and that it will be accompanied with gastronomical plenty for all the inhabitants of the land.

TOVA GANZEL, Director of the Midrasha at Bar Ilan University, has a Ph.D. in Biblical Studies from Bar Ilan, and is one of Israel's first trained *yo'atzot halakha* (women's halakhic advisors). A former Tikvah Fellow, Tova is the recipient of a number of academic awards and grants. She has published many articles, book chapters, and encyclopedia entries, and is the author of *A Visionary's Oracles – From Destruction to Restoration, Studies in the Prophecies of Ezekiel* (2012).

And of Naphtali he said: O Naphtali, sated with favor and full of the LORD's blessing . . . (Deut 33:23a)

It's not surprising that the feeling of being completely satisfied, of having everything we need and could possibly want, is so often expressed in language associated with food and drink. Eating and drinking is the realm of everyday life in which most of us – the readers of this book – are most likely to experience the uncomplicated emotion of being utterly "catered for."

DIANA LIPTON

Postscript

Tracking the Talmudic Bread Crumbs

TIKVA BLAUKOPF SCHEIN

Exhibit One – Soured milk, moldy bread crusts and a splash of salt: not a forgotten Roald Dahl special or a feast for Jerusalem's cats, but 4th century Babylonian local fare, known as *kotaḥ*, palatable only to Babylonian Jews; repugnant to natives of the land of Israel. Used as medicine as well as blamed for infirmities, a source of halachic dispute (Babylonian Talmud, Pesahim 42a).

Exhibit Two – The humble cabbage, extolled in Babylonian Talmud, Berakhot 57a – as by Cato the Elder*, 15th century French monks**, and the eponymous Russian house-wife – as the panacea for all physical ailments. Together with spinach, honey, chamomile, veal, and liver, the yeshiva recommended it, alongside standard halakhot, as the recipe for healthy living.

Exhibit Three – Rabbi Meir's sensitively filtered learning from his heretic teacher, Elisha ben Abuya, appraised as the actions of someone who is able to eat succulent pomegranate seeds yet discard the rind, presenting food as ripe for metaphor (Babylonian Talmud Hagiga 15b).

Where the Bible provides color, the Talmud discerningly paints

---

* *De Agri Cultura*, 156–7

** Wright, C., 2001, *Mediterranean Vegetables: A Cook's ABC of Vegetables and Their Preparation*, Harvard Common Press, p.79

a spectrum of nuanced shadings – often not so neatly, featuring daubs and splatters. When it comes to food laws, these visuals, as above, can be graphic and direct. At first glance, the Bible seems to speak of food incidentally or in terms of agricultural laws. Talmudic discourse is overt, forming a wild yet rigorous reckoning with legalistic imaginations that outdo any "create your own adventure" obstacle course. Endless talmudic weavings of Torah, halakha, and daily life – food – form a tapestry of interconnectedness. Here follow several illustrations of the Talmud's relation to food in general and bread specifically.

The agricultural seasons and their varying produce govern biblical life, from marking the seven year cycle, allowing the land to rest, to bringing the first fruits to the Temple every Shavuot. For the talmudic Jew, the food laws manifest additional dimensions. As a universally understood motif and a source of metaphor, food is exploited for halakhic application. Length, height, and depth are measured by the experience of eating with others, "Great is eating for it distances those who are near, and brings close those who are far" (Babylonian Talmud, Sanhedrin 103a). Time is measured in halakhic units using food – the "as long as it takes to eat a portion of food" yardstick (*kdei akhilat pras*) – such that the minimum time possible for consummation of marriage is the time it takes to eat three eggs (four if you're lenient, Babylonian Talmud, Avoda Zara 67a; Sotah 4a). Functionality of object is deemed according to food-storage ability (Babylonian Talmud, Shabbat 112b) – earthenware vessels are considered broken if they no longer store pomegranates. Humans also are measured by food-guarding ability, (Babylonian Talmud, Baba Kama 85b) – the minimally functional worker is made watchman of a cucumber patch!

Food's significance is all-consuming, tangibly delineating interactions, person with God; with environment; with other; with one's own being and with love. The dimension of ethical responsibility, person with other, is seen in Babylonian Talmud, Shabbat 140b, where food is seen as the measuring stick of miserliness or profligacy. Rav Hisda judges as wasteful one who eats wheat bread when he'd be satisfied by barley bread, and Rav Papa (a brewer by trade), one who drinks wine when he would be satisfied by beer. Examples of talmudic food appropriation for understanding and sustaining social mores are as countless as the number of *ḥametz* crumbs in a Pesah nightmare.

Talmudic conceptions of food's importance extend even to the defining of presence and absence. Akin to determining pixilation size in an image to standardize visibility levels, beyond which something is officially invisible, the *kezayit* measurement, Hebrew for "olive-size," is the halakhic threshold for what constitutes the act of regular eating. The *kezayit* also creates a super-intellectual objective reality, wherein the presence of both consumer together with her consumed is recognized only when a *kezayit* or more is internalized. For the Talmud examines both the nature of the consumed and also the act of consumption. "Rabbi Yohanan said [in reference to his difficulty in understanding a 'well-chewed over' Mishnah], 'Look, we have a table, we have the meat, we even have a knife, but we don't have a mouth to eat it'" (Babylonian Talmud, Kiddushin 46a). The ability to consume in an appropriate manner is vital to the correct ingestion of the food. Extra-rationally, foods augur fortune, says the 4th century CE Babylonian sage, Abbaye, in Babylonian Talmud, Horayot 12a – gourds, fenugreek, leeks, beets, and dates, ingested on Rosh Hashanah, act as omens of good for the year ahead.

So far, food in general; continuing to bread specifically:

> *Four things were said regarding bread: One should not place raw meat on bread, one should not pass a full cup over bread, one should not throw bread, and one should not prop up one's bowl with a piece of bread. (Babylonian Talmud, Berakhot 50b)*

Although I may be convinced to make a meal out of the confectionary aisle, Pooh-Bear style, there are staples and bread is one of them. Not just a complex carbohydrate, bread's value exceeds the nutritional in its accessibility and variety of forms. With bread as the keystone to any meal, halakha will hardly deign to respect a full banquet which lacks bread as being a halakhic "meal." With the universality of food as a trope for the Talmud's exploration of biblically-regulated life, bread stands foremost. In its (desired) ubiquity, bread is the nexus for all demographics, poor and rich, kebab van and haute cuisine, hungering and satiated, public and private. Moreover, across the smorgasbord of the Talmud, bread is claimed as the remedy for many deficiencies, e.g. What if you are grievously ill, not clever enough, need to be a fast runner, sweat too much? (Babylonian Talmud, Bava Metzia 107b).

"When the Holy Temple was in existence, the Altar atoned for Israel; today, a person's table atones for him" (Babylonian Talmud, Berakhot 55a). Two loaves at every person's table form the gustatory flag for celebrating Shabbat and hagim. The bread is crafted (in my house at least) to resemble *leḥem hapanim*, two loaves of six braided strands each, which were placed in the Temple daily, representing the twelve tribes of Israel and ceaseless presence before God. Bread is thus a tool for demarcating the times at which we are apparently closer or further away from God. If our relationship with God is made tangible in one form through the matrix of bread, then how fitting to use this matrix to explore the elements of our godly relationships.

Having bread in your basket (Babylonian Talmud, Sotah 48b; Ketubot 62b) is a metaphor for having personal access to sexual relations. In this spirit, one can read the prohibition in Babylonian Talmud, Sotah 4b against having wet hands while making a blessing on bread and consuming it. The force of the veto lies in the abhorrence regarding transmitting ritual impurity through water still on one's hands. Just as bread must be handled with respect, so too should one's bread, a term for one's wife, be handled with purity, care, and wholesomeness.

These talmudic explications on the biblical limitations concerning bread consumption enhance our conception of the most intimate delights of the marital bedroom together with the standard fare of societal negotiations. Pesah dessert suggestions ("sponge cakes and honey cakes," Babylonian Talmud, Pesahim 120a) give us a cultural appreciation of what was considered fine-dining, what traditional, and what ploughman's grub.

The etymology of "diet" is the Greek for "way of life." Talmudic discourses on food tell us what others' life looked like, what ours can look like, and how to live it – by emphasizing the strict regulations governing interactions with people as much as by emphasizing food.

The preceding picnic menu of samples gives you a taste. As a recipe book for living healthily and fully, the Talmud contains one rich feast.

Betayavon!

TIKVA BLAUKOPF SCHEIN read Classics and Oriental Studies at St. Anne's College, Oxford, and went on to teach Classics and English at private schools in the UK and Israel. Since making *aliya*, she has worked in the non-profit arena, focusing especially on Israel-Diaspora relations, and taught Torah at Limmud and in various Jerusalem contexts. She is working towards a graphic novel of Herodotus, a Talmudic cookbook, and a doctoral degree at Bar-Ilan University, in the world of Classical and Jewish connections.

Works Cited

Ashkénazi, Yéhouda Léon, *Foi et morale, Ki Mitsion II Le calendrier hébraïque – (les mo'adim)*37–41. Foundation Manitou (Jerusalem: 1999)

Auerbach, Eric, *Mimesis: The Representation of Reality in Western Literature*, Princeton University Press (New Jersey: 1954)

Ben Shmuel, Gabrielle, Israel Pibko (ed), *Sod ha-Ivri: Yesodot ha-Emunah L'Ohr Pesukei ha-Torah, Vol I* Foundation Manitou (Bet El: 2005)

Childs, Brevards, *The Book of Exodus: A Critical, Theological Commentary*, Westminster John Knox Press (Louisville: 1974)

Greenberg, Moshe, *Ezekiel*, Doubleday (New York: 1983)

Hertz, Joseph, *Commentary on the Pentateuch and Haftorahs,* The Soncino Press (London: 1960)

Kennedy Fisher, Mary, *"Foreword," The Gastronomical Me,* Duell, Sloane & Pearce (New York: 1943)

Levi, Primo, *If This is a Man*, The Orion Press (New York: 1959)

Lockshin, Martin, *Rabbi Samuel ben Meir's Commentary to Genesis: An Annotated Translation* Edwin Mellen Press (New York: 1989)

Pollan, Michael, *The Omnivore's Dilemma*, Penguin (New York: 2006)

Proust, Marcel, *Remembrance of Things Past. Swann's Way: Within a Budding Grove,* tr. C.K. Scott Moncrieff and Terence Kilmartin, Vintage (New York: 1982)

Reichel, Ruth, *Why Food Matters*, The Tanner Lectures on Human Values, Yale University, New Haven, Connecticut (2005), http://tannerlectures.utah.edu/_documents/a-to-z/r/Reichl_2007.pdf

Safran Foer, Jonathan, *Eating Animals*, Penguin (London: 2009)

Slackman, Michael, *Egypt's Problem and Its Challenge: Bread Corrupts,* New York Times, January 17, 2008

Zisquit, Linda, *"Porous," Return from Elsewhere,* Outriders Poetry Project (New York: 2014)

Tanakh. The Holy Scriptures, Jewish Publication Society (Philadelphia: 1999)

Further Reading

Here follow a small selection of books and articles I found helpful while writing this commentary and teaching a related course at Hebrew University's Rothberg International School.

Memoirs

Abu-Jaber, Diana, *Language of Baklava: A Memoir*, Pantheon (New York: 2005)

Hemingway, Ernest, *A Moveable Feast* (1994)

Kingsolver, Barbara, *Animal, Vegetable, Mineral: A Year of Food Life*, Harper Perennial (New York: 2008)

Kramer, Jane, 'Spice Routes: Claudia Roden's culinary diaspora', *The New Yorker*, September 3 2007, http://www.newyorker.com/magazine/2007/09/03/spice-routes

Kramer, Jane, 'The Philosopher Chef: Yotam Ottolenghi's ideas are changing the way London eats', *The New Yorker*, http://www.newyorker.com/magazine/2012/12/03/the-philosopher-chef

Volk, Patricia, *Stuffed: Growing Up in a Restaurant Family*, Bloomsbury (London: 2003)

Von Bremzen, Anya, *Mastering the Art of Soviet Cooking: A Memoir of Food and Longing*, Black Swan (London: 2013)

Anthropology and Culture Studies

Counihan, Carol and Penny Van Esterik (eds), *Food and Culture: A Reader*, Routledge (London: 2012)

Douglas, Mary, *Purity and Danger: An Analysis of Concepts of Pollution and Taboo,* Routledge (London: 1966/2012)

Gow, Peter, 'The Perverse Child: Desire in a Native Amazonian Subsistence Economy', *Royal Anthropological Institute of Great Britain and Ireland,* New Series, Vol. 24, No. 4 (Dec., 1989), pp. 567–582

Levi Strauss, Claude, *The Raw and the Cooked: Mythologiques vol. 1*, University Chicago Press (Chicago: 1983)

Mauss, Marcel, *The Gift: Forms and Functions of Exchange in Archaic Societies*, Norton (New York:1954/2011)

Mintz, Sidney and Christine Du Bois, 'The Anthropology of Food and Eating', *Annual Review of Anthropology* 31, 2002, pp. 99–119

Watson, James and Melissa Caldwell (eds), *The Cultural Politics of Food and Eating: A Reader*, Blackwell (Oxford: 2004)

Academic Biblical Studies

Brenner, Athalya,"The Food of Love: Gendered Food and Food Imagery in the Song of Songs," *Semeia* 86, 1999 [the whole issue is devoted to food]

MacDonald, Nathan, *Not Bread Alone: The Uses of Food in the Old Testament,* Oxford University Press (Oxford: 2008)

MacDonald, Nathan, *What did the Ancient Israelites Eat? Diet in Biblical Times*, Eerdmans (Grand Rapids: 2008)

Schafer-Elliot, Cynthia, *Food in Ancient Judah: Domestic Cooking in the Time of the Hebrew Bible*, Equinox (Sheffield: 2013)

Politics and Economics

Naylor, Rosamond, *The Evolving Sphere of Food Security,* Oxford University Press (Oxford: 2014)

Patel, Raj, *Stuffed and Starved: From Farm to Fork – The Hidden Battle of the World Food System*, Portobello Books (London: 2013)

Moss, Michael, 'The Extraordinary Science of Addictive Junk Food', *The New York Times*, February 20 2013, http://www.nytimes.com/2013/02/24/magazine/the-extraordinary-science-of-junk-food.html

Literature and Culture

Barbary, Muriel, *Gourmet Rhapsody*, Europa Editions (New York: 2009)

Ben-Yossef, Noam, *Bread: Daily and Divine*, The Israel Museum, Jerusalem (Jerusalem: 2006)

Dinesen, Isak/Karen Blixen, *Babette's Feast and Other Stories*, Penguin (London: 1950/2015)

Fisher, Mary Frances Kennedy, *The Art of Eating*, Houghton Mifflin Harcourt (Boston: 2004).

Kafka, Franz, Joyce Crick (tr), *A Hunger Artist and Other Stories*, OUP (Oxford: 2012)

Morais, Richard, *The Hundred Food Journey*, Scribner (New York: 2011)

Shalev, Meir, *Four Meals*, Barbara Harshav (tr.), Canongate (Edinburgh/London: 2000)

Young, K., (ed), *The Hungry Ear: Poems of Food and Drink*, Bloomsbury (New York: 2014)

Cook books

Ottolenghi, Yotam, and Sami Tamimi, *Jerusalem,* Ebury Press (London: 2012)

Roden, Claudia, The *Book of Jewish Food*, Viking (London: 1997)